Aircraft Down!

Aircraft Down!
Evading Capture in WWII Europe

Philip D. Caine

BRASSEY'S
Washington

First paperback edition 2000

Library of Congress Cataloging-in-Publication Data

Caine, Philip D., 1933–
    Aircraft Down! : evading capture in WWII Europe / Philip D. Caine.—1st ed.
      p. cm.
    Includes bibliographical references and index.
    1. World War, 1939–1945—Aerial operations, British. 2. Escapes—Europe—
    History—20th century. 3. World War, 1939–1945—Personal narratives, British.
    4. Great Britain. Royal Air Force—Airmen—Biography. I. Title.
    D786.C317   1997
    940.53'21' 0922—dc21   97-19667
                                                 CIP

ISBN 1-57488-234-1 (alk.paper)

Printed in Canada on acid-free paper that meets the American National Standards Institute Z39-48 Standard.

Brassey's
22841 Quicksilver Drive
Dulles, Virginia 20166

10 9 8 7 6 5 4 3 2 1

To Barbara, Virginia, and Jennifer

Contents

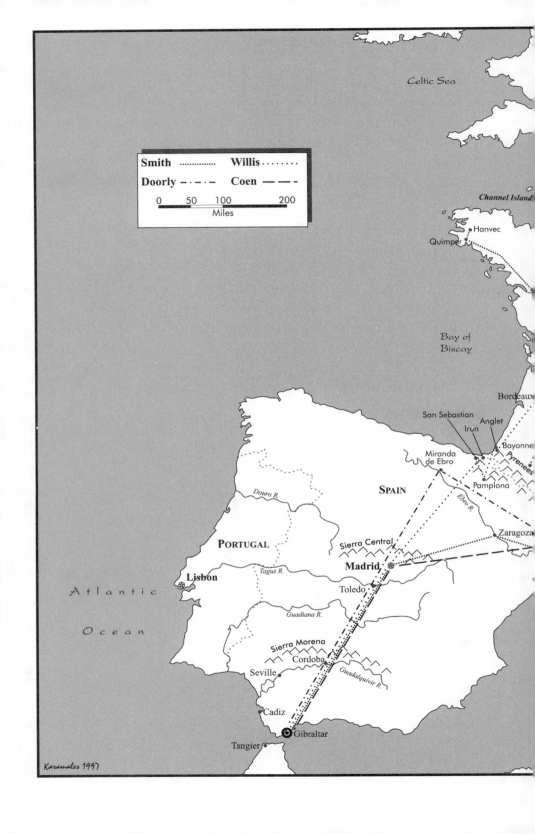

Celtic Sea

| Smith | .... | Willis | .... |
| Doorly | — · — · — | Coen | — — — |

0   50   100   200
Miles

Channel Islands

•Hanvec
Quimper•

Bay of
Biscay

Bordeaux

San Sebastian   Anglet
        Irun
                    •Bayonne
Miranda   Pyrenees
de Ebro
                    Pamplona•

SPAIN

Douro R.

Zaragoza

Sierra Central

Ebro R.

PORTUGAL

Tagus R.

Madrid ⊗

Lisbon ⊗

Toledo•

Atlantic

Guadiana R.

Ocean

Sierra Morena
            Cordoba•
Seville•   Guadalquivir R.

•Cadiz

⊚ Gibraltar

Tangier•

Karamales 1997

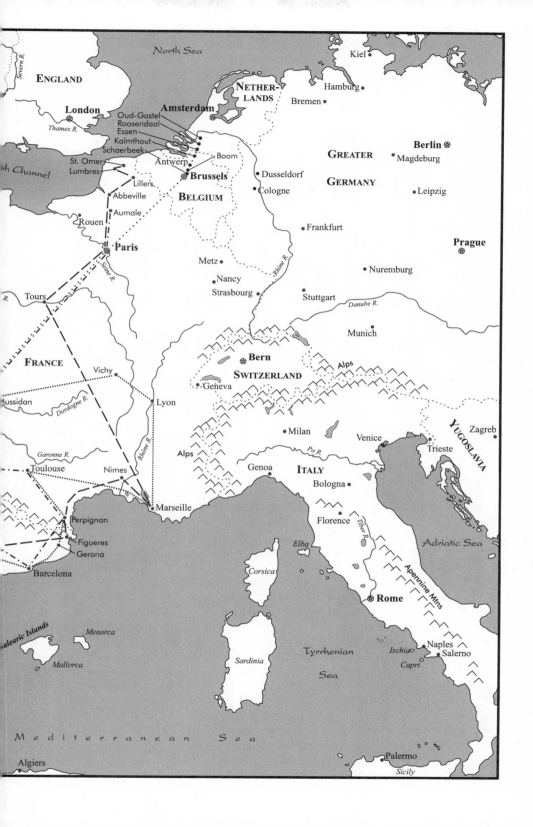

Preface

My interest in writing a book about evasion and survival really came
from two sources. First was my position during the last twelve years
of my military career. Among my other duties, I was responsible for
SERE (survival, evasion, resistance, escape) training at the Air Force
Academy and was involved in determining the course of training for all
the services under the Department of Defense. In that capacity, I became
acutely aware of the challenge, stress, and hardship that survival and evasion place on an individual. While I saw this in a training scenario, I
could only imagine how difficult it must be in a real wartime situation.
And it was very difficult to find good examples of survival and evasion
experiences for use with the cadets at the Academy. This book is an effort to relate to that specific audience the courage, confidence, self-
reliance, and ingenuity that are needed to evade and survive successfully.

My second motivation was provided by Eric Doorly when I interviewed him in conjunction with my first book, *American Pilots in the RAF*.
As he recounted his weeks and months of evading the Germans in France
and then his horrible experience at the hands of the Spanish, I realized that
his story needed to be told since it represented a chapter in the history of
World War II in Europe with which most people are not familiar. I became
further convinced of this as I interviewed more survivors about their evasion experiences. The stories in this book are those I considered the best
and most instructive of all the ones that came to my attention.

No author can write a successful book without the help of a number of people. This book is no exception. Leading the list are the men whose stories I have told: Oscar Coen, the late Eric Doorly, Robert Smith, the late Donald Willis, Robert Priser, Joseph Cotton, Fred Glor, Ernest Skorheim and S. G. Fassoulis. Brad and Zita Hosmer and Maria Couvaras not only put me on the trail of S. G. Fassoulis, but Zita also translated an extremely important document from French to English. Pat Willis provided information, hospitality, and a host of records to help in my chapter about her late husband. Ralph Patton, chairman of the Escape and Evasion Society, gave me permission to use material from his collection, located at the Air Force Academy, and volunteered any other help I might need. Duane Reed, the Air Force Academy archivist and a good friend, opened the Special Collections Division to me and gave constructive counsel and advice. Don Barrett, recently retired as the deputy director of the Academy Libraries, provided information on both World War II bombing in Europe and the activities of the underground. Colonel Dick Rauschkolb, commander of the Air Force Historical Research Agency at Maxwell Air Force Base, searched his archives and obtained copies of many escape and evasion reports from World War II. John H. Dortmans graciously undertook the extremely difficult task of translating material from Dutch to English while Horst Richardson did the same for German as did Larry Hoffman for French. My questions about the physical impact of high G forces and the effects of diseases such as malaria and jaundice on an evader were answered by Dr. Wayne Kendall. And Nick Aspiotis interviewed several people on Corfu and took a number of pictures for my use during his annual trip to that island.

I owe a special debt of thanks to Peter Kummerfeldt, the most knowledgeable survival instructor in the Air Force, who taught me about SERE over the years and whetted my appetite for the subject. My good friend Lee Gover not only read the entire manuscript but also offered innumerable suggestions that enhanced the book. My editor, Don McKeon, was always ready to offer his expertise. Finally, my wife, Doris, once again spent countless hours reading and rereading the manuscript, making suggestions and corrections, taking notes during countless interviews as only she can, and providing the encouragement and advice that are essential to success. I offer my thanks to each one, but I alone am responsible for the final product.

Monument, Colorado
December 1996

The Situation

Almost every day during the last three years of World War II, the inhabitants of most of the countries in Europe had their attention diverted from their daily tasks by the drone of aircraft engines. As they turned their gazes skyward, they might see a single airplane or a formation of a thousand. The sight could be punctuated by hundreds of vapor trails etched against the blue sky, following the straight lines of a bomber formation, or by the crazy patterns created by fighters darting in and out of formation or engaging others in dogfights as two opponents fought literally to the end. And although these formations of various types and sizes of planes often brought death and destruction, they also brought countless American and British airmen who were forced to abandon their crippled aircraft and parachute to safety or crash-land their machines in a nearby field. The number of survivors of such an incident could vary—from a single fighter pilot to an entire bomber crew of ten spread over several miles.

As the war progressed, activity in the sky over Europe increased proportionately. During 1942, for example, there were about 10,000 sorties flown by American aircraft against targets on the Western Front. (A sortie is one takeoff and one landing by a single aircraft. A fighter sortie of two to five hours of flying was typical; for bombers, sorties often lasted more than eight hours.) By July 1944, a month after the Normandy invasion, the American effort hit a peak of 130,000 sorties.

During 1944, there were nearly 12,000 aircraft lost over western Europe, 1,200 in July alone, not to mention thousands over the rest of the continent. Although a significant number of these losses were fighters, which had only a pilot aboard, about half were heavy bombers, each carrying a crew of about ten. And these are figures for American aircraft only; the British had nearly as many losses. It is generally accepted that about half the crew members of aircraft that were lost were either killed in their aircraft or died before or shortly after reaching the ground. The other half were either captured immediately or became evaders. This translates to nearly 30,000 American airmen in western Europe during 1944 alone (100 a day), most of whom landed in Holland, Belgium, France, and Germany.[1]

Nearly all of those who landed in Germany were taken prisoner almost immediately, but a good number in the other three countries became evaders. The success of these evaders was varied. Most were eventually captured and sent to German prison camps; only about a fourth of them were able to avoid capture and either return to England or remain in western Europe until the end of the war. The impact of these numbers is obvious. Almost every day, there were American and British airmen, in various states of physical and mental condition, trying to figure out how to evade the Germans. For nearly all of those who were able to avoid capture for the first few hours, this meant making themselves known to a native and hoping for the best.

While the initial contact by a downed airman put the person to whom he made himself known in a difficult situation, it was no less traumatic for the victim himself. Almost without exception, the evaders in Europe were airmen, and most of them had to face the initial evasion experience alone. The flier was unique in this regard, for most of the foot soldiers in Europe in World War II fought as a group, and those relatively few who were captured were generally taken with a group. The same holds true for the sailors who fought the German navy. Thus, when faced with an evasion situation, members of the group could take counsel among themselves and discuss a course of action, give help to an injured buddy, and give each other moral support. This situation was true for the few bomber crews that were able to crash-land their wounded aircraft and thus stay together. But most fliers spent the first few days in their strange circumstances relying solely on themselves. Probably no word more characterized the evader—when he had time to sit and think for the first time about his situation—than *loneliness*.

It was not as though they were not aware of this possibility. After all, fighter pilots went to war by themselves. But it was nonetheless a traumatic experience to have to leave the relative security of their aircraft—generally with only seconds' or, at the most, a few minutes' notice—and become an evader. In addition, the transition from flier to evader was almost always a violent one. The airman found himself bailing out of a crippled aircraft that often was on fire, or making a forced landing in a field or on water and hoping to survive the often-fatal process. Most of the time decisive action was required as soon as the airman set foot on the soil, for he had to rid himself of identifying items such as his parachute, his rank insignia, and his life vest. To complicate matters, a large number were either wounded in the air or got injured when they landed, and so movement was often difficult. For many, the situation was such that they had only seconds to get moving and find a place to hide if evasion was to continue.

If the flier was successful in meeting these initial challenges, he then had to begin to move through a strange and hostile countryside without any food or water, relying on the few basic items he carried with him in his small escape kit and what little training he had received. Unlike his fellow aviators in more recent wars, he also knew that there was no way for him to be rescued by his own forces, not only because he had no radio with which to contact anyone but also because there was no search-and-rescue force with the capability of going into hostile territory to pluck him out. Eventually he would have to make himself known to someone and ask for help.

While there were many Allied airmen who were contacted by native farmers or workers almost immediately after they landed and were spirited away from the Germans, most surprised those to whom they made themselves known. Imagine the shock of the French farmer answering a tentative knock on his door and coming face-to-face with a man he had never seen before who was speaking English, which the farmer probably couldn't understand, and was asking for food, shelter, and help. And there was little doubt that the farmer was aware of the many missives that were being circulated throughout the occupied countries of western Europe:

WARNING

All males who come to the aid, either directly or indirectly, of the crews of enemy aircraft coming down in parachutes, or having made a forced landing, help in their escape, hide them, or come to their aid in any fashion, will be shot on the spot.

Women who render the same help will be sent to concentration camps in Germany.

Persons who will capture or detain landing crews or para-chutists or who will contribute by their attitude to their capture will receive a reward up to 10,000 francs. In certain particular cases this compensation will be increased.

Paris
September 22, 1941
The Military Commander in France

[Signed] *Von Stulpnager*
General of Infantry[2]

This was not a hollow threat by any means. In Belgium, the entire male population of the village of Menseel-Kiesegem was deported *because a Canadian airman was found there.*

The dilemma faced by the farmer, or any other native contacted by an evader, was obvious. Should he aid this desperate airman—who, after all, was fighting to defeat Germany and restore freedom to his country—and, in the process, risk his life and the lives of his family? Or should he take the safe course and chase the airman off, or worse yet for the evader, detain him and call the Germans or local authorities? Although a significant number turned hapless airmen over to the authorities, a very large proportion helped them in some way and thus put themselves in a potentially deadly position. The help was often just a bowl of soup, a piece of bread, or a night in a haystack, but it could also be a room for a few days, substantial meals, native clothing to disguise the evader, and possibly help in moving to another town or in making contact with the underground. The latter circumstance was a red-letter day for any evader, for each pilot had been briefed, time and again, that there was no way to contact this mysterious group. You simply had to evade capture and wait for the underground to contact you.

Most of the farmers and residents of small villages to whom evaders made themselves known, particularly during the early years of the war, did not know anyone in the underground and had little idea of how to make such a contact. (This situation had changed by 1944, when most people in the countries of western Europe knew at least someone who might be able to make the contact.) Thus, the farmer or villager who gave an airman food and shelter had no idea of what he was going to do with this stranger. He only knew that the man needed help and that he was willing to take the chance to give it. As many an evader aptly put it, "Greater love hath no man than these people showed for me."[3]

For the evader to have any chance of returning to his base, it was almost essential that he be taken into custody by the underground. Although being taken in by the underground did not guarantee that an Allied airman would be returned to England or another friendly or neutral country, not being in the underground network meant that he had little chance of getting back before the end of the war. As a result, a number waited for many months, were never able to effect a contact with the underground, and were still evading the authorities at the end of the war.

Underground became almost a magic word to those airmen who were trying to evade capture and eventually escape from German-occupied territory. Almost every evader would breathe a huge sigh of relief when he found he was under their control. But it is important to distinguish between the underground and the resistance. The terms are often used interchangeably, even though the primary purpose of the resistance was to confound the German occupation of a particular country, destroy military targets, and prepare for the day when the citizens could help the Allies crush the Germans. Although many members of the underground were also involved in the resistance, the purpose of the underground was to care for and eventually move Allied personnel out of occupied Europe to a location where they could be evacuated to England. Almost ninety percent of those who were returned to England during the war were evacuated across the Pyrenees and through neutral Spain.

Several underground networks were active at various times in western Europe. Probably the most famous was the Comète Line, which began in Belgium and ran to Marseilles, on the Mediterranean, or to Biarritz, on the Atlantic. It was founded in 1940 by a twenty-four-year-old Belgian woman, Andrée de Jungh. Although both de Jungh and her father were eventually taken prisoner by the Germans, the line operated effectively for nearly four years. Its last group of evaders was taken over the Pyrenees on June 4, 1944. There were hundreds of Belgians and Frenchmen involved in this organization, and they were able to not only move the evaders but also provide them with identification cards, clothes, safe houses, and other necessities.

Aside from the Comète Line, the other main underground organization in France was the Pat O'Leary Line, which took the operational name of its founder, Lieutenant Commander A. M. Guerisse, a doctor in the Belgian army. This organization was based in Marseilles and took evaders from northern France to Marseilles for evacuation by sea or over the Pyrenees. One of the main safe houses for this group was the flat of Louis Nouveau in Marseilles, through which Oscar Coen passed on his way out of France. Nouveau was betrayed in 1943 and was sent to a concentration camp. The Greek doctor Rodocanachi, with whom Bob Smith stayed in Marseilles, was also a key member of the Pat O'Leary Line. He was eventually executed by the Germans for his activity, but the Pat O'Leary Line continued to operate on a reduced scale through 1944. There were no organized underground systems in either Italy or Greece, the other countries in which stories in this book took place.

The risk involved for and the price paid by members of the underground who were caught ranged from deportation to a labor or concentration camp to being shot on the spot. There is no way of knowing how many members of these organizations paid with their lives for helping Allied airmen escape occupied Europe, but estimates range as high as two underground lives for every successful evader returned to England. These people are the real heroes of every story of escape and evasion.

At Mount Valarien in Paris there is a monument to these brave people. Just behind the monument is a place known as the Killing Grounds, where thousands of underground and resistance members were shot, six at a time, during the war. One story says that a German Catholic priest said he gave the last sacrament to nearly 4,700 Frenchmen before they were shot—and executions had been under way for two years before the priest was assigned to duty there.[4]

Henri Michel summarized the contributions of the underground and the resistance:

Keep in mind that the resistance (and underground) was made up of ordinary people, not supermen. Some cracked under pressure and talked under torture; some betrayed their fellows to save a family or a loved one; some refused to help and some became collaborators; but they were a force that tied up tens of thousands of German troops, destroyed countless critical facilities, transportation systems, etc., and helped return hundreds of Allied airmen who, although most did not fight again, went back to duties which freed another man to take his place in the fight against Germany.[5]

My objective in this book is to illustrate different evasion scenarios by telling the stories of American airmen in several survival situations. The first, Oscar Coen, became an evader even before the United States entered World War II. He was moved from northern France to Marseilles, where he stayed with Louis Nouveau, and then across the Pyrenees by the Pat O'Leary Line. Eric Doorly was aided for much of his evasion by individual Frenchmen who had no connection with the underground but who felt it was their duty to help an Allied pilot in his time of need. Bob Smith had a similar experience but for a much shorter time. Both were eventually turned over to the Pat O'Leary Line and were evacuated across the Pyrenees. Their experiences in Spain in late 1942 and early 1943 are illustrative of a most difficult period when evaders were treated as criminals by the Spanish.

Donald Willis covered as much of western Europe as almost anyone who evaded during World War II. After crashing in Holland, he made his way to Belgium, where he was picked up by the Comète Line, which had him under its control during most of his evasion. Rather than go across the Pyrenees on the Mediterranean side, as did Coen, Doorly, and Smith, Willis went across the western end of the mountains as a member of the last group moved into Spain by the Comète Line. The treatment he received after being intercepted by the Spanish authorities illustrates the different situation that Americans found in Spain in 1944 as opposed to 1943.

Robert Priser was in contact with the underground from nearly the beginning of his evasion experience, but they were able to do little with him. His adventure in Belgium began after the Comète Line had been compromised by the Germans and was no longer effective. Therefore, he evaded through the combined help of the remnants of the underground, ordinary Belgian citizens, and an informal network that gave aid to a huge number of airmen who could not get out of Belgium and had to wait to be liberated by Allied forces.

The fate of the B-17 crew that crashed on the island of Corfu illustrates still another survival and evasion situation. Since there was no organized underground on the island, crew members were initially sheltered and kept away from the Germans by the people of the town of Lefkimi. It was they who organized the move of the Americans to Albania and then to Greece. Throughout their time in Greece, the Americans were not in the hands of an underground unit whose objective was to get them safely out of the country, but were rather aided by a resistance movement that got its support from the British and had vowed to sabotage the German occupation of Greece. Still, the members of this resistance group were able to engineer the eventual escape of the ten Americans.

Finally, the adventures of Satiris Fassoulis are quite unique. Fassoulis evaded in the hills of Italy with the help of a number of Italians who had no organization other than that put together by friends and various townspeople. Since he could not be evacuated, he chose to get through the lines to the Allied side after the invasion of Italy.

All of the men whose stories appear in this book were motivated by one primary desire: to evade capture so they could return and fight again. And none of them was ever able to repay the debt he owed to countless individuals, many of whose names he never knew, who took the risks and paid the price to help facilitate that desire.

Notes

1. Office of Statistical Control, *Army Air Forces Statistical Digest* (U.S. Government Printing Office, Washington, D.C., December 1945), pp. 220, 254.

2. English translation of a German army proclamation in French. Original in Ralph Patton File, SMS 923, Addendum 1, Box 2, Special Collections Division, U.S. Air Force Academy Library, Colorado.

3. Clayton C. David, *They Helped Me Escape* (Sunflower University Press, Manhattan, Kansas, 1988), p. 18.

4. Richard M. Smith, *Hide and Seek with the German Army* (Defense Printing Service, Fitzsimons Army Medical Center, Aurora, Colorado, 1955), pp. 36–37.

5. Henri Michel, *The Shadow War* (Harper and Row, New York, 1972; translated from French by Richard Barry), p. 355.

· T W O ·

"The Drinks Are on Me!"

Under an early Monday morning overcast in late October 1941, two RAF Spitfires flew unnoticed. Their pilots, Oscar Coen and his flight leader, Chesley "Pete" Peterson, searched the railroad tracks below for the ammunition train they were expecting. Although it was barely dawn over German-occupied France, from his position just below the base of the clouds, Coen could make out some of the fall foliage of red, russet, gold, and brown that decorated the trees lining the hundreds of small fields. Having to crash-land in one of those fields was far from Coen's mind, but he subconsciously kept his eyes open for emergency landing areas—as did every fighter pilot over enemy territory. It was obvious to the two aviators that it would be almost impossible to crash-land successfully in the wet, muddy fields bordered by the rows of high trees and dense hedges.

The two American pilots of RAF Fighter Command Number 71 Squadron had been awake for several hours. They had decided the day before that they would fly a low-level search mission over France to see if they could find a good target to destroy. The squadron intelligence officer had told them about the possibility that a German ammunition train would be going toward the coast between St. Omer and Calais, so that became the target they wished to find. The pair had taken off into the weather and been in the clouds all the way across the Channel, but, as had been forecast, there was room to maneuver below the clouds and the drizzle over France.

"I have the train at eleven o'clock," called Peterson. Both pilots immediately gave their full attention to the task at hand: stopping the train and then destroying as much of it as possible with their two Spitfires. The pair flew parallel to the train, checking the terrain and looking for obstacles, such as power lines, that could bring down their fighters on a low pass. Satisfied, Peterson pointed toward the train and rolled into a shallow dive for his attack.

Coen, flying about two hundred yards to Peterson's right, waited a couple of seconds and then rolled into a screaming dive after his leader. Picking out a car near the middle of the train and more toward the rear than the one Peterson was attacking, Oscar concentrated on the gun sight that would ensure that his two cannons and four machine guns would do maximum damage. He pushed the center firing button when he was about two hundred and fifty yards from his selected target, and his Spitfire bucked as all the guns responded with devastating fire. He continued his shallow dive as he poured his shots into the train. When he was about twenty-five feet above the ground, he leveled off and flashed over the top of the smoking car. The attack had forced the train to stop, and both pilots confidently relished the thought of being able to tear it apart on their next few passes.

Suddenly Oscar's blood ran cold as he felt a huge thump under his right wing and his Spitfire was lifted from its flight path. Immediately the cockpit filled with the acrid smoke of the superheated glycol that cooled the huge Merlin engine and the pilot's visibility went to zero. But just as rapidly as the smoke had come, it disappeared. Coen poured over his instruments, trying to determine what damage had been done. The seriousness of the situation became apparent as the needle on his engine temperature gauge advanced like the second hand on a clock, indicating that the cooling system for the Rolls-Royce V-12 had been seriously damaged. Oscar swore at himself as he realized he had gone too low on his strike. Just as he had passed over the car he had been attacking, it must have exploded, and since he was so low, debris tore the entire cooling radiator off his wing. Oscar knew he had only about one minute before his engine would seize and catch fire. During that time he had to gain as much altitude as possible so he could successfully bail out of his stricken craft. He hoped the plowed fields below were as soft as they looked since he was going to have to parachute into one of them.

Coen kept his wounded engine going at full power as he pulled sharply back on the spade grip and fought for altitude before the inevitable bailout time came. Just as the Spitfire broke into the early morning sunlight above the shallow cloud deck, his engine started to misfire and run roughly, and he knew the end of his flight was near. On the way up, he had called Peterson to tell him of the problem and that he was going to have to abandon his Spitfire. Peterson climbed above the clouds with him, and when the smoke started to pour from Coen's engine, Peterson told him to get out and wished him good luck.

Oscar had mentally gone through the bailout procedure countless times on the ground, but this was the real thing. He pulled the release handle for the canopy and was relieved as the front of it lifted and the force of the air tore it away, for that system had been known to fail on the Spitfire and leave the pilot trapped in his aircraft. The noise was deafening with no canopy and Coen systematically disconnected the oxygen hose and the radio cords from his leather helmet. Finally, he opened the small door on the left side of the cockpit and began to climb out onto the wing, staying as low as possible to miss the tail. As he tried to bend farther to get hold of the trailing edge of the wing, the slipstream caught him and he was gone, tumbling headfirst into the air. He caught a glimpse of the tail going by and was relieved that he had missed it by a good foot. He marveled at how trim the Spitfire looked from the rear as the pilotless craft flew on to its doom. As he entered the clouds through which he had just climbed, Coen had no idea what position his body was really in. His instructor at the operational training base in England had told him that if you put out your arms you would fall feetfirst. "Then you can just watch the ground come up, and when you are fairly low, pull your rip cord," he had said. "You don't want to open your chute too soon, since that gives those on the ground more time to watch where you land." Coen dutifully put his arms out for a few seconds to stabilize his fall, felt his body rotate and then stabilize, and began looking between his legs for the ground.

Oscar estimated that the base of the clouds was at about a thousand feet, so he should have time to open his chute after he broke out. But as he waited and waited and dropped and dropped, Coen decided he had misread his altimeter, for it couldn't take that long to get through the clouds. Panicked that he was much lower than he had thought, he gave the rip cord a mighty tug and watched his chute deploy between his legs! He had been falling headfirst and looking between his legs at the clouds. He was violently jerked from his headfirst fall and saw the ground scarcely more than a couple of hundred feet beneath him. Coen looked up, checked his chute, looked down, and hit the ground hard, cringing as pain shot through both ankles.

Instinctively, he looked skyward for the friendly sight of Peterson's Spitfire, but then he realized that if his friend came down to circle him he would be giving away his position to anyone in the area. So Coen turned his attention to his own situation. He had landed in a small, muddy field that appeared to have been recently plowed. Not far away was a line of rather tall trees, whereas in the other three directions he saw only dense hedgerows marking the boundaries of the field. There were no buildings on the gray horizon, and his activities apparently had not roused any interest that early in the morning, since no other people could be seen. Sensing no real urgency to act, Coen, still surprised at how calm he was, gathered up his parachute, sat down, and took stock of his situation.

Although flight training instruction on how to bail out was detailed, there had been no discussion on what to do after you landed. Oscar realized that the first step was to get rid of anything that might identify him as a downed RAF pilot and then get away from the area as quickly as possible. As luck would have it, he spied a large rodent hole nearby, so he quickly stuffed his parachute, helmet, and gloves into it, then ripped off his RAF insignia and wings, which also went into the hole. He began to remove his boots to see what might be done about his painful ankles, but the pain caused by his efforts was intense. He knew he would really be in a mess if he got the boots off and then couldn't get them back on, so he decided to just walk off the pain, as he had done with an ankle injury he'd suffered when he was in high school.

Fortunately, Oscar knew he was somewhere between St. Omer and the coast, and he decided that the Germans would probably look for him between the wreckage of his aircraft and the Channel. He decided to go in the opposite direction, east. Coen had looked at his escape kit dozens of times back at his base at North Weald, but this time his need was real. Going through the contents, he took out the small compass, sighted east, and then put the compass in his pocket along with a map and the new French francs that he found in the kit. He kept his identification card so he could prove who he was if the need arose, as well as his .38 Wembley pistol. The rest of the items from the kit went into the rodent hole. Covering the hole to make it look as natural as possible, he set out across the field toward the east in the gray light of dawn.

Almost as soon as he began to walk, it started to drizzle. Although he might get cold as he got wet, the rain would erase his tracks and make him that much more difficult to follow. Despite his painful ankles, Oscar actually found that the farther he hobbled across the muddy furrows in the absolute silence of early morning the more convinced he became that he was going to be able to evade capture. He knew he had to make contact with the French underground, which he had no idea how to do, but he could just imagine the boost it would be for everyone's morale if he could walk back into the RAF officers' mess in a few weeks and say "The drinks are on me."

After walking for about an hour through plowed fields and fighting his way through the dense shrubbery of the hedgerows, some of which had been planted by the Normans four centuries earlier, he came to an asphalt road that ran at an angle to his path but still basically east. The trek thus far had reassured him that he had not been seen, for there were still no people or vehicles. He had heard nothing but the sounds of the soft drizzle and his boots sloughing through the muddy fields. Coen made his decision and started to walk down the asphalt. Being on the road bothered him at first, since he had been told that it was best to stay away from the main lines of communication. Still, he was glad for the asphalt surface because his ankles had been twisted constantly by walking in the fields and he feared that if he was limping he was sure to raise someone's suspicion. He also thought he would be more suspect walking through a field on a rainy day than on a road anyway.

Coen's first challenge was not long in coming. After a half hour, a small cluster of houses appeared in the distance. Nothing seemed out of the ordinary, but as he got closer, Coen saw that on the far side of the tiny village the road crossed a railroad track that, to his dismay, was guarded by a German sentry. His concern was heightened by the black-and-white-striped gate lowered across the road and the presence of a military staff car whose occupants were apparently talking to the guard. "My God, this is it," was his initial thought. He was sure the officers were telling the guard that there was a downed RAF pilot in the area. He wanted to turn around and run, but he couldn't leave the road or go back the way he had come because the Germans might already have seen him and that would be sure to arouse their suspicion. No sooner had he begun to feel the gnawing panic in his stomach than he saw a possible way out. Just ahead, in the cluster of buildings, he spied a bistro, which, fortunately, was on the opposite side of the road from the guard post. And although Coen didn't know if the French drank at that time of the morning, he saw no way out but to go into the pub. So, shaking from head to toe, he walked directly to the small building and pushed open the door.

He found himself in a dimly lit room, about fifteen by twenty feet, with a bar running down the left side, away from the door. There was no one behind the bar, but fortunately, four or five men were sitting around a table in the far corner of the room. As soon as Coen opened the door the group of men stopped talking and looked at him. Avoiding their eyes, as the sweat ran down his back, Coen walked over to the bar and rapped on it with his knuckles. Almost immediately a teenage girl came out of an adjoining room and, much to his relief, the men began talking again. Coen pointed to a bottle and put one of his ten-franc notes on the bar. The young girl looked closely at him, obviously realizing that he was not a regular customer, poured his drink of what proved to be fairly good cognac, and then studied him again. The more she looked at him, the more he was sure she suspected he was a downed airman. After a few seconds, she took his money and gave him back a few coins in change. Coen shoved a couple of the silver ones back at her. She said "*Merci*" and, much to his relief, turned and disappeared into the room from which she had come.

Trying to appear as just another French farmer, Coen slowly sipped his drink. The liquid was warm on his throat, and he found that his shaking gradually subsided. For several minutes he simply stood at the bar while his mind raced as he thought about what to do next. He knew he had to find out what was happening at the railroad gate, so he picked up his drink and wandered over to the window at the front of the small building. A glance at the men talking around the table confirmed that they were still not paying any undue attention to him; apparently they thought he was looking for someone. What met his eye outside was reassuring. The staff car had departed, the gate across the tracks was up, and the guard was leaning on his rifle next to his hut. It seemed like as good a time as any to move, and Oscar reasoned that if he waited there would only be a greater chance that the alarm would have been sounded for an RAF pilot. With that, he downed the rest of his drink, returned the glass to the bar, opened the door, and walked out onto the road.

Any confidence Oscar had gained while in the bistro about getting past the railroad guard vanished as soon as he got outside. He found himself on the opposite side of the road from the guardhouse with about a hundred feet to walk to get to the tracks. As he mulled over his next action, he reasoned that if he tried to pass on the side of the road he was presently on, the guard would certainly say something to him, motion him to come across the road, or in some way ask for his identification. If any of those occurred, he was sunk. So he decided to take a chance and beat the guard to the punch by crossing the road and walking right past the German like it was an everyday occurrence. So, his stomach in knots, he angled to his left, crossed the road, and approached the guard, trying not to limp. As he passed the sentry, Coen simply nodded to the German, who responded with an uninterested "*Guten morgen.*" Coen nodded again and walked on down the road. A minute later, both the guard and the little cluster of houses were fading in the distance and Coen's breathing had once again become normal.

As he continued down the road, Coen noticed that the drizzle had stopped, but there was still no traffic and no other walkers. This gave him some time to both think about the crisis he had just surmounted and plan what he was going to do next. Since he had not been stopped at the train crossing, Coen concluded that the Germans had not yet found his plane or his parachute and had not put out the alarm. This gave him added confidence and the impetus to get as far away as possible from the area where he had bailed out, so he determined to keep walking as long as he could. At the same time, he could not help but think about the crisis at the railroad crossing. For a long time, he'd had a theory that guards in any army of any country had one trait in common: they did not want any trouble on their watch if they could help it. So if you didn't give them a reason to question you or to think there was a major problem, they were happy to let you go on past, making their tours as uneventful as possible. Although it had worked once, he hoped that he would not have to test the theory again.

As he continued to walk, he remained surprised that he met no one and saw few vehicles on the road or workers in the fields. After a couple of hours, however, he noticed that the fields, with their boundaries of trees and hedgerows, were giving way to more houses and a few shops. He knew that St. Omer was not too far from where he had abandoned his Spitfire, but he thought he could hardly be in the town so soon. In any case, he had planned to go around St. Omer if he could. He knew from his squadron briefings that it was an important location for the Germans, so there were bound to be a large number of soldiers garrisoned there. After walking a few more minutes, however, the buildings and activity around him made it obvious that he was indeed in St. Omer. What to do? There was no way to get off the road without going back into the fields, which he thought would make anyone who saw him more suspicious than ever, and there were no crossroads onto which he could turn. As he had back at the railroad crossing, he just kept walking. Soon, the neat one- and two-story stone houses began to have small gardens in the front or at the sides and the barns and animal pens disappeared. Actually, he was surprised at how well kept the area was, given the German occupation. He still wondered why there were so few people about, but the smells in the air reminded him that it must be near noon. By now, he was so far into the town that he had no choice but to keep going right on through it.

Doing his best to blend in with the few people who were walking on the sides of the road, he continued walking. It was hard to not look around at both the people and his surroundings, but he managed to keep his eyes glued to the road—as it appeared most of the French were doing. He remained surprised at the few people and the complete lack of any children outside playing, especially since the rain had stopped. Fortunately, he saw no German soldiers.

As is the case with most roads in European towns, the one that Coen was traveling soon came to the last place he wanted to be—the town square. Without any warning, he found himself in the almost deserted square, and immediately the surge of near panic that he had felt at the railroad crossing returned. His stomach knotted and sweat formed on his brow—for, about a half block ahead of him, in front of one of the buildings, was a German guard leaning on his rifle. Coen was confronted by the same dilemma as before. If he tried to pass on the other side of the street, it would raise suspicion, and he certainly couldn't turn around. Unfortunately, there were no people to divert attention from the lone walker. It was time for his guard theory once again.

When he got closer to the sentry it became obvious that the place he was guarding was more important than a remote railroad crossing. The German flag hanging in front indicated a major military building, and Oscar's heart sank. Resisting the impulse to turn and run, once again he simply walked past the guard and nodded, keeping his eyes downcast. The guard did nothing to acknowledge Coen's presence, so he kept walking. When he reached the corner, the evading airman couldn't resist glancing back over his shoulder. The sentry was looking right at him. But by then it would have been hard for the guard to stop him. Coen quickly turned the corner and briskly departed the square on a road going toward the south. He was amazed that there still was apparently no alarm out for him, which reinforced his desire to make every minute count and get as far from St. Omer as possible before dark.

With few residents of St. Omer on the street, and almost no Germans about, Coen had a better chance to take in his surroundings. He had noticed a large cathedral off the square, but the houses were pretty much alike: relatively small, many two stories high, made out of stone, earth-colored brick, or ochre-colored stucco. Most were set back only a few feet from the road. One big difference from England was the lack of flowers in front of most of the houses. And embracing everything was the absolute silence of the scene, not even a dog barking to break the tranquility.

He continued walking. The houses began to thin out, and once again small farms were evident. Just at the outskirts of St. Omer, Coen walked past a small shedlike building with an open front door. He knew he shouldn't, but he looked in—straight into the eyes of two German soldiers. Apparently intent on lighting a fire to cook their noon meal, the soldiers simply looked at him and went back to their work.

By midafternoon, Oscar was getting tired. He had been on the road for nearly nine hours without any food or water and figured that he must be over twenty miles from where he had bailed out of his stricken Spitfire. As he walked on, he realized that he had to take the step that could well determine if he was to successfully evade the Germans or be captured. He had to get help.

The word around the squadron was that the French were generally friendly and would try to help you, but you had to realize the terrible consequences for them if they were found out by the Germans. So, if it was obvious that they wanted you to just go away, you should go without further efforts to encourage them to aid you. One of Coen's instructors had also told him, "You can't find the underground; they will find you when and if they want to." Above all, you should never try to deceive anyone about who you were. Once you made yourself known, it was essential that you did just what they told you to and did not ask any questions. Oscar remembered that it had all seemed to not make very much difference when he was sitting around the warm fire in the mess drinking a beer and talking with his squadron mates. But this was the real thing, and the rest of his life was on the line.

He believed it would be safer to try to get help in the countryside than in a populated area, so when he heard church bells ringing in the distance, he decided to act before he found himself in another town. Not far from the road, he saw a small farmhouse with a barn a short distance away and a haystack in back of the barn. Since no one was around, and because the farm looked very typical of those he had seen along the way, Coen sat down on a culvert and began to watch the house. He had not been sitting there long when three people left the house and began walking toward the sound of the bells. Assuming that it must be a holiday of some sort, since there were so few people about and the church bells were ringing, Oscar thought he would have at least a couple of hours to look over the house and try to figure out if it was a good place to make contact with the French. With every nerve on edge, he cautiously approached the house and confirmed, as best he could, that there was no one about. Satisfied that he was alone, he walked to the door and, holding his breath, knocked. To his relief, no one answered, and since the door was open a crack, he pushed it open and went in.

Coen found himself in a small, warm kitchen. An involuntary shudder made him realize that he was not only tired and hungry, but he was also cold. Had he been thinking more clearly, he would have realized that the pot of potatoes cooking on the stove indicated that he did not have a lot of time to look around. But the aroma was so good, and the room so comfortable, that he sat down for a while to rest and think. To him, the logical place to be when the residents of the house came home would be sitting in the kitchen, for then they would surely know that he meant no harm. But believing that he had ample time to look over the house before the family returned, he set out. He was particularly interested in finding some other clothes, since he thought his were far too obvious. He didn't know that one reason he had failed to attract any attention during the day was that when the British evacuated the coastal areas of France they'd left thousands of uniforms behind with all their other equipment. It hadn't taken long for the hard-pressed Frenchmen to start to wear various parts of the uniforms for everyday use. Thus, walking around in an RAF flight jacket and pants was not as unusual as Coen thought.

He was also curious about the farmhouse. It was obvious that the kitchen was the main room, for it contained, in addition to the warm stove and an adjacent counter area, a good-sized table around which were six chairs. Other chairs occupied two corners of the room. Next to the counter area was a small pantry and storage room, with a dirt floor; the room contained a few cans of food, a couple of hams hanging from the ceiling, and a large bag of potatoes. Coen was impressed with how clean and orderly everything was.

He moved from the cozy kitchen and entered a small living room set with two overstuffed chairs, a couple of small tables, and a cabinet containing several nice dishes and a number of photographs. There were a few pictures on the walls, and as he looked around the room, his gaze was drawn to a framed poster that depicted the French and English flags with crossed staffs. He thought that was a sign that the family was friendly to the British cause—or even had relatives in England—so he was satisfied that he had picked the right house to enter. Adjacent to the living room was a room he took to be the master bedroom, so he assumed that the other bedrooms were up the stairway that occupied one corner of the kitchen. Oscar was so intent on looking in the bedroom closet to find some other clothes to wear that he lost track of what was going on in the house. He really was not concerned with his situation because of the flag poster he had seen. But suddenly he felt the back of his neck burning and knew someone was watching him. He turned around and found himself face-to-face with, and less than three feet away from, a large middle-aged man who wore a dark mustache. Oscar's heart stopped.

The youthful Oscar Coen (*front*) with RAF intelligence officer Roland Robinson (*left*) and a fellow American Eagle Squadron pilot, Michael G. McPharlin (*right*).

Oscar Coen

But the farmer was looking at Coen in a puzzled manner. He was faced with a person in RAF flight clothes but whose features and physique—five feet six and a hundred and twenty-five pounds—were so youthful that he could be taken for a teenager. Further, his light brown hair and blue eyes indicated that he was probably not French. Coen desperately searched for a way to show the farmer that he was a downed RAF pilot who needed help rather than simply a thief. After all, he had been discovered going through the man's bedroom, not sitting in the kitchen as he had planned. Suddenly he thought of the cigarettes in the pocket of his flight jacket, cigarettes that would have given him away in a moment as an American but that he had forgotten about when he was burying his parachute and other gear. As the farmer watched, Oscar reached into the outside pocket of his flight jacket, pulled out his pack, and offered a cigarette to the farmer.

"Oh, Camel!" exclaimed the Frenchman as he took the offered smoke and casually lit it. He then studied the pilot closely. Oscar hoped that the Camel cigarettes would let the farmer know that he at least had some connection with the United States, although America was not yet in the war, and that he needed help. The Frenchman apparently realized his plight and was satisfied that Oscar meant no harm, for he led the still shaking airman back into the kitchen and finished his cigarette. He then indicated that Oscar should stay in the kitchen while he went to get someone who could speak English so they could talk.

Before the Frenchman could leave, a woman and a teenage girl arrived at the house. As far as Oscar could tell, they were the farmer's wife and daughter. Probably because he was a stranger and the two ladies were either frightened or, at least, ill at ease, neither responded to Coen when he attempted to talk with them. And although Oscar thought there was a chance that the farmer might be going to get the Germans or the French police, he reasoned that the man would hardly leave his wife and daughter alone in the house with him if that was the case. Hoping that it would all work out, he waited.

About thirty minutes later, the farmer returned with a tall, thin woman who looked to be in her early forties. She was able to speak a reasonable amount of English and identified herself as the local schoolteacher. As the questioning began, Oscar remembered the admonition to give truthful answers because this might be the information the French relayed to the underground. The first question the farmer asked, after the teacher established that Coen was indeed an American flying for the RAF, was what President Roosevelt and the American people thought of the French for having given up so rapidly to the Germans. Oscar thought this was a logical question in October 1941 but didn't know how to answer it. He just said that he knew the French had had a difficult time with the Germans and that the United States had always seen France as one of its great friends in Europe. Fortunately, his answer seemed to satisfy his questioners. It was apparently easy for the farmer and his family to understand Coen's flying for the RAF since many French pilots had gone to England and were doing the same. Coen tried to keep his answers simple and did not go into detail as to why he'd joined the RAF since he thought the idea of an American going to Canada to fly for the British could easily confuse everyone.

Coen's ability to concentrate on the labored conversation was impeded by hunger pangs and the smell of cooking. After what seemed like an eternity, the schoolteacher exclaimed, "Oh, you must be hungry." He acknowledged that he was and expected that everyone would sit down and shortly have dinner. He was shocked when the lady of the house gave him a bowl of potatoes from the pot that had been cooking on the stove and the farmer went into the pantry and came back with a piece of ham he had carved from the family's precious supply. He also brought a glass of red wine. Oscar felt very self-conscious as the entire group sat and watched him eat, since he was sure he was eating their dinner. Still, he thought it was an important part of supporting the war to them, and he was famished, so he ate enough to look good but tried to leave as much as he could for the family. He was sure that they would divide up what was left and probably go to bed hungry.

After Coen ate, the teacher said that she might know someone who could help him. She told him to wait in the house and then departed into the October twilight. After a few minutes of silence, the daughter spoke hesitantly to Oscar in very basic English. He was surprised, for she had said nothing during the previous conversation, and he had assumed that she did not speak or understand English. She first wanted to know about his home in the United States. He told her that he was from Illinois, which she immediately associated with Chicago. She was surprised to learn that he had been a schoolteacher before he decided to try flying, because his youthful appearance belied his age. Apparently the girl had noticed his slight limp, probably brought on by the stiffening of his ankles from his having sat so long, and asked him if he was all right. Although he had initially thought he could make it without any treatment for his sore legs, the past couple of hours had made his ankles swell against his boots, and they were indeed bothering him. "I'm fine," he told the girl, thanking her again for the dinner, "but my ankles seem to be swelling and they are sore." The farmer's wife motioned that he should take off his boots, and through the daughter's hesitant translation, he told them how he had hurt his ankles in the landing after bailing out of his stricken Spitfire.

Another potential crisis came as he pulled off his right boot: his pistol, which he had stuck in the top of that boot after he landed to try to keep it hidden, fell to the floor. Amazingly, none of the family seemed at all surprised. The farmer explained, through his daughter, that Oscar should give him the gun since he would know what to do with it and that Oscar should not be caught with a gun by either the Germans or most Frenchmen. Coen hesitated as he looked the Frenchman in the eyes. Then, in the ultimate test of confidence in his new benefactors, he gave up the weapon. He was now completely committed to them and whatever they wanted to do with him.

The farmer and his family had thus far shown none of the apprehension about helping that Coen had been told by his instructor to expect. It appeared to him that their attitude, and the poster of the flags they had hanging in their living room, demonstrated that they not only didn't fear the Germans but even had contempt for them.

As the farmer's wife was looking after Oscar's ankles, rubbing them a bit and binding them with some strips of cloth, the schoolteacher returned. She stayed only a minute, telling Coen that he would be moving outside to the haystack and someone would come by for him by morning. After helping him get his boots back on, the farmer led the young flier into the night behind the barn to the haystack that Coen had seen earlier from the road. He indicated that Coen should remain out of sight and wait for his next contact. Confident that the French were committed to helping him, an exhausted Coen snuggled into the warm hay and promptly went to sleep.

A few hours later, he was abruptly awakened by someone scratching around in the hay. Not knowing what else to do, the panicked Coen just remained quiet to see what would happen. If it was the Germans, he thought, they might just poke around a bit and then go away. When it became apparent that whoever was there was not going to give up, Coen took a deep breath, pushed back the hay, and quietly said "Over here." A man appeared and motioned Coen to get out of the haystack and follow a short distance behind him as he slowly rode his bicycle. At first, it was hard for Coen to walk fast enough on his sore ankles to keep up, but after a few hundred yards, he began to feel better.

After traveling for about fifteen minutes, they came to a small, dark village that Coen assumed was the source of the church bells he had heard the preceding evening. His mysterious guide stopped and went to the door of a house. He knocked, indicated to Coen that he should remain there, and rode away on his bike. No sooner was his escort swallowed up in the night than an elderly woman came to the door and motioned Coen to come into the house. He was very surprised that, rather than being in her nightclothes, she was dressed and obviously expecting him. She motioned to him to follow her to a second-floor bedroom, where she gave him some soap and a towel, showed him the bathroom, and left. He promptly washed his face, took a big drink of water, took off his outer clothes and his boots, climbed into bed, and, marveling at his good fortune and the dedication of the French to help him, went to sleep.

Just as it was getting light, Coen awoke with a start. Initially disoriented, he sat up in panic. The lady was sitting beside his bed, talking to him in French. He wondered if he had been talking in his sleep or had done something else to cause the lady to be concerned. But she was not at all flustered. In very halting English, she told him he was in the small village of Lumbres, offered him a drink of water, and indicated that he should try to sleep some more.

A much more rested, but famished, Coen awoke about midmorning and hobbled downstairs. He discovered that there was a petite woman who looked to be in her forties also living in the house. She could speak a little English and told Oscar she was the daughter of his hostess. Her husband, a French army officer, was a prisoner of the Germans. Upon hearing this, Coen was confident that he was with another family dedicated to his safety. After a breakfast of coffee, bread, and a little cheese, the women wanted to talk with him. Being a naturally outgoing person, he was excited at the prospect. He found that both women were able to read and write English very well, so the easiest means of communication was written notes, which were promptly burned when each paper was full. They began by asking what the Americans thought about the war and when the United States would enter, but the topics rapidly became more personal.

They asked about his family, why he was in the RAF, what experiences he'd had before being forced to bail out, and just about every other question one could think of. In response, he told them that he had a college degree and that during the course of his college experience he had taken two years of ROTC training. Because of his youthful appearance, the two ladies, like the schoolteacher, found it hard to believe that he had been a high school agriculture teacher in Thompson, Illinois, but he soon convinced them. He told them that he had always wanted to fly, so when it looked like war was coming to Europe, he had enlisted in the

Army Aviation Cadet program. When he arrived at Randolph Field in Texas for advanced training, he was in part of the class that was picked to train as navigators rather than pilots. Coen wanted to be a pilot or nothing at all, so he was allowed to resign from the cadet program, he went to Canada, and he joined the Royal Canadian Air Force. After completing that training, he was assigned to instructor duty in Canada but, not wanting to spend the war there, went directly to the RCAF Headquarters in Ottawa and applied for a transfer to the RAF as a fighter pilot. He passed the required flight check with flying colors and soon found himself in Halifax ready to transit the hazardous North Atlantic.

It took half the first day to write all of this information for the inquisitive ladies, and Oscar thought that would certainly satisfy their curiosity. Such was not the case, however, and after a lunch of bread, cheese, and wine, he was back writing notes again. The two were fascinated with the account of his crossing the Atlantic on a Dutch cruise ship that was making its last voyage before being converted into a troop carrier. He told them about the Asian waiters, the piano bar that was almost always open, and all the other accommodations. They were most interested in accounts of the high-spirited Australian fliers who were also on the voyage. Aside from being able to drink seemingly endless quantities of beer, the Aussies almost always had a new card game every day.

In January 1941, Coen had arrived in Glasgow, Scotland, and promptly made the train trip to London, where he was outfitted with the uniform of a Pilot Officer in the RAF. In a matter of days, he was assigned to the operational training unit at Sutton Bridge, flying Hurricanes. It was at Sutton Bridge that Coen, along with two other Americans, was picked to become a member of the relatively new Number 71 Squadron of Fighter Command, the Eagle Squadron. Both women were quite impressed with his account of changing from the Hurricane to the Spitfire and the mission on which he had been forced to leave his aircraft. Still, he wondered why they were prying so much into his background.

When there was a lull in the questioning, Oscar decided he would try to learn some French from the ladies. He found that he was not very good at it, and although he worked at it all during his time in France, he never really got very proficient. He was also allowed to wander about the house but was cautioned to not look out of the windows. He was encouraged to go outside, into an area behind the house that was surrounded by a high brick fence, where he could walk and get a little exercise. Although he welcomed the fresh air, he always felt more comfortable and secure when he was inside the house. The house was very similar to the farmhouse he had just left. On the main floor was the living room, a combination kitchen and dining area, and one bedroom. Upstairs were two bedrooms and a bathroom. It appeared to Coen that the younger lady and her husband had not been living there when he went into the army, but he never found out for sure. He remembered his instructor's admonition to not ask any questions of the French so you would not have any information about them if you were captured by the Germans. And although there was not very much food available, the ladies seemed to find enough to feed Coen adequately. During his stay in the village of Lumbres, he ate lots of potatoes, plenty of delicious bread, and at least one piece of meat each day, but no fruit.

It was a much more confident and calm Coen who went to sleep the second night. But once again, he awakened with a start sometime during the night, and once again, the older lady was sitting beside his bed. This continued for the five nights he was there, but he never figured out why, and he puzzled about it during his entire stay.

It was not long until Coen began to have visitors. The first was a photographer, who took his picture wearing typical French garb. When Coen inquired, the younger lady told him it was for his identification card. This brought the questioning on his first day in Lumbres all into focus as he realized the women were finding out as much as possible about him so the underground could verify who he was. It all fit into place.

One of his most interesting visitors was a tall, well-dressed, red-headed woman who stopped by during his second day in Lumbres. It turned out that she was a cousin of Charles de Gaulle, the leader of Free France in exile in the United Kingdom. She talked a bit about the family and asked Coen to relay that they were all well to de Gaulle when he got back to England.

After de Gaulle's cousin departed, the younger lady brought him her husband's razor and a few extra blades and told him that he would have to shave every day. Young men eighteen and older had to be in the army, she told him, and since Coen looked like a teenager, she thought he would not arouse suspicion. She also told him how to bleach and scrub the first and second fingers of his right hand so the nicotine stains from his heavy smoking habit would be removed. Coen was instructed on the French way to take a cigarette out of his mouth using his thumb and first finger.

All this preparation became worthwhile the next day when the photographer brought Coen's identification card. It was official down to the proper German stamps, which, the ladies told him, had been duplicated from the original. A member of the resistance had stolen the original seal from the office where she worked so it could be copied. Coen's name was now Victor Thomas, and he was a Flemish laborer. He was not told why they picked that name, but the ladies did inform him that Flemish was the best nationality for him since he didn't speak either French or German and few Frenchmen or Germans could speak or understand Flemish. They told him that he would have no trouble, but if he did, he could always play that he was deaf and dumb. As part of getting his new identity, Coen's RAF identification card was burned. And although he was concerned that he now had no way to prove his real identity, he was relieved that the Germans would not assume he was Jewish if they did capture him. He had been bothered about his last name ever since he began to fly combat missions, for he had no way of proving that his family name was German rather than Jewish. The photographer also brought the news that Coen would be leaving the next day to begin his move toward freedom. The older lady had spent a lot of time treating his ankles with alternating hot and cold cloths, so he could now walk much more comfortably with no sign of a limp.

That evening the ladies, whose names he never learned, put on a special meal featuring what they said was roast rabbit. Coen enjoyed the meal with his new friends, and they drank a toast to their mutual health and success, his safe return to England, and the defeat of Germany. They also gave him a St. Christopher medal to wear, and although he was not Catholic, he wore the medal throughout his ordeal. It was only after he went to his room that Coen realized that the cat, which had been sitting on the window ledge most of the time, had disappeared that day. But his thoughts were on the future as he lay in his bed. The next morning he would begin to move toward freedom by whatever means the underground wanted to use. Still, he could not help but think that the sacrifice of the cat showed the lengths to which the French were willing to go to help anyone who was fighting for their freedom.

Early the next morning, a van pulled up in front of the house and, after emotional good-byes from his hostesses, Oscar was hurried out and put into the back of the vehicle. There he found himself among a bunch of welding equipment. The owner, Coen was told, worked on the German base at St. Omer, so he had gasoline for his truck and the movements of the van were not questioned. Coen was not told who the other passenger in the front seat of the van was, but he was dressed in a business suit. Without any acknowledgment from the two occupants of the front seat, the van moved off. Again, as he bounced along on the floor of the van, Oscar could not help but think of the sacrifice that was being made for him. He knew that if he was captured the worst that would happen was that he would go to prison camp, but the other two occupants of the van would probably be shot. And whereas the two ladies had never seemed completely at ease with him in their house, the men in the van appeared relatively nonchalant about the whole thing as they drove down the road. Oscar reasoned that the women were not part of the underground, and since one woman was a widow and her daughter's husband was in a German prison camp, any man around the house would raise suspicion. He was also quite sure that they had never had a downed airman in their house before. The driver of the van and his friend, on the other hand, apparently were experienced at moving such contraband.

Just as Coen had settled down in his new surroundings and begun to think about where the van might take him, the driver slowed down, stopped, and picked up a German soldier who was hitchhiking. Oscar's heart skipped a beat as he envisioned the German getting into the back of the van with him and immediately wanting to enter into some kind of conversation or seeing something that might make him suspicious. But the soldier got into the front with the other two men and paid no attention to him. It even appeared to Oscar, from the way the driver and the soldier conversed, that they knew each other. It did not make him breathe any easier, however, when, in a few minutes, he saw the German base at St. Omer come into view. The van was driving directly to the one place in the entire world that Coen had been intent on avoiding a few days before. The old feeling of panic returned, and once again the sweat broke out on Oscar's neck as they approached the base. Coen had no idea what to do, so he just sat and sweated. The driver stopped at the front gate, let the soldier out, and turned back onto the road. As Oscar breathed a sigh of relief, he began to wonder where they were going and why the businessman was in the van.

After about an hour, they entered a small town, which Coen later found was Lillers, located about forty miles west of the city of Lille. They stopped in front of a two-story stucco building in the middle of the village. The bottom floor of the building was a restaurant, and the well-dressed man took Coen inside. Since it was about noon, Coen assumed that they were simply going to have some lunch. He was flabbergasted when he found himself in the middle of what appeared to be a party with at least twenty people in attendance. It soon became obvious to Coen that the businessman who had been in the van was the owner of the restaurant and that the party was some kind of local celebration. Although he was both ill at ease and frightened, Coen took advantage of the several kinds of cheese and bread on the table, as well as the delicious red wine. He judged it probably the nicest restaurant in the town since all the tables in the large room had white tablecloths and most of those attending the party were fairly well dressed.

Coen was soon introduced to two British soldiers who had been left behind in France when the British evacuated Dunkirk. One had found a French girlfriend and planned to stay in Lillers until the war was over. The other had been in the village for nearly a year but was trying to get back to England. He told Coen that there really wasn't any plan to get them out of France, but since Coen was a pilot and there were already two other RAF pilots in the town, the underground would have more motivation to devise such a plan. As the party progressed and people came and went, Coen found himself talking with the other two British pilots. One, George Barkley, was a flight commander who had been shot down in his Spitfire. The other, Squadron Leader Henry Bufton, had been forced to bail out of his Blenheim bomber. Oscar soon noticed that he stood out in the crowd since he was the only person not in civilian clothes. (The ladies with whom he had stayed in Lumbres did not have any clothes that would fit Coen, so he was still in his British battle jacket and pants. They had given him a pair of ill-fitting shoes since they thought his flying boots would be too obvious.) The restaurant owner had already considered the problem and accumulated some rather nice civilian clothes—a jacket, shirt, and pants—that fit him fairly well, but no shoes. (Coen didn't give any thought to changing from his uniform into civilian clothes, but the ramifications were significant. Under the rules of the Geneva Convention, a captured soldier had to be accorded humane treatment. As soon as Coen destroyed his identification card and put on civilian clothes, he ceased to be a downed airman and could be legally executed as a spy if he was captured.)

Still, the change of clothes did nothing to quell his anxiety about the situation. He thought it was ridiculous to have so many people coming and going to the restaurant and that it would only be a matter of time until some German would happen by, especially since it was by then well after noon. He finally got the proprietor aside, pointed at all the people, and tried to tell him that it was too dangerous. The Frenchman apparently thought Coen was saying he was tired and wanted to be alone, so he took him upstairs to a small bedroom. Although that was not what Oscar had had in mind, he still felt more secure out of the bustle of the party—and also thought he could hide if the need arose. The evading airman was apparently more tired than he'd thought, and while he pondered the events of the day and what might lay in store for him, he soon fell asleep.

When Coen awoke all was quiet and it was dark. Unsure of what to do, he lay in bed and dozed. He wondered why he had been brought to the restaurant but decided that maybe it was the only place where there was enough food to take care of an evader without raising suspicion. He also thought that the party had been a great cover for moving someone like himself in or out of the restaurant without attracting attention. Just at it was beginning to get light, he heard noises in the kitchen, directly below his room. He dressed and shaved, as he had been instructed, and cautiously went downstairs. He was enthusiastically greeted in the now-deserted restaurant by the owner, who set out a magnificent breakfast of eggs, ham, bread, cheese, and coffee.

A few minutes after he finished breakfast, the welder's van in which he had ridden the day before pulled up in front of the building. The restaurant owner indicated to Coen that he was being taken to where he was going to live and that there would be another pair of shoes waiting for him when he arrived. With that, Coen was hurried out and again found himself in the back of the vehicle. After driving around Lillers for a short time, the van rolled into a walled yard behind another two-story building and stopped. The driver took him into the back room of the building and immediately up two flights of stairs to a small, windowless room that had been set up in the attic. It was furnished only with a bed. Coen found a good hiding place for his few possessions, his razor and his sunglasses, putting them where the rafters went into the roof, and then sat down on his bed.

Shortly, a teenage girl appeared at the door. After greeting him in English, she led him down the stairs into a rather large kitchen. There he met Madame Blanchard and her daughter, the girl who had come for him, and was told that he was being housed above their business, a meat market that fronted on the town square. The women tried to make Coen feel welcome and set out a lunch of bread, cheese, a little ham, and a glass of water. The kitchen adjoined the meat market, which occupied the space of the living room in most houses. Madame Blanchard and her daughter seemed friendly enough but were not disposed to much conversation, and Coen decided to just be quiet and eat. After lunch, he was escorted to his room by the teenage girl and instructed to stay there until someone came to get him for supper.

As Coen sat in his ten-foot-square attic room, he could hear the sounds of the activity in the square and was curious about what was going on. He marveled that he could be hidden so well and be so close to the activity of the town. And as he sat on his bed his thoughts skipped to the risks that the Blanchards were taking in hiding him. It was

incredible to him that a family would hazard being shot, or at least having all of their property confiscated and being sent to a concentration
camp, just to help an RAF flier. The more he thought about the circumstances, the more he came to appreciate all that had been done for him
thus far. And while he assumed that he was in the hands of the underground, it was still difficult to sit still in his room and put all of those
people at risk. For the first time in his life, Coen felt completely helpless and unable to do anything to control his destiny.

The afternoon was long and boring, and Coen was glad when the
young lady again came for him and told him that he was going to meet
her father. Upon arrival in the kitchen, he was introduced to Monsieur
Blanchard, a wiry Frenchman about fifty years old, and his son, who
was about twenty. The two men had apparently known that Coen would
be there when they arrived home from work, and they did not seem
surprised to see him. The daughter explained that the two worked in a
sugar factory, a fact that became obvious to Oscar when the men opened
their lunch buckets and emptied out the sugar they had smuggled from
the factory. They divided the sugar into small containers, and periodically throughout the evening a neighbor would come by and pick up a
parcel of sugar. At first, Coen was very apprehensive and wanted to
hide, or at least sit off in a corner of the room, when the neighbors came
by, but he soon found that they didn't pay any attention to him. As he
spent more time with the Blanchards, it became obvious to him that a
number of people knew he was there anyway, and no one was giving him
a second thought.

During Coen's first evening with the Blanchards, they explained,
with their daughter translating, that he was to stay in the house or the
enclosed backyard all the time. He was not to go into the meat market
part of the building unless he was with one of the Blanchards, since
everyone knew that both the men in the household worked and he would
immediately arouse suspicion if the authorities saw him. When he was
outside, he was not to look over the fence, and if he heard or suspected
anything out of the ordinary, he was to immediately go into the house
and to his room in the attic. He surmised that most houses in the town
did not have a room in the attic, so no one would think of looking for
him there. Any search would be confined to the cozy kitchen and the
master bedroom on the main floor as well as the two bedrooms, occupied by the son and the daughter, on the second floor. It was easier for
him to accept these rules than it had been in Lumbres, because he now
realized the danger so many people were putting themselves in for his
sake. Thus, Coen was surprised when, just as it was getting dark, Mrs.

Blanchard told him that he could go for a walk in the square if he wanted. Her only caution was that he not talk to anyone, and if he suspected a problem, he was not to come back to the house until he was sure it was safe.

Oscar was certainly not ready to go out the first evening he was in Lillers, but after spending a day sitting in the Blanchards' house, he ventured out the second evening. Although his main concern was German soldiers, he saw none, and he soon began to enjoy the quaint French town. The first thing he noticed, as he walked out onto the cobblestone street, was that there were very few people moving about. Strange, he thought, for the town square. The buildings were just as he had imagined they would be: stone, brick, or stucco; two stories, well kept, fronting on all four sides of the square. Most, it appeared, had businesses on the ground floor and living areas above. He was also impressed with the cleanliness of the streets. Coen repeated this walk nearly every night he was with the Blanchards; fortunately, he never saw a single German.

As he talked more with the Blanchards, still using their daughter to interpret, he found that the meat market had been a thriving business before the German invasion. As the war dragged on, there was less and less meat available, which had forced both Monsieur Blanchard and his son to go to work in the sugar factory. Any meat that did become available had to be distributed quietly, or the Germans would take it away in a flash.

Coen became a butcher himself on his fourth day at the meat market. A man brought a calf into the enclosed backyard. Its legs were tied together and its mouth was tied shut so it could not make any noise. Madame Blanchard was out getting bread and visiting the neighbors, so it fell to Oscar and the daughter to butcher the calf. When they were finished, the young lady had Coen bury the head, hide, entrails, and other nonedible parts in the backyard, whereas the rest of the animal was taken into the meat market and was divided for the neighbors. The Blanchards kept a portion for themselves. Soon, the same neighbors who periodically came for sugar began to arrive to buy meat, and within a couple of hours the entire calf had disappeared. Oscar was sure that the Blanchards welcomed and needed the meat, especially with an extra mouth to feed, for it soon became obvious that food was hard to get. Unlike the owner of the restaurant, who had given Oscar a huge breakfast, the Blanchards offered a bowl of porridge, some bread, coffee, and an occasional egg as the usual breakfast fare. Lunch and dinner were generally potatoes, bread, and maybe a little ham, unless an animal had been freshly butchered. Again, in contrast to the restaurant, the Blanchards had very little wine, an occasional glass with dinner at the most, and generally drank water or coffee with their meals.

Whenever anyone came to the meat market, the Blanchards made sure that Coen was not seen if it could be avoided. If he was noticed, he was not introduced, nor was any attention paid to him. Initially, this struck Oscar as odd, given the party he had been involved in when he'd arrived in Lillers. But as the days went by, he realized that the restaurant owner had evaders for only a day or two and that the group of people at the party were very familiar with that business. The Blanchards, on the other hand, were committed to keeping Coen until some arrangement could be made to get him out of the country, which could be weeks, and the people who might come to the meat market were not all necessarily enthusiastic about having an American flier in their midst. The Blanchards were also extra cautious because Coen was the first Allied airman they had kept and they realized the risk was tremendous.

As the days passed, Oscar came to feel very much at home with the Blanchards and quite comfortable with his surroundings. However, his complacency was shattered and his knees turned to jelly one morning as he was sitting alone in the kitchen. A strange man walked into the room without knocking, a tactic he had heard the Germans often used. The man did not acknowledge Coen, but simply went over to the stove and poured himself a cup of coffee, as did most other visitors to the house. Oscar knew that the man had to be familiar with the house, but still, who was he and what did he want? After a few minutes of saying nothing but simply sitting and looking at one another, Oscar felt he had to do something, for this was no ordinary visitor. Trying to appear non-chalant, he went to the stove and got the coffeepot, walked over, and gave the stranger a refill. On the way back across the room to the stove, he was able to detour past the door that opened into the meat market, where Madame Blanchard was working. Fortunately for Coen, she saw him, and he discretely motioned to her with his head to come back to the kitchen.

Oscar's apprehension was not relieved until Madame Blanchard recognized the stranger and introduced him to Coen simply as Paul, a British agent charged with getting groups of evaders to Marseilles, in southern France. Coen could have guessed Paul was British, given his blond hair, rather long face with a large, pointed nose, and somewhat crooked teeth. (Members of the underground were never referred to by other than a first name, which was generally fictitious anyway. The evader was instructed to never ask for a full name or to make any note of even the first name of a contact. This way, if either an underground member or an evader was captured and tortured, he or she could not compromise the entire system by giving the Germans the names of the participants. Marseilles was in Vichy, or unoccupied France, and at the time housed many evaders, refugees, and others attempting to stay out of the hands of Nazi Germany.)

"Why did you scare the hell out of me? You could have at least said something rather than let me sit here and shake in my boots," Coen blurted out.

"I just wanted to see what your reaction would be," was the reply.

"Did I pass the test?" Coen asked, suppressing his desire to punch the guy in the nose.

"Very well," replied Paul. "I needed to see if you would panic or use good sense in the situation."

In the ensuing discussion, Paul told Coen that he would probably meet his helpers, a Frenchman named Roland and a Frenchwoman named Suzanne, after the journey began. In the meantime, Coen was to be patient and wait for Paul to contact him—in a week or so, if all went well.

Oscar was elated, and for the first time since being shot down, he found himself humming a tune as he sat in his small room that night. Two days later, a light-complected man of average height showed up with Flight Lieutenant Barkley and Squadron Leader Bufton, the two British fliers Coen had met at the party at the restaurant. The man turned out to be the Frenchman Roland. Although it appeared on the surface that the purpose of the visit was for Coen to get to know the two RAF officers better, as the conversation developed Oscar was quite sure that it was really the final effort to ensure that he was not a German infiltrator. In the course of the conversation, the two talked with Coen about flying, his training, where he had been stationed, and some of the pilots they all three might know. The fact that the three had several mutual friends ensured in everyone's mind that all were legitimate. When the meeting was over, Roland again told Oscar to be patient. Things were slowly coming together, and they should be moving in another few days.

True to his word, about three days later Roland stopped by the meat market to tell Coen that they would be going the next day. Coen was to practice saying "A ticket to Abbeville, please" in French until his hosts were confident he would not give away his nationality by his accent. Roland also told Coen that there would be seven people in his group. In addition to Coen, Barkley, and Bufton, there would be the two sergeant pilots that Coen had met at the party in the restaurant, a Belgian pilot, and a Belgian poet. Roland told Coen that the seven would seldom be together, but they would all be on the same train.

In order to not arouse suspicion, each of the evaders was to buy his ticket at a different time and each was instructed to sit in a different compartment on the train. All the new French money that had been in Coen's survival kit had been exchanged for old money by the underground, and Coen had been instructed on the exact amount to give the ticket agent so that he would get change. The underground made a practice of getting rid of the new money that was in pilots' escape kits because it would attract attention too easily.

After an emotional farewell to the Blanchards, Oscar, with a knot in his stomach and shaking knees, went, by himself, to the ticket window at the station in Lillers and asked for his ticket to Abbeville. The operation went smoothly, and Coen found himself on the train, seated in a compartment with four other people, none of whom he knew. He had been given a book and told to act as if he was so deeply engrossed in reading that no one would try to engage him in conversation, but Oscar was so apprehensive that any word from one of the other occupants of the compartment made him jump. Roland had reassured him by telling him that there would be someone nearby to help out if there was a problem and also to tell him when to get off the train since he could not read French with any reliability. The first test came a short while after the journey began when the conductor came by to check the passengers' tickets. "Just keep acting like you're reading your book when you hand the conductor your ticket and he won't bother you," Madame Blanchard had said before Oscar left the meat market. That proved to be good advice, and so Coen sat in the compartment, pretending to read, ignored by the other occupants, and waited apprehensively for the next phase of the plan to unfold.

All the members of the party had been briefed that they would have to get off the train and walk across the bridge spanning the Somme River, which separated the Abbeville restricted area from the surrounding countryside. They had also been told that this was the most dangerous part of the journey and were warned to be very careful. As the train slowed, then crept onto a siding, and everyone prepared to get out, Coen's heart began to pound and he began to sweat. Once again, he was facing a situation over which he had no control. He just had to do what he had been told and hope for the best. One false move and his freedom was gone for the rest of the war, or he could be shot as a spy!

The sight that greeted Coen when he alighted from the train reinforced his anxiety. The occupants had already begun to line up to walk across the old stone road bridge, nearly a city block long, and show their papers to the German guard posted at the top of the curved structure. Oscar had no idea how to even begin to get across or what papers to show the guard. Trying to remain calm, he looked anxiously around for a friendly face and soon spied Roland, who gestured with his head for Coen to follow him. But rather than going to the bridge, Roland led the bewildered Coen to a house a short distance down a side street. When they entered the apparently deserted structure, Oscar expected to find the other members of his group, but he was by himself. Any concern for the others vanished as the complexity and planning that had gone into the operation became apparent. First, Coen was introduced to Suzanne, a pretty, petite blonde who appeared to be about nineteen years old. Roland then explained the plan.

Coen was given papers that identified him as a lay priest with permission to pass freely into and out of the restricted area because of the nature of his work. The plan was that he would use the priest's identification to cross the bridge and that Suzanne, who had her own papers, would precede him. There were two underground members posted as lookouts at each end of the bridge to see if the guard looked closely at the papers. If he did not, Suzanne was to get them from Coen, bring them back across the river, and they would be used by another evader, who was hidden somewhere else, to cross. Although the plan sounded good, Coen was cautioned that if anything went wrong he was on his own. With that Suzanne left and walked toward the bridge.

After waiting a few minutes, Coen and Roland set out on the most critical part of the journey thus far. Coen could not help but wish he was back in the security of the Blanchard home. He tried, unsuccessfully, to keep his knees from shaking and the sweat from showing on the brisk day as they walked back toward the main street. Roland stayed with him only until they were in sight of the bridge, and then, suddenly, he was on his own. The bridge looked like it was a mile across to the frightened American as he began the climb to the middle. He noticed that the arch of the bridge was greater than he had thought and that he would be at least thirty feet above the water when he reached the guard. If anything went wrong, he had absolutely no place to go and no avenue of escape. For the first time in his evasion experience, he had no options at all.

As Coen approached the top of the bridge and the guard post, a horse-drawn wagon loaded with hay pulled up beside him. He immediately slowed down so the wagon would get to the guard post first and he could see just what the procedure was. What he saw encouraged him. The guard simply glanced at the wagon driver's papers, poked his bayonet into the hay to ensure that there was no contraband being hidden in the wagon, and waved the driver on. Coen was next. He pulled out his pass and gave it to the guard. The German simply said "*Danke schön*," glanced at the pass, gave it back, and motioned him on across the bridge. Relief flooded Coen's entire body as he heaved a big sigh and, suppressing the desire to run, walked briskly down the other side of the bridge. The first major hurdle of his trip to freedom had been successfully crossed. (Over the course of several months, a large number of evaders crossed the bridge at Abbeville using the priest's identification. Coen found out several years later that someone was eventually stopped, and the papers were confiscated. The Germans were easily able to find the priest, and he was shot for helping the evaders.)

Coen's instructions were to turn right after crossing the bridge and just continue to walk. He had not been out of sight of the bridge for more than thirty or forty feet when Suzanne stepped out of a doorway and began to walk beside him. He gave her the pass. She told him to continue on for two more blocks and go into a restaurant he would find on the corner. She then turned down a side street and disappeared. His feeling of well-being was short-lived, for when he arrived outside the restaurant he did not see anyone he knew. He entered, as instructed, and sat down amid some of the other customers. He thought it strange that no waiter came to take his order, but he was relieved at the same time, for he did not relish the thought of having to order something in French when the waiter approached him. After what seemed like an hour, but was really only about ten minutes, Paul, the British agent who had come to the Blanchards' meat market many days earlier, arrived, and soon the entire group had assembled in the restaurant. By this time, Oscar was so impressed with the way the underground was moving the group that he was not surprised at the absence of a waiter and no sign of anyone in charge of the establishment. For the first time since he had left the meat market in Lillers, he felt confident that the plan would succeed.

Still, Coen could sense that the underground members were very uncomfortable with the situation, and as soon as the entire group was accounted for, Paul told them that Abbeville was much too dangerous a place to be and that they would have to get away from the town as rapidly as possible. As the group soon found out, that meant walking. Oscar was surprised at the size of the group of which he was a part. Eventually, seventeen people, rather than the previously mentioned seven, assembled in the restaurant. Each of them had made his way there by a different route and means from somewhere in occupied France. There were no introductions and no chances to get to know others in the group, for as rapidly as they had assembled, the evaders were lead away, one by one, through the streets of Abbeville. And although Coen didn't know his guide, he dutifully followed as they walked down crooked streets and through mazes of homes in their trek out of town. As dusk began to fall, the group was reassembled in a deserted field and the serious walk began—a walk that lasted all night. Their goal was a small town about twenty miles from Abbeville where they could get a train that would take them to Paris. At about three o'clock in the morning, the exhausted group stopped at a large barn near a little milk train stop to get a few hours of sleep before beginning their next move.

Shortly after dawn, Coen was awakened by another stranger and, with two other members of the group, was taken to the tiny hut that served as a train station. Again, he bought his own ticket and, after a short wait, boarded the train for Paris. Because there were few people on the train, he had no trouble finding a seat by George Barkley where he could pull out his book and pretend to read during the trip.

The journey was uneventful until Barkley fell asleep with his legs sticking out into the narrow aisle. A short time later, a woman, her arms loaded with parcels, wanted to pass, so Coen gave Barkley a nudge. He awoke with a start, apparently thinking it was the conductor who was nudging him, stood up straight and tall, and said "I beg your pardon, sir" while producing his ticket. The pair immediately attracted considerable attention because of Barkley's use of English, so Coen and Barkley got off at the next stop. Fortunately, they still had their tickets and there was another train for Paris in a few minutes. The two were soon on their way again.

For the evaders, the biggest boost in their confidence came with their arrival in Paris. Both Coen and Barkley had a more nonchalant attitude as they emerged into the streets and became part of the ever-changing scene that is any big city. And while Oscar marveled at the beautiful buildings and the wide boulevards, he was also relieved to see few German soldiers among the crowds on the streets. There was little traffic, but he paid particular attention to the occasional German staff car that drove by. Those Germans he saw were obviously concerned with what they were doing and, Oscar thought, not very interested in whether he was evading or not. Being British, Barkley had been to Paris several times and knew both the city and the French language fairly well. He led the way to a restaurant, where he ordered for both of them. Oscar was very uneasy while they were eating and had the feeling that the waiter knew they weren't French. He was relieved when they finished eating and again emerged onto the street. Fortunately, Barkley was able to find the place where they were to stay.

The pair were told that the door at their destination would be unlocked. When they arrived at the designated address, they found themselves in a flat that evidently belonged to an artist, for down one wall were several racks of drawings and paintings in various stages of completion. They had also been told that the owner would not be there, and they never met him—nor were they ever told who he was. After they were secure in their lodging, Barkley, who had apparently been given a fairly complete briefing about their travel plans, told Coen that they would be going by train to Tours the following day. He did not tell Coen why they were going to that city, and Oscar decided it would be best not to press him for more information.

Early the next morning, the pair left the artist's flat for the train station. En route, they stopped for a typical French breakfast of bread and coffee, and upon arrival at the station, Barkley bought two tickets for Tours. Although the train was fairly crowded, the two evaders again began to "read." The trip proved to be uneventful, but Oscar was not able to relax, for at each city the people in his compartment would change, and he was always fearful that one might be a German soldier or official who would find out his identity.

As soon as they arrived in Tours, Barkley and Coen went directly to a restaurant where the entire group, which had last been all together in Abbeville, was reunited. As soon as they were finished with their lunch, Suzanne, Coen's guide at Abbeville, told him that she was to be his escort to Marseilles. Since the members of the group left the restaurant at different times and with various guides, it was apparent that each evader was again traveling by himself or, at the most, in a group of two or three. A few hours after leaving Tours, just at dusk, the train crossed from occupied France into Vichy France, that portion of the country not yet occupied by the Germans. Finally, Oscar could breathe a sigh of relief, and apparently Suzanne did also, for she sat beside him for the remainder of the journey into Marseilles. Not only did Oscar not have to worry about the Germans now, but he also had an attractive young lady as a traveling companion. Unfortunately, the two could not converse in English because that would have aroused the suspicion of the others in the compartment. So, although Oscar was bursting with questions, he simply had to continue to "read" his book and occasionally doze through the long night as the train trundled toward its destination. As he looked at Suzanne, he thought again of the tremendous risk assumed by each of the underground members who had gotten him out of occupied France. And while he marveled at their spirit, especially Suzanne's, his mind dwelled on the character of each of those who were on the trip.

Oscar hadn't really trusted Paul from the start. He hadn't liked the way Paul had burst into the kitchen at the meat market that first day, or his aloof nature. Barkley had told Coen that he also didn't trust Paul. As the pair observed the three underground agents who were their escorts when the trek got under way, it appeared that neither Roland nor Suzanne liked Paul, either. He was often gone for long periods of time with no explanation of where he had been, and when he returned to the group, Roland and Suzanne watched him very closely. Still, he was obviously in charge, and the others abided by his decisions. Roland was an outgoing chap, but he seemed to be just learning all of the intricacies of moving evaders through the country. He was often nervous and never made any decisions without consulting Paul. Suzanne was the favorite of everyone in the group. She was always happy, outgoing, and considerate, and instilled confidence in the entire group with her positive attitude and optimism. Oscar felt very lucky to have her escorting him on his journey to Marseilles. During one of the few short conversations they were able to have when they were alone in the compartment, he learned that she had a Polish father, who had been either killed or put in prison by the Germans, and an English mother. Suzanne had grown up in France.

The following morning, as Oscar gazed at the French countryside drifting by, he also continued to wonder what would happen to him when he arrived in Marseilles. He had no idea how he was to get out of the country. The only logical solution was a boat, and he couldn't figure out where such a vessel would come from or how it would make it through the Mediterranean, since the Germans controlled the entire sea. The thought of going over the Pyrenees never even entered his mind because he didn't think they could be crossed on foot in late November. Oscar's frustration with these questions was only heightened by having Suzanne next to him and not being able to ask her. Given the compartmentalized nature of the underground, Suzanne probably did not know the plan, either. Her job was simply to get him to Marseilles; someone else would take him farther.

It was early afternoon when the train arrived in Marseilles. The first order of business was to find a place for lunch. Suzanne picked a bistro on a side street not far from the station. Much to Oscar's relief, they were the only two patrons. Suzanne then led him to the area of the old harbor, where there were several shops and a small amusement park.

Probably because of the time of day and the cool November weather, there were relatively few people around. As they walked through the streets and past the multistoried stone buildings in the area surrounding the harbor, Oscar began again to think that they were proceeding to a rendezvous with a boat that would take him to Spain. He was absolutely stunned when, as they came to the street that bordered the harbor, Suzanne told him that someone would meet him soon, kissed him on both cheeks, said "Good-bye," and departed.

Oscar was devastated as he waited in the carnival area where Suzanne had left him. Not only had the attractive young lady, whose company he had come to enjoy, departed, but also no one appeared to help him. He then decided that something must have gone wrong with the plan and that he was on his own. "At least I'm better off than I was when I was in occupied France," Oscar thought. He wandered down to an area of the harbor a block or so away that appeared to be the pier for private boats. In the back of his mind, he thought he might find someone in one of the boats who would take him to Spain. He soon decided that it was unlikely he could find someone to undertake the twenty-four-hour round-trip through German-infested waters, and he didn't have enough money to pay for such a trip anyway, so he abandoned the idea. His concern heightened as the sun began to sink in the west. All the large buildings surrounding the harbor looked nearly alike, and he had no idea where to go or what to do next. Still, he maintained a faint hope that the underground would get to him, because he was sure that Suzanne would not have left him if a contact had not been arranged.

After Coen had wandered about for nearly an hour and a half, a rather distinguished-looking gentleman strolled out to where he was and simply said, in English, "My name is Nouveau, are you Oscar Coen?" Oscar was flabbergasted but managed to give a relieved reply, and the two set off for the gentleman's flat. "I'll never again underestimate the underground," thought Oscar as they climbed the stairs to the harborside apartment. On the way, Monsieur Nouveau told Coen that he had been watching him since Suzanne left and was just waiting for the right time to contact him without raising any suspicion. But Coen had another surprise awaiting him, for when he walked into the flat, he was given a guest book and was asked to sign in. As Coen looked at the thirty or forty names ahead of his in the book, two of which he recognized, he realized that this was indeed a big operation and that there had to be very specific plans for what he was to do next.

After a very good dinner, complemented by wine, Coen and Monsieur Nouveau sat and talked for several hours. Coen found out that his host had relatives in Los Angeles, and Nouveau asked Coen to look them up and say hello. He told Coen that all the members of his group had arrived safely in Marseilles and were being housed in various areas of the city. Nouveau also confirmed that they were suspicious of Paul and suspected that he might be stealing some of the underground's money. During the course of the evening, Coen suggested to Monsieur Nouveau that he might be able to get out of France simply by going through the American Embassy in Marseilles. His host immediately told him no. When Coen pressed Monsieur Nouveau a bit on the subject, he found out that several people had approached the embassy for help, only to be turned away and then arrested. Nouveau believed that the embassy was working closely with the Vichy government on several very important international issues and that trying to get military personnel out of France simply complicated matters. Coen also mentioned trying to go to Portugal, particularly since there was a fairly universal fear that Germany might occupy Vichy France at any time. But to that suggestion, Monsieur Nouveau simply said "No good, no good." Oscar soon realized that the trip from Paris, the dinner wine, and the stress of the past few days had taken their toll, and he could no longer stay awake. After being shown his bedroom, Coen was soon asleep.

The following morning, during breakfast, a stranger arrived and Monsieur Nouveau told Coen that this man would take him to the city of Nîmes, about seventy-five miles northwest of Marseilles. Although his driver spoke only a little English, Coen was able to determine that he was going to the area of the ancient coliseum, commonly called the bull ring, in Nîmes. He spent the trip through the rolling, scenic countryside of southern Provence trying to figure out why his destination was Nîmes. After all, that city was miles from the sea. How could he get to Spain from there? His attention was often diverted by a farmer doing his final harvest of corn or by someone in a vineyard preparing for the coming grape harvest. He even caught a glimpse of the ancient Roman coliseum in Arles and wondered if it was similar to the structure that was their destination in Nîmes. As they entered that city, Oscar was impressed by the beautiful tree-lined boulevard that led to the ancient bull ring. True to his word, the driver pulled up to the curb on a narrow street lined with old stone houses near the back of the bull ring and indicated that Coen was to get out. As Coen stood on the curb watching the car pull rapidly away, he was greeted by a very pleasant, rather dark-complected Frenchman who instructed him, in excellent English, to follow him. Near the bull ring, his guide opened a door beside one of the buildings, and Coen found himself on a stairway that led to a fairly large, well-furnished apartment. They were greeted by a middle-aged woman whom his host introduced as his housekeeper.

To Oscar's continuing amazement, rather than taking him to his room or showing him where he was to live, his host immediately took him to the room of which he was the most proud—his wine cellar. A sample was in order, and it was quite some time before the now relaxed Coen was shown his room. Again, to his surprise, the housekeeper brought him some pajamas, the first he had seen since he left England, some other fresh items of clothing, and a few toilet articles.

After a couple of hours of sleep, Coen was awakened for dinner. It wasn't until he sat down with the man who owned the apartment that he realized he had not eaten since he left Marseilles. The dinner was, as were all the meals during his stay in Nîmes, excellent, with various meats and sauces complemented by different wines. After eating, Coen and his host again retired to the wine cellar, where they spent the evening talking. During their conversation, Coen found out that his host had been to the United States on several occasions. He was very proud of a picture of himself on a motorcycle in Chicago. The good food and variety of wines were available because Coen's host was a smuggler who moved goods between France and Spain. Thus, he was able to get about anything he wanted. But the biggest bombshell to Coen was his host's announcement that he and the rest of his group would be hiking over the Pyrenees Mountains into Spain. Coen was naturally full of questions. His host was not ready to give out any information about the route or timing, so the conversation turned to other subjects.

The following evening, Coen's host suggested that they go to some of the taverns in the old quarter of Nîmes. Since they were in unoccupied France, Oscar felt reasonably safe going out, but Suzanne had cautioned him that there were a number of German agents and sympathizers about, so he still had to be careful. His host, however, assured him that there would be no problem, and away they went into the narrow stone streets lined with old two- and three-story stone and stucco houses, a variety of shops and restaurants, and several bars. At the first stop, Coen's host ordered absinthe, which Coen had never heard of. When the waiter asked Coen what he wanted, he replied, "The same." His host immediately chimed in with "Not for you, not for you," and changed the order to beer, explaining that absinthe was a very powerful drink that he was afraid Coen couldn't handle.

At one of the first taverns they visited, Coen's companion got into a long conversation with one of his friends. Bored, Oscar blew a couple of smoke rings and watched them float out over the table. His host immediately took him by the arm and stood up with a rather gruff "We have to get out of here." Once they were on the street, Coen asked about their sudden departure. "People here do not know how to blow smoke rings," was the reply, "and they will ask you to blow more. You won't understand what they are saying and then we will have big trouble."

As the pair walked about the city, Oscar marveled at the almost complete lack of any signs of the war. There were no soldiers about and no military activity of any sort. He was particularly impressed by the ancient Roman amphitheater, temple, and other ruins. The people were even happy and appeared little concerned with the war, in sharp contrast to those he had seen in northern France.

After a few hours of going from tavern to tavern, Oscar began to worry that they would attract too much attention, given his host's condition, and that he would not be able to find his way back to the apartment of his hard-drinking companion. Fortunately, the man could hold his liquor very well, and he never got so drunk that he was a problem. Still, the ritual went on every evening of the week that Coen stayed in Nîmes. Whether his host followed that procedure when he had no guest, Oscar didn't know, but the man mentioned several times that it was so special to have an American staying with him that Oscar thought he was just trying to be a good host.

During the course of their many conversations, as they walked about town or sat in the wine cellar, Oscar discovered that the other members of his party were staying in various towns and houses in the area, waiting for the details of their trek across the mountains to be finalized. His host confided in him that it would be one of his men who would lead the group over the Pyrenees. "The trick of getting across the mountains anytime, and especially in the winter, is knowing the trails, passes, and where the Spanish authorities are located," his host told him. "My men are the best there are, and they will be able to get everyone safely into Spain." Oscar could only hope that these claims were more than just idle boasting.

Early one morning in mid-November, Coen was awakened by his host, who told him that it was time to leave for Spain. After a hurried breakfast, Coen and his benefactor got into a car with another man, whom Coen had never seen before. As they drove south, Oscar could see the Pyrenees looming ever larger in front of him and to his right, and the ocean glistening in the early morning sunlight to his left. After driving south for nearly three hours, they passed through the port of Perpignan and immediately entered the foothills. Several miles later his host pulled off the narrow dirt road and told Coen they had driven as far as possible, so this was where they would part. He gave Coen a loaf of bread to put in one pocket and a flask of brandy for the other, and with an admonition not to use it all up too soon, he drove away, leaving Coen with the other man who had been in the car.

The two left the road and began walking into the hills. Before long they came upon the fifteen other members of the party, already assembled and waiting for Coen and his companion, who was the guide for the entire group. The group was quite diverse and included, besides Coen, George Barkley, Henry Bufton, a sergeant pilot, the two soldiers left over from Dunkirk whom Coen had first met at the party in the restaurant at Lillers, a Belgian poet, a Belgian Spitfire pilot named Alex Nitelet who was flying with the RAF, and several others whom Oscar did not know. All of the delays, he rapidly figured out, had been caused by trying to get this large a group to the same place at the same time without being discovered. When he thought about the complex arrangements that it had taken just to get him to that point, it seemed miraculous that the entire group had successfully been assembled.

With Coen's guide in the lead, the group began its single-file trek into the foothills of the Pyrenees in the morning sunlight. By the middle of the day, they had reached the snow line and the terrain had become steep, rugged, and barren, with few trees and little other growth. And still they climbed, legs aching and lungs crying out for more air. They encountered no other people and paused only long enough for an occasional rest, to take a bite of bread, or to ensure that everyone was still with the group. As the afternoon wore on, Oscar was thankful for the shoes that had been given to him at the meat market, but the ideal shoes were those worn by the guide—they had rope soles that enabled him to climb anywhere without slipping. When the sun began to set, the pleasant temperatures of the day dropped and Oscar wished he had some kind of outside coat. He was not alone, however, since most members of the group were dressed like him, with only a suit coat as an outer garment, and they all shivered in the cold air. When it got dark, the group bunched up even closer as they tried to follow the small trails that led through the passes and around any police outposts in the moonless black. Oscar didn't know when the group crossed into Spain, and no one even broached the question as the cold and exhausted hikers continued their silent trek, thankful that their guide seemed to know every inch of the terrain by heart.

Around midnight, the trail began to descend, and before long there was again some vegetation and the path became smoother. At the same time, a light rain began to fall, and soon the hikers were soaked and chilled to the bone. Shortly before sunrise, the miserable evaders reached an area with three or four houses and a number of vineyards. Their guide told them to find whatever shelter they could and to be quiet since they were waiting for a train that would come along about dawn. Remaining quiet was easy since each member of the group was fearful of being found by the authorities and put in jail. While he had been staying in Nîmes, Coen had been told by his host that the Spanish were not friendly to anyone coming across from France and that, if you were caught and arrested, the initial sentence would be six weeks in a jail that was worse than anyone could possibly imagine. The concern was reinforced by their guide. Shortly before they got to the vineyard, he had each member of the group go through his pockets and get rid of all of their money and anything else that it might be illegal to bring into Spain. Having anything illegal with you, if you were arrested, would add another six weeks to your jail sentence.

As Coen lay shivering and shaking in the vineyard, he was thankful he had listened to his former host's advice to save some of his food. He finished what little bread he still had and then basked in the warmth created by the remainder of the brandy, which he slowly drank. Exhaustion and cold took over and he dropped off into a fitful sleep.

In what seemed to be only minutes, the group was awakened by their guide. Every muscle in Oscar's body ached, and he began to shiver again in the damp cold. One by one the group cautiously moved toward the small platform that marked the train stop at the village of Vilajuiga. Each of them was given a ticket by their guide and told he was to get off the train at Figueres, about an hour's ride. The exhausted travelers were pleased to see that they and their guide were the only ones on the train. Although a few other people boarded at the few subsequent stops, no one paid any attention to the group scattered throughout the car.

As the train approached Figueres, Oscar suddenly realized that he didn't know what to do when they arrived. He had assumed that someone would tell him, so he had not thought about a plan of action. Now he was about to be dropped in a small Spanish town to fend for himself. His stomach was churning as the train came to a halt and all the members of his group, mixing with the few other passengers, got off the train. Coen followed. No sooner had he alighted on the platform than the guide who had been with him since Nîmes motioned for him to follow, and they started to walk east, toward the outskirts of town.

When they got some distance from the station, the guide told Coen that they were going to the British Consulate, a comment that made no sense to Coen. He had always assumed that the consulate would be a rather substantial structure in a busy part of town, and they were walking through an area of very small houses, many of which were in poor repair, bordering on the fields. As he looked at the weed-infested yards and the need for paint on many of the structures, Coen was convinced there was some mistake. When they turned down an alley, his apprehension mounted as the guide pointed to a house beyond a small garden and said, "That door, there." Coen took a couple of steps toward the house and stopped, convinced that something wasn't right. But when he turned around to question his guide again, the man was gone. "I have never felt so alone in all my life," thought an absolutely panicked Oscar. "This can't be the house where the British Consulate is located." But as he thought about his situation, Oscar realized that he had no better alternatives, so he approached the house and knocked on the back door.

To his surprise and relief, the door was answered by a lady who identified herself as Rose, the wife of the British consul at Figueres. She looked Coen over and immediately said, "Take those filthy clothes off and I'll get you a bathrobe." Coen did as he was told, left his clothes in a pile on the back steps, and followed her into the bathroom, where a bath had already been drawn, complete with some kind of disinfectant to take care of fleas, lice, and whatever else he might be carrying. As he sat in the warm water, Oscar was once again amazed at the underground system, not only for getting him into Spain, but also for taking care of such details as letting the wife of the consul know when he was arriving and asking her to have a bath ready. Coen also realized that the house was not the consulate at all but just a safe house that must be used regularly to move refugees, such as himself, on to freedom while keeping the real consulate free from suspicious activity.

After his much-needed bath, Coen put on fresh clothes and was able to spend a few minutes talking to the consul's wife. She confirmed his suspicions about the use of the house and told him that food was very difficult to get in Figueres. She and their maid spent almost all of their time trying to get enough just to take care of the needs of the consulate and its staff. After those remarks, Oscar was not surprised that he was not offered anything to eat. In fact, his conversation was cut short by the arrival of the consul's car in back of the house and his hurried departure. The consul's wife told Coen that he was being taken to the railroad station to get the train for Madrid. She gave him directions on how to find the British Embassy when he arrived in the Spanish capital, as well as a ticket for the trip and enough Spanish money to buy food on the train. After a few more words of caution about his situation, especially since he had no identification of any sort, Coen got in the car and was on his way.

Thankfully for the tired Coen, the overnight trip to Madrid was uneventful and he was even able to get several hours of sleep on the sparsely populated train. His hunger rapidly disappeared because he was able to buy food from vendors that lined the sides of the track at every stop. Still, he was not able to completely relax since he was without a guide or anyone to help him if there was a problem.

The directions to the embassy were very clear, and Coen found himself standing outside the compound, in the late November afternoon sunlight, with a lump in his throat as he saw the Union Jack flying in the breeze. The guard at the gate was expecting him, and as he stepped into the embassy compound, Oscar felt safe for the first time since that fateful day, over six weeks earlier, when he took off in his Spitfire for his ill-fated mission over France. When he walked into the dormitory on the embassy grounds, there was more to smile about, since he was reunited there with Barkley, Bufton, and the rest of the British members of his evasion group, who had arrived earlier in the day.

Life for the group in the embassy compound was certainly better than they had been used to during the preceding weeks. They were given some back pay so they could buy food, and the embassy assigned them a Spanish cook. Since each had lost weight during his ordeal, the tasty food she produced was eaten with relish. Each man was told not to leave the embassy compound since he would be subject to immediate arrest. However, several ignored the rules and went out on the town on several occasions. Since all of them were in the country illegally and none had any valid identification papers, Coen decided that a night on the town just wasn't worth the risk. To help combat the boredom, the ambassador met with them occasionally and even had a small party in their honor.

But problems remained, and as the days dragged by, Coen became more and more impatient. His unique situation made his travel difficult. It was impossible for the British embassy to get him an exit visa to leave Spain because he had no entry visa. Although he was a member of the RAF, he was an American citizen, and so any legal documents had to come from the American Embassy. But since the United States was still technically a neutral country, it was unwilling to officially acknowledge the presence of an American in the RAF. Coen's British companions Barkley and Bufton, on the other hand, got the necessary paperwork through the British Embassy and were soon on their way to Gibraltar and England.

A few days after Coen's arrival, the U.S. military attaché from the American Embassy came to visit. The officer left him a carton of cigarettes and several back issues of *Life* magazine, but Coen got the impression that the visit was primarily to make sure he was really Oscar Coen. In any case, the attaché told him that the U.S. Embassy was not able to do anything to help him because of America's neutral status. (The Germans had eventually found Coen's parachute and the other items he buried in the rodent hole and had reported that he was a prisoner. Since there was no other communication from him, his squadron mates doubted the German report, but his family had no way of knowing that the German report was not true. After the visit of the American military attaché, Coen's family was notified that he was safe in the British Embassy in Madrid.)

Unknown to Coen, his entire status changed on December 7. Early the next morning, an embassy official woke him up and told him to get his things together because he was leaving right away. In less than an hour, the mystified Coen was in an embassy car, with a guide, headed out of Madrid. Shortly after leaving the city, they came to a small town where he and his guide were let off at the railroad station. Since the guide spoke little English, Coen was unable to determine why they had departed the embassy in such a hurry, but he did understand that they were going to La Linea, the Spanish town that adjoined Gibraltar. During the overnight train trip, Coen tried to relax and enjoy the countryside. At every stop, there were local people selling fruit and other foods. Although he had no money, his guide kept him well supplied with fresh fruit and anything else he cared to eat. But even though he had been told that the Spanish government had given permission for him to travel, he could not completely quell the uneasiness he felt because of the hurried nature of the trip. All during the day, his guide tried to tell him something about Pearl Harbor, but Coen was not able to understand what had happened. In reality, the bombing of Pearl Harbor had put Coen in a completely different status with the Spanish, and they were anxious to get him out of the country since they were sure the United States would enter the war against Germany immediately.

When Coen and his guide arrived at La Linea, they hurried to the border between Spain and Gibraltar. They arrived just at the beginning of the period when the Spanish workers who were employed in Gibraltar were crossing into the British possession. Coen's guide indicated that he should just join the workers and walk across. Oscar was not reassured by what he saw, however. There was a Spanish and a British guard at the border, and he certainly didn't want to get stopped this close to freedom.

TELEPHONE: HOLBORN 3434

Extn.................

Any communications on the
subject of this letter should
be addressed to :—
THE UNDER SECRETARY
OF STATE,
and the following number
quoted :—

P363099/41/P.4.Cas.

AIR MINISTRY,

LONDON, W.C.2.

22nd November, 1941

Sir,

    I am directed to confirm the information already conveyed
to you that according to news now received from a confidential
source, your son, (Pilot Officer Oscar Hoffman Coen,) Royal Air
Force Volunteer Reserve, has reached Spain.

    Until further information is obtained, no attempt should
be made to communicate with him, neither should any mention of
the matter be made to the press or over the telephone, as this
might prejudice his chances of safety.

    Should any further news be received in this department
it will be communicated to you immediately.

           I am, Sir,
           Your obedient Servant,

               J. G. Shreeve

    for Director of Personal Services.

A.B. Coen, Esq.,
1803, Elm Street,
Murphysboro,
Illinois,
U.S.A.

Letter from the British Air Ministry to Coen's parents notifying them that their son had
reached safety in Spain, but warning them not to notify anyone because that might jeopardize his safety.   *Oscar Coen*

As he approached, both guards looked right at him, but, employing his
tried-and-true guard theory, he just kept on walking. In a few steps he
was a completely free man standing on British soil. It was December 9,
1941. As he looked at the flag and finally realized that his evasion adventure was over, tears came to his eyes. He thought about all those people who had given so much—for some, it would turn out that they gave
their lives—to get him and others back to friendly soil.

During the next few hours, as he was processed into British control, Coen learned about the attack on Pearl Harbor and realized why he had been so hurriedly moved from Madrid. Speed was not the case in Gibraltar, however, and he was left to his own devices to get back to England. The British officials simply said that he would have to wait his turn, for there were so many people with reasons to get to England and so little airlift available that no one knew when he would get out. With little else to do, Coen would often frequent the pubs in the town. On one occasion, he surprised a couple of his old squadron mates from England, who were on their way to Singapore and thought he was a prisoner of war. There were also some Americans on Gibraltar studying gun emplacements, and Coen spent a couple of evenings with them, but still no transportation back to England.

Coen's most fortuitous visit to the pub came on December 23. He'd no sooner walked into the pub than he heard, "Hey, Oscar, what the hell are you doing here?" It was one of the Australian air crews that had been on the ship from Canada with him. They were flying a four-engine Sunderland amphibious aircraft and were returning to England the next day. Over a few beers, Coen relayed his adventures and that he was trying to get to England.

"Are you qualified as an air gunner?" the pilot asked.

"I sure am," was Coen's reply.

"Then you are a part of the crew, so be down at the dock at five in the morning."

Coen couldn't understand why he had to be a member of the crew to fly on the Sunderland, but the pilot told him that no passengers were allowed on warplanes if they were on an official mission—in this case, looking for submarines. But as a crew member, Coen could be taken along.

Early the next morning, Air Gunner Coen reported to the dock and was soon in the air and on his way to England. The long but pleasant flight ended as Coen arrived in London on Christmas Eve. During the next few days he was interviewed by the intelligence officers, got his uniforms back, and spent a couple of days in London getting reacquainted with the town. On December 29, Coen took the train back to Martlesham Heath and reported to his new commander, Chesley "Pete" Peterson, on whose wing he had been flying when he'd had to bail out. The official theme of the New Year's Eve party in Number 71 Squadron of the RAF for 1941 was "Happy New Year, Oscar." True to his thought from more than two months before, Coen bought the first round of drinks. Within a few days, he was again flying his Spitfire over France.

Coen transferred to the U.S. Army Air Forces on September 29, 1942, and was assigned to the Fourth Fighter Group of the Eighth Air Force. He was seriously injured when he was again forced to bail out of his stricken aircraft in 1943. This time it was a P-47, but fortunately he was over England. In 1944, he returned to the United States and was assigned to the Fighter Branch in the Pentagon. Coen was sent to the Pacific in 1945, but he arrived too late to see any action. He ended the war with six German aircraft to his credit, the Silver Star, two Distinguished Flying Crosses, the Air Medal, the British Distinguished Flying Cross, and the French Croix de Guerre. After World War II, Coen remained in the Air Force. He retired as a colonel and presently lives in Oregon. He has three daughters and three grandchildren.

After the war, Coen and his wife visited England twice, in 1986 and 1990. Both times they visited with Suzanne and her husband, who lived in London. Suzanne told them that Paul was really a double agent who had infiltrated the French underground. She didn't know what happened to him, but did hear that he had been severely beaten in Marseilles for some of his actions. His information was also a key in the arrest and execution of a number of the Frenchmen who had helped Coen and others escape. Suzanne herself was eventually picked up by the Germans, released, arrested again, tortured, and sentenced to death. She managed to escape and survived the war. Louis Nouveau, Coen's benefactor in Marseilles, was also arrested and imprisoned but survived the war. Coen never returned to the scene of his evasion experience in France, nor did he ever see any of the others who had helped him. He still has pangs of sorrow about the fate of those who aided him. He has always believed they were the bravest people in the war.

• THREE •

"My God, I Thought You Were Dead!"

Pilot Officer Eric Doorly, RAF, had a lot on his mind as he settled his lanky, six-foot-two, one-hundred-seventy-five-pound frame into his Spitfire on a sunny September afternoon in 1942. Not that there was anything unusual about the flight—escorting American B-17 bombers on another raid over northern France. Nonetheless, he knew there were sure to be German FW-190s and ME-109s lurking high above the bombers waiting for the opportunity to strike. And just the thought of the combat to come was enough to cause any fighter pilot to break a light sweat. Still, the soft-spoken and often introspective Eric could not help but think some lighter thoughts as he waited for the mission to begin. His mind wandered to Sunday afternoons at home, when he would wash the car and then join his friends cruising down the main street of Garden City, New York. He thought of his impending transfer to the U.S. Army Air Forces and the tripling of his monthly pay, which would certainly change the way he lived when he went into London. Just as exciting was the change from British rations to American food that he hoped would accompany the transfer. The thought of London brought memories of the previous weekend, when he'd wandered the town and spent an unforgettable evening with a young lady he had met at the Crackers Club. He was to call her again tonight, after his mission. And, like all his squadron mates, he continued to be impressed with how the Spit IX, the first new airplane he had flown since joining the RAF, performed. It had two hundred more horsepower than the older, war-weary Spit V, which meant it could outperform the German FW-190, a welcome thought to any Allied fighter pilot.

But all the random thoughts immediately ceased for Doorly as the red flare was shot high into the air and the action began. "Throttle open, tail up at about sixty, and let her fly off at ninety. Gear up, flaps up, trim her for climb, and let's see just what this Spit IX will do." Doorly looked over at his wingman, Dick "Goody" Gudmundsen, and could see that he, too, was pleased with the way this new plane performed. In what seemed like no time at all, they were at 25,000 feet. Almost immediately, there were the white vapor trails that marked the B-17s against the clear, blue sky as they trundled over the French coast, each bomber's engines straining to keep their load at that altitude. In contrast, Doorly's V-12 Rolls-Royce engine seemed to be almost loafing along as the squadron of Spitfires weaved back and forth, covering the bomber formation. Doorly and all his squadron mates took comfort in knowing they were flying the most advanced fighters in the world.

Escort flying could be very boring. Just weaving back and forth to keep the Germans at bay if they tried to get to the huge, lumbering B-17s made it difficult not to get complacent. On recent missions the squadron had seen few German fighters because, for some reason, the Germans had not been challenging the bombers. Rather, they had been sending up terrific flak barrages, and that was even worse. The fighters could dodge and move about, so their chances of being hit by the anti-aircraft fire were small, but the bombers were not very maneuverable, and their large, tight formation kept them from being able to avoid the flak. Every fighter pilot had nothing but admiration for the courage of the ten-man bomber crews as they droned toward the target.

"Blue Section, looks like e-a [enemy aircraft] at six o'clock high." The flight leader's voice was calm as he reported the enemy fighters. Almost instinctively, Doorly and Gudmundsen pulled a hard right turn, and as the tremendous G forces sucked them into their seats, they looked for the German planes. As the FW-190s came thundering through the bomber formation, Doorly slammed the spade grip all the way to the left and in a second he was on the tail of the last 190. His adrenaline was flowing as the German filled Doorly's gun sight. But when he pushed the firing button, anticipation of shooting down the enemy aircraft turned to disgust and his elation with his new airplane evaporated. His guns jammed after firing only a few rounds! Doorly's only alternative was to break off his attack and wait for his wingman to rejoin him in the hope that Gudmundsen's guns were working properly.

Eric Doorly and his mates from Squadron 133, RAF Fighter Command, at Biggen Hill, England, in summer 1942. Standing are (*from left*): Dick Gudmundsen (Doorly's wingman who was killed when Doorly was shot down), Gilbert Omens, Doorly, Bill Slade, and Colburn King (killed in action). Kneeling are (*from left*): Don Lambert and Don Gentile, the famous ace.   *Donna Livingston*

Doorly looked around for the rest of his squadron and could see other Spitfires here and there. And although he couldn't see behind his Spitfire very well, he was sure that the wing he saw out of the corner of his eye was that of his friend Goody. Doorly retarded his throttle slightly and waited for Gudmundsen to get in position so they could get back to the business of escorting the bombers. The next second Doorly's world literally blew apart. Unbeknownst to him, an FW-190 had just shot Gudmundsen down and was now on his tail. In seconds, he proceeded to blow Doorly's Spitfire to pieces. The first cannon shells shot the tail off the Spit. The next volley came over Doorly's right shoulder and into the instrument panel and the engine. The September sun was immediately blotted out as the canopy was covered with oil and Doorly lost all sense of up or down. At the same time, the control column went limp and banged from front to rear as the now-cut control cables simply blew about in the wind. The mortally wounded plane pitched violently forward, and Doorly was slammed against his lap belt and shoulder harness with his arms and head plastered against the top of the canopy by the negative G forces. The terrified pilot fought to get his hand to the canopy release, but he was helpless, and he suddenly realized that he was going to go right into the ground with the front part of his plane. But almost as if to give the fighting airman another chance, the Spit stalled, and suddenly Doorly was weightless in the cockpit. "If it will just do this again," the panicked Doorly thought as he was once again slammed against the top of the canopy, "maybe I can get out." Sure enough, the plane stalled again, and in one lightning-quick move, Doorly pulled the canopy release, opened his seat belt and harness, and was immediately thrown free of the plane.

Doorly had no idea of his altitude when he was thrown from his oil-soaked fighter into the early evening sunshine, so all he could think of was to get the parachute opened. He was rudely reminded that his chute had deployed, because he had borrowed a friend's chute and hadn't bothered to fit it properly, leaving too much slack in the straps that went between his legs. Doorly would always remember the pain he felt when the chute opened and those straps suddenly snapped tight. For the moment, however, it was enough to just be alive.

Suddenly Doorly realized that he was not alone in the sky. The FW-190 that had shot him down was coming straight at him, and the guns in its wings looked huge. For a moment the panicked pilot thought that he should have stayed with his ship, for meeting death in it would be easier than just hanging in his parachute while his adversary shot him to pieces. Every American pilot knew of stories, sometimes true, of German pilots who shot airmen while they were descending in their parachutes—even though such action was against Luftwaffe policy. But Doorly's German adversary apparently had no intention of shooting him, and after two or three circles, the FW-190 broke off and went back to the fray. Eric was so relieved that the plane was gone that he forgot about his pain and started to think about landing. He had plenty of time, since he had been so high when he opened his parachute. His attention was immediately attracted by what appeared to be a group of soldiers and several trucks on the road toward which he seemed to be drifting.

As he watched the trucks on the road he tried desperately to recall the instructions he had been given on steering his parachute. He remembered that pulling on one of the risers would make the chute go faster in one direction, but he could not remember which side to pull for which direction. After a couple of experimental pulls, he got the chute moving in the direction he wanted and began to drift away from what he assumed were Germans. For the first time, he thought about possibly evading capture—after all, the Germans had to stay on the roads. As he got lower, Doorly lost sight of them. Realizing that if he couldn't see them, they couldn't see him, the elated airman prepared to hit the ground. Time and again in survival briefings, RAF pilots had been told that contact with the ground would be hard and that they could be seriously injured if they weren't careful. But Doorly's landing in a plowed field was surprisingly soft. "Get out of the area where you land as rapidly as you can," was the rule the RAF instructors had repeated over and over again, so Doorly just dumped his parachute on the ground and was off to find a place to hide as fast as his pained body would let him run.

Fortunately for Doorly, the field where he'd landed was only a short distance from a large stand of trees and a fairly dense hedgerow. As he made his dash for the cover of the forest, his mind was going a mile a minute. He thought of climbing a tree but dismissed that as too obvious, too difficult for his sore body, and impractical since he couldn't stay up in a tree all night. A few yards into the forest, Doorly stumbled and fell in a shallow ditch he hadn't seen because of the dense cover of fallen leaves. He was relieved that he hadn't sprained an ankle but cursed the delay in getting away. Suddenly, the idea hit him that if he hadn't seen the ditch, maybe the Germans wouldn't see it either, and if he could get into the deepest part and cover himself with leaves, they just might not find him. Burrowing down into the leaves, the downed airman was soon completely out of sight.

Seconds became minutes and minutes became hours while Doorly lay as motionless as possible under his pile of leaves. Periodically he would hear voices, and on two occasions he even heard the leaves crunching under German boots. His tension was heightened by the stories he had heard about the way the Germans searched any suspected hiding place to see if it was occupied—by jabbing their bayonets into it. While it would have been a good time to plan his next move, Eric was so afraid he would be discovered that he used every bit of his effort just to stay quiet. Still, it seemed to him that the leaves were palpitating with his heart as he waited for what seemed to be an eternity. His muscles ached from being in the same position, but still Doorly didn't move. After all the sounds of searchers had long since ceased, he cautiously moved a few leaves. Thankfully, he found that it was dark. He knew that he had to use the cover of night to get as far away from the area as possible, since he was sure the Germans would return and possibly bring dogs to find his hiding place. The problem was that he didn't know exactly where he was or in what direction to go. All he knew was that he had been about fifty miles northwest of Paris when he bailed out.

Judging direction as best he could, Doorly began to walk away from where he had landed. After a short distance he emerged from the forest, and in the partial moonlight, he could see a rather large expanse of farmland. He remembered his survival instructor telling the class that haystacks were good hiding places since there were so many of them and they made it easy to keep warm and remain out of sight. After walking what he thought was several miles, he found a small barn that was partially filled with a new crop of hay. After a brief investigation to ensure that he was alone, Doorly burrowed into the hay. He began to formulate a plan for the next day, but despite the desperate nature of his circumstances, his dramatic escape from his mortally wounded fighter, his run into the forest, the hours of remaining motionless, and his hike to the barn took their toll and he soon fell asleep.

It was not daylight but a young farmhand who woke Doorly the next morning. It took a moment for him to remember being shot down, but about the same time he got his bearings he was confused again, because the young man was speaking German. Doorly assumed that the man was some sort of German agent and would turn him in immediately, thus ending his brief attempt at evasion. But since there was nothing Doorly could do about the situation, and it was obvious from his clothing that he was a downed airman, he tried to remember some of his high school German. Amazingly, he was able to communicate a bit. He soon found out that the young German had left his homeland to keep from being drafted into the army, so he too was trying to stay out of sight. After assuring Doorly that he was not going to call the police or the Germans, he indicated to the flier that he should stay in the barn, and then left.

Eric was surprised when, in a few minutes, the young man returned, accompanied by an old woman who was carrying some French clothes and a hat. And although Eric couldn't speak French, he managed some communication with the lady through the German-speaking farm helper. It turned out that Eric was actually quite safe, since the last people in the world the German farmworker wanted to see were German soldiers. So, after changing from his RAF uniform into the old gray suit coat and pants and putting on the typical French farmer's cap, he followed the lady into her house.

It was clear to Eric that the old lady and her worker did not like having him on their farm and that they wanted him to go away as fast as he could. Doorly had heard countless stories that entire French families had been shot for harboring downed pilots, so he understood their concern. Nonetheless, the lady gave him a breakfast of eggs, toast with butter, and coffee, after which she pointed to the road and made it clear that he was to begin walking. So Doorly set off down the lane, not knowing where it led or where he was going. And if he had any confidence that his civilian clothes would help him blend in with the populace and appear to be a typical Frenchman, it was tempered by a look in the mirror at the farmhouse. He was shocked to see that his normally clear blue eyes had been made bright red by the force of the blood rushing to his head and rupturing the capillaries in his eyes while he was pinned in his airplane.

Doorly didn't get even a hundred yards down the lane before the old woman started yelling at him and walking briskly in his direction. He imagined the worst, but the woman just went through his clothes again to make sure there were no labels or other marks that could link them with her if he was captured. Satisfied that all was in order, she again motioned for him to move off down the road.

Doorly had found out from the farmworker that the lane led to the nearest village, Aumale, which was about ten miles away, and was nearly midway between the port of Dieppe and Paris, about thirty-five miles from each. Since he had not made any evasion plan the night before, it was time to decide what he was going to do. One thing was clear to him: he couldn't survive on his own, so he would have to make himself known to a Frenchman sooner or later. His first contact had been really accidental, so he had no idea how to proceed and he didn't remember his survival instructor addressing the subject. Still, Doorly found that walking helped him think, and besides, it was a beautiful fall day, the leaves were changing color, and he was just glad to be alive.

When he set out down the country lane, his primary concern was what he would do if he was stopped by German soldiers. Much to his relief, however, Doorly passed very few people on the road and saw no Germans during the day. And even though he was still wearing his fur-lined flying boots on his size-twelve feet, the people he passed seemed to pay no attention to him. Around noon, the road descended into a beautiful valley. Not knowing what else to do, Doorly wandered off the road and down by a stream, where he got a drink of water and then simply sat for an hour and enjoyed the scenery as he rested. But as he sat, a sudden sense of loneliness came over him. He had never been that alone in his life. Here he was, a fugitive in a country he knew little about, where he couldn't speak the language and where he didn't know anyone. He was sure that if there were two or three others with him, they could come up with a good plan, but it was hard by himself. Fortunately, the depression brought on by these thoughts didn't last long. As the sun descended toward the horizon, an anxious Doorly realized that he still had no plan, that he did not really know where he was or where he was going, and that he had no idea of how to get any food or shelter. It was clear that he was going to have to find some help.

For some time, the road on which Doorly had been walking paralleled a small stream. As he rounded a bend, he saw a small stone bridge and the little village of Aumale on the other side. Given his rather desperate straits, he was not deterred by the presence of a young man, dressed in typical knickers and shirt, who was positioned at the end of the bridge. Although the young man was not visibly armed, he was evidently guarding the bridge. With his heart in his throat, Doorly approached him. Although he knew no French, Doorly was able to communicate to the young man that he was an RAF pilot who had been shot down and needed help. The young Frenchman apparently understood and indicated, by a nod of his head, that Doorly should follow him. After walking only a few hundred feet, they came to the young man's home, where he lived with a younger brother and his widowed mother. And although Doorly's stomach was in knots as they walked into the village, he could only hope for the best and accept whatever came.

As they approached the small, single-story stone duplex in which the young man lived, Eric was surprised that there was no effort made to sneak him into the village or the house. Although they had passed no Germans, Eric felt sure there must be some in the area. Still, he found himself shaking as they approached the front door. The boy's mother opened the door and showed no apparent surprise upon seeing Doorly. She asked him to come in and took him directly to a small bedroom adjacent to the living room and indicated that he was to remain there. Through the door, he could hear a very serious family discussion taking place, and although he didn't understand what the family was saying, he assumed they were talking about him. Once again a feeling of loneliness came over him as he sat in an unfamiliar room in a strange town and listened to a family he didn't know debate his fate. Because the penalty for housing or helping a downed airman was generally the firing squad, Eric feared they might decide to turn him over to the Germans. On the other hand, he hoped that they had a contact in the underground and could help him escape. In any case, he knew that he could not live off the land, so he had to wait and see what happened. He had already made that decision when he contacted the young man at the bridge.

Several anxious minutes later, the young man appeared and communicated to Doorly that he was to stay in the house for at least the next few days. A supper of soup, bread, and red wine followed. Doorly's three hosts tried to talk with him, but because they knew little English and he knew even less French, the conversation didn't get very far. He was able to learn that the family's name was Ranson and that the two young brothers were Jean, about nineteen years old, the one Doorly had contacted at the bridge, and Robert, about seventeen. As soon as the meal was finished, Doorly was taken back to the bedroom where he had been kept earlier. The food, the luxury of having a bed and a blanket, and the fatigue of the day took their toll, and Doorly was soon asleep.

After a breakfast of bread, cheese, and coffee, Mrs. Ranson and both her sons departed for work after giving Doorly strict instructions to remain in the house and stay out of sight. If anyone came to the door he was to ignore the caller and try to hide. There was bread and cheese for his lunch. After the family left, Doorly decided to explore the small house. He found that it consisted of a kitchen, in which the family ate their meals, a sitting room, and three bedrooms, one of which he had been given. It was clear to him that one of the two brothers had moved into the other's room to make space for him. Probably the biggest shock about his new accommodations was the typical French toilet—two iron foot plates and a hole in the concrete floor. Soon the day began to drag by because Doorly could find nothing at all to do but sit. So after a couple of hours, curiosity got the best of him, and despite Madame Ranson's charge, he peeked out the front window. He noticed little traffic on the residential street and few people about. Thankfully, there was no apparent activity in the other half of the duplex. Eric's confidence was certainly reinforced as he viewed his surroundings. Although the accommodations were not very plush, at least the family had decided to keep him for a few days, and he still hoped that they could put him in contact with the underground.

Suddenly, his thoughts were interrupted by a jolt of absolute terror. Two German soldiers walked up the street and turned in at the walk leading to the duplex. Eric was frozen at the window as his mind raced. All his confidence evaporated as he feared that the Ransons had kept him just one night to be nice and had then contacted the Germans to come and get him. Panic seized him and he tried to think of where he might hide. As the soldiers drew nearer, Doorly stepped back from the window—just as they took the right fork of the sidewalk and went to the other half of the duplex. Eric's thoughts made another quick turn, and he decided that he had not been turned in but rather that the Germans were making a house-to-house search for him. He ran to his little room and climbed under the bed, covering himself as best he could, and waited for the inevitable knock on the door or, more likely, a rude opening of the door and a search of the house. As had occurred in the woods, Eric could hear his own heart pounding. But the minutes went by and nothing happened. He began to realize that the Germans really had no way of knowing he was in Aumale, so they probably weren't looking for him at all. For all they knew, he'd walked in the opposite direction when he left his landing area. Eventually, he crawled from his hiding place and moved around the house, keeping a good distance from the windows. Still, the rest of the day went slowly as he continued to think about the German soldiers and tried to figure out what they had been doing.

It was with great relief that Eric welcomed the Ranson family back home that evening. During their supper of chicken, potatoes, bread, and coffee, Doorly told them about the day as best he could through a little English, some German, and a lot of hand gestures. He was surprised when they all laughed about the German soldiers. As he eventually figured out, the other half of the duplex was occupied by two ladies in their thirties who entertained German soldiers on a regular basis, both day and night. The Ransons' only concern was that Doorly might be seen by one of their neighbors' German "customers," so they again emphasized staying away from the windows.

By the time he had been in the Ransons' house for a week or so, Eric found it increasingly difficult to do nothing all day long. The problem was not made easier by the periodic sound of large formations of aircraft overhead, the occasional noise of the antiaircraft guns, and the thuds of bombs in the distance. He was not concerned that the village would be bombed, but oh, how he wanted to at least watch the B-17s and Spitfires go over. And his thoughts would often wander to his days in the RAF and the ones before he ever left home.

Flying had been part of Eric's life for as long as he could remember. As a young man he'd built model airplanes and read everything about flying that he could get his hands on. Reading and music were always important in the Doorly household. His mother was an English teacher, and his father, who had been born in England, was the editor of a newspaper. Eric had learned to enjoy reading while he was still very young, but his first love was mathematics, and he decided quite early that he would become an engineer. After graduating from high school in 1938, he had enrolled in the engineering college at Rensselaer Polytechnic Institute in Troy, New York.

The specter of war in Europe brought a marked increase in the need for Americans who knew how to fly—just in case the United States ended up going to war. The primary vehicle for this training was the Civilian Pilot Training Program—the CPTP—which focused on recruiting young men to learn to fly as part of their college experience. This was ideal for Doorly because CPTP flying instruction did not cost very much and he could learn while he continued his studies. He enrolled in the program in the spring of 1940, and before the semester was over he had become a licensed pilot. He immediately signed up for the advanced program and learned to do some aerobatics. The flying bug made its fatal bite on Doorly that summer, and he got a job at a flying school so he could get more instruction. He didn't go back to RPI, but instead went to work as an apprentice aircraft mechanic making fifteen dollars a week, part of which he spent to get additional flying time.

The German conquest of France and the subsequent threat of invading England, which was thwarted by the RAF in the Battle of Britain, brought the reality of the war home to Doorly. He read daily of the heroic exploits of the RAF pilots in their Hurricanes and Spitfires as they faced the mighty Luftwaffe. The topic at work each day seemed to be the fighting and the shortage of pilots for the RAF. With his love of flying and his admiration for England, the latter at least partly because of his British father, he decided to try to join the RAF.

The desperate shortage of pilots brought on by the losses in the early days of the war had caused the British to expand their recruiting efforts, and the United States was a prime market. In 1939, they had contacted an American artist and former pilot in World War I, Clayton Knight, and asked him to set up the machinery to recruit American pilots for the RAF. By mid-1940, Knight had his organization functioning and recruiting began. Because of the U.S. Neutrality Laws, Knight was not able to recruit openly, but his organization was extremely effective in spreading information throughout the country, especially at airports.

The twenty-year-old Doorly heard about the Clayton Knight Committee at work and went to the Waldorf-Astoria Hotel in New York City to sign up. His biggest problem was convincing the interviewing officer that he had the required two hundred hours of flying time rather than the one hundred or so he really had. The need for pilots was obviously great, so Doorly was given an evaluation flight, was accepted, and in early 1941 found himself at an RAF Refresher Training School in Tulsa, Oklahoma. He completed that school in May 1941, took the train to Canada, and set sail for England. He arrived there in June 1941.

But daydreaming could last only so long, and Doorly continued to try to find ways to occupy his time. Back in England, he would have listened to classical music, which he had learned to love from his mother, who was a very talented musician. Because he loved to read, he was terribly frustrated that all the books in the Ranson house were in French. He wished he had paid more attention to his father, who had urged him to take French, rather than German, in high school. He tried working mathematics problems but that soon got boring as well. As time went by, Doorly began to wonder why nothing was being done to get him on his way to Spain, or wherever he might be taken on the road back to England. What he did not know was that the Ransons had no connection with the underground and that there was concern on the part of the town officials as to who Doorly really was. It was not uncommon for the Germans to try to infiltrate various underground units by having someone pose as a downed pilot to learn just how the organization operated and who the key people were. Thus, there was much discussion about Doorly and what should be done with him.

About two weeks after his arrival in Aumale, Doorly could see a definite change in the Ransons' attitude toward him. Apparently, they had accepted the fact that he was an American in the RAF, although he did not know why. This first became evident when the two boys took him to a friend's house one evening to play cards and drink wine. A cold sweat ran down Doorly's back when he was led out of the house. Once again the specter of being turned in to the Germans raised its head as he tried to figure out why he was being taken outside in plain view of anyone walking down the street, especially since he had been cautioned so often about staying out of sight. The shock at being taken to another house, introduced as "our American pilot," and being dealt a hand of cards was almost as traumatic. This proved to be only the first of many such evenings.

It wasn't long until one of the older men would occasionally come by and take Doorly to play cards during the day just to ease his boredom. Fortunately, during these walks to other houses he was never stopped and the few German soldiers he saw paid no attention to him. Evidently, Robert and Jean were also confident that there would be no problem. One other benefit of playing cards and talking with several of the townspeople was Doorly's rapidly improving ability to understand, and even speak, some French.

Eric gathered all his impressions of Aumale during these few walks to play cards. The village was situated in a beautiful valley and consisted of no more than forty houses and other small buildings on both sides of the road for about five hundred yards. The only businesses were those that were necessary for daily life, such as the produce market, meat vendor, baker, and a general store that carried about everything else. Doorly was never allowed to go into any of the businesses because that would have been too risky. "I can see why there are so few Germans here," he told Jean one evening. "They must just pass through the village and maybe stop to see the women next door"—his comment brought a laugh from both brothers.

Doorly had actually become fairly comfortable with his surroundings after just a few days, and aside from the boredom of being alone all day and wanting to get back to England, he was not anxious to leave his safe situation for the hazard of traveling in a hostile country. For one thing, Madame Ranson was a great cook. She would pick mushrooms and make delicious omelets; there was chicken and rabbit and lots of eggs. Actually, Doorly was eating better than he had been in England, and he rapidly realized why the French were famous for their culinary talents. He also had come to like the family, and he and the boys spent hours communicating about the United States, France, the war, and any other subject that came to mind. Although Madame Ranson seldom participated in the small talk, for she had less patience with the mutual struggle to communicate, she remained curious about Eric's background and his life in the RAF.

Doorly's rapidly improving ability in French soon made him an active partner in the discussions, which began a few weeks after his arrival in Aumale, about how to get him out of France. Madame Ranson's brother was a smuggler in southern France, which, at that time, had not yet been occupied by the Germans. He lived in Lourdes and so was less than fifty miles from the Spanish border.

A plan was finally conceived for Doorly and the two boys, both of whom wanted to get to England so they could fight for the Free French, to travel first to their uncle's house. Madame Ranson's brother would then smuggle them across the Pyrenees Mountains into Spain, and from there, by unknown means, they would get to British Gibraltar and to England. Since the uncle was a very successful smuggler, the plan seemed workable. Doorly was uneasy all the same, because it was obvious to him that the underground was not involved and that the three young men would need a lot of luck to succeed.

About a month after Doorly's arrival in France, when his eyes had returned to normal, the mayor of Aumale came to the house and filled out a number of papers. Doorly also had his identification picture taken—through the window, so he would not have to go outside the house. A few days later Doorly's identification papers arrived and, along with Robert and Jean Ranson, he began the harrowing journey through German-occupied France to Lourdes.

It was difficult for Eric to leave the Ranson house and Aumale. He had become used to his surroundings and felt safe with the Ranson family. And although he knew he had to move on, he was grateful that Robert and Jean were going with him. Without them, he knew, he probably would have little chance of making it to Lourdes. Still, he had a difficult time sleeping the night before they were to leave. He thought of the terrible price the entire Ranson family, and possibly the entire village of Aumale, would pay if the Germans found out that he had been sheltered and aided there in his effort to evade capture. And he thought, for the first time, about how he could repay them for all they had done when he got back to England.

England! Eric would always remember the anticipation he'd felt as his ship neared England in the early summer of 1941. He was impressed with the beautiful countryside, the flowers, the quaint villages, and the hustle and bustle of the great city of London. He immediately admired the British for their ability to carry on their daily lives in the face of German bombings and to get along despite the shortages brought about by the war.

Doorly's first stop in Britain had been at the Air Ministry in London, where he had been sworn in to the RAF and given a book of clothing coupons so he could get his uniforms. And what pride he'd felt as he walked out of Moss Brothers Clothiers in the uniform of an RAF pilot with wings on his chest. After a few days of processing at Bournemouth, a resort town in southern England, he was sent to an operational training unit where he came face-to-face with the airplane of his dreams— the Spitfire. "What a beautiful airplane," he remembered thinking at the time. "It looks like it is going four hundred miles an hour just sitting on the ground, and it is so much bigger than anything I have ever flown. I hope I can fly it." But fly it he could, and in late August he was assigned to 133 Squadron of RAF Fighter Command, ready to do battle with the Germans.

As Doorly and the Ranson boys waited the next morning for the train to take them to Paris on the first leg of their trip to the south, Eric was sure that everyone at the tiny Aumale train station could see him shaking. He had a hard time believing that he was really going to get on the public train to go to a city where there were thousands of Germans. And he was terrified at the thought that someone on the train might try to talk to him and find out that he was not French. Still, there was no other way out of France, but he didn't stop shaking even after the three were safely on the train. The uneventful ride to Paris took only an hour, and Eric actually began to enjoy the scenery along the way. He even thought about returning to France after the war to tour the country and thank the Ransons.

But Eric's fright reached new heights as he and his companions stepped from the train in Paris. Not ten feet away were three German soldiers who were probably waiting for a train. That was the closest Doorly had ever been to a German soldier, and he just knew that all three of them were looking at him. Although Robert and Jean had told him to act normal, to not look at anyone, and to keep moving, he seemed frozen to the spot. At any moment they would ask him for his papers and his evasion would be over. A tug on his sleeve by Robert got Doorly moving, and a moment later the three were out of the station and on the street, moving at a brisk pace, for the Ranson boys had found out that they had to walk a number of blocks to another station in order to continue their trip and reach their next stop, Bordeaux.

As he walked through Paris, Eric found himself thinking of the number of times he had looked down on the city as he flew over it, escorting bombers on raids in France. He also remembered his father's descriptions of the city as one of the centers of art and culture of the Western world. Now he was walking down the wide boulevards, looking at the beautiful buildings, the statues and monuments, and the quaint sidewalk cafés. Once again, he felt almost like a tourist. But he was always abruptly jerked back to reality by the sight of German soldiers on the sidewalk, a German vehicle among the relatively large number of cars on the streets, or a large flag bearing the swastika hanging from one of the stately buildings. He couldn't help but think about what a tragedy it would be if such a beautiful city were to be bombed because of the Germans. The effect of the occupation was also apparent to Eric when he noticed that the

Parisians—who, he had always heard, were lighthearted and happy—did not smile very much and that their conversation was muted as they hurried from place to place. Still, he sensed an attitude of arrogance and defiance on the part of the French when they met a German on the street.

After a few blocks, it became apparent that no one on the street, French or German, was the least bit interested in Doorly and that his appearance didn't cause any second glances. He began to lose some of his fear and actually believe he was going to be able to get through Paris and on the next train without being caught. He even found himself looking at people he met and trying to figure out if any of them might be evading airmen just as he was.

But Eric's confidence suddenly disappeared when he and Robert and Jean entered a little restaurant to get some lunch. Doorly had no idea how to read the menu and didn't know enough French to order. Again, he needn't have worried, because Jean simply ordered for all three of them and the young waitress paid no attention to Doorly. Suddenly he remembered a movie he'd seen just before he flew his last mission. In it, the Germans caught a spy because he used his eating utensils differently than the French did. To add to his tension, two young German soldiers came into the restaurant and sat down at a nearby table. Eric was sure that his hands were shaking as he picked up his knife and fork. As it turned out, he had unconsciously adopted the French way of holding his utensils—and the Germans ignored the several restaurant patrons anyway. Although the food was very good, Doorly was glad to finish eating and be back on the street.

Money was not a problem during the trip since the escape kit provided to every RAF pilot contained several thousand French francs. Doorly had kept part of the money, but he had also given some of it to Madame Ranson during his stay and some to Robert and Jean before they began their journey. The value of the francs became obvious when the Ransons told Eric that without his money there would be no way they could make the trip to Paris, much less to southern France. Doorly had wondered if the Ransons were part of the French underground ever since he was taken in by them. And although he had seen no evidence of any formal or organized activity during his time in Aumale, he still wasn't sure. He had become convinced that they were acting independently when Mrs. Ranson told him they needed his money to get to southern France. In addition, the actions of his companions during the trip to the south made it obvious that they had no contact person or knowledge of one either in Paris or on the train. They were simply three young men traveling to southern France.

The next Paris station was also crowded, and as usual, there were large numbers of Germans. Although Doorly remained on edge, he was not as nervous as he had been when they'd arrived in the City of Lights. No one questioned Robert when he bought their tickets, and they were fortunate that the train was not crowded so they could find a compartment to themselves, which gave them room to stretch out and occasionally doze. Doorly slept little during the long but uneventful trip to Bordeaux because he could not risk waking from a sound sleep and not knowing where he was, even for a few seconds. During the daylight hours, he was able to enjoy the beauty of the French countryside, but the night seemed to drag on forever. Robert told him to remain in his seat and be as inconspicuous as possible when they went through a large town, but other than that, Doorly acted like any other passenger. The only fear he had was that another passenger might try to engage him in conversation. This had happened a couple of times on the way to Paris, and on each occasion one of the Ranson boys had immediately joined in so Doorly did not have to speak to anyone. If he was stopped while on his way to the bathroom or walking around the train car, he realized, he would be in trouble. Jean also anticipated the potential problem, and so Doorly was always accompanied by one of the boys whenever he left his seat.

About ten miles outside of Bordeaux the train stopped in a small village and the trio got off. They had decided not to go into Bordeaux because it was occupied by the Germans and, even though they had fared perfectly well in Paris, why push their luck. They also knew that, although they were still in the occupied area, the line of demarcation was only about fifteen miles to the east, and it would be easier to get into unoccupied France by staying in the countryside.

So the three simply started trudging down the country road in the morning sunshine, with Jean and Robert carrying their suitcases. Still, Eric was concerned, because he was sure that if anyone saw them it would be obvious that they were trying to get to unoccupied France. The Ransons had a valid excuse—they were going to Lourdes to visit their uncle—but Eric thought his fate would be sealed if they were stopped. Once again, luck was with him. They walked for about five hours without meeting anyone. Eventually they were seen by a farmer who called out to them and motioned that the unoccupied zone was just across the road. So the three crossed and, in theory, Doorly was out of danger. (The occupied area of France included northern France and all of the Atlantic Coast to the Spanish border. The remaining southern part of France, including all of the Mediterranean Coast, was not occupied, so once Doorly reached that area he was relatively safe. Following the Allied invasion of North Africa in early November 1942, the Germans and Italians occupied all of France, although their control in many areas of the south was marginal.) After a quiet celebration, the trio continued on to find a town and a way to get to Lourdes. Little did Doorly know that the hardest part of his journey back to England was yet to come.

After another hour of walking, they came to Mussidan. It was a fairly large town, and as the trio walked along the narrow streets, Eric was taken by the quaint houses and the large town square. Although the Ranson boys told him to relax, it was impossible as they brushed shoulders with people in the square and looked at the buildings and shops. Doorly was struck by the seemingly normal pace of life in the town as opposed to that in the area occupied by Germany. It almost seemed as if they had arrived in a different country—one not yet affected by war. Finding that they had to wait for the bus to Lourdes, the Ransons decided to visit a war museum just off the square. Even as they walked through the practically deserted building, Eric found it hard not to look around for unseen German agents waiting to turn him in. Their brief stay at the war museum was plenty long enough for Eric; he could breathe easily for the first time during the entire trip only when they were on the bus to Lourdes and the Ransons' uncle's house.

The bus trip to the small, picturesque city of Lourdes, in the foothills of the Pyrenees, took only six hours. About thirty minutes into the ride, Doorly suddenly felt very weak. A few minutes later he broke out in a sweat and everything suddenly started to swim in his vision. At first he thought it was food poisoning, but it soon became obvious that the problem was a lot greater than that. Eric's world crumbled, for he knew that if he passed out on the bus or became so sick that he attracted attention, someone would surely find out that he was not a Frenchman and then the police would get involved. Fortunately, the bus was not crowded and he was able to lay down on the seat. But he had no control over the situation and he got worse with every passing moment, rapidly becoming more sick than he had ever been in his life. Despite his most valiant efforts, he continued to get weaker and weaker until he was not able to even sit up and could scarcely talk.

By the time the bus reached Lourdes, Doorly was incoherent and his two companions felt sure that he was going to die. He was only partly conscious and barely able to stumble through the streets. The situation was not made any easier by the fact that it was late in the evening and the Ransons did not know exactly where their uncle lived. Had it been earlier in the day, the three could have simply passed themselves off as pilgrims who were coming to Lourdes so the miraculous waters could make Doorly well. But there were no visitors still on the streets, so they didn't think they dared take a taxi and arouse any extra suspicion, given Doorly's condition.

Jean and Robert managed to eventually find their uncle's home, and luck was again with Doorly. The large stucco house was situated on a quiet residential street, and several people, mostly refugees from Germany and occupied France, rented rooms there. Among the boarders was a German Jewish doctor who, after being aroused from a sound sleep, evaluated Doorly's symptoms, observed his yellow pallor, and immediately diagnosed him as having severe jaundice. Doorly's chances of survival, he said, were very slim. Nonetheless, the doctor made him comfortable and, lacking any medicine, fell back on an old remedy of giving the patient periodic enemas to flush out the system.

Early the next morning, the Ransons went to the famous shrine, where in 1858 a fourteen-year-old girl had a vision of the Virgin Mary, to get water to keep Doorly hydrated. (Because of the supposed miraculous healing powers of the water, several million people make the pilgrimage to the city each year.) For several days, Doorly hung between life and death. His pulse rate got as low as forty, and he periodically lapsed into unconsciousness. During one of the most serious of these lapses, the neighborhood priest was summoned to give him the last rites of the Catholic Church. Although none of the other boarders came near him because of the disease, each took time to inquire about his progress and several took turns getting water for him from the shrine. Eventually he began to recover—due primarily, as far as the French were concerned, to the miraculous powers of the water he had been drinking. Still, he was confined to his bed, and it was several weeks before he was strong enough to continue his journey to freedom.

When he had been in Lourdes about a month and was judged fit to continue traveling, two men from the underground at Toulouse came to Lourdes to interview him. Since he had thrown away his dog tags and any other identifying material when he had changed out of his uniform, he had no way to prove his identity. Although the people in Aumale were sure that Doorly was an RAF pilot and those at the house in Lourdes accepted that fact, this was not good enough for the underground—and it was they who would have to get him out of the country. The identification process could often be lengthy, but it was not as long as it might have been for Doorly. The Ransons' uncle had already told the underground as much as he knew about Doorly, and the French had determined, from coordinating with the British by secret radio, that Doorly was indeed missing and that his plane had crashed in the vicinity of

Aumale. Fortunately, by this time, Doorly could speak some French, but it proved to be unnecessary since his two interrogators spoke a little English. Doorly was able to convince them of his identity, and the plan for his escape was put into motion. He would go to a safe house in Toulouse and wait there, with other downed fliers and refugees, until there was a sufficiently large group to be taken to the coast and put on a British submarine for the trip back to England. Unfortunately, the underground had very limited resources and there were too many people with essential skills waiting to get out of France, so the Ranson boys had to stay behind and were never able to fulfill their ambition of fighting for the Free French.

After saying his emotional good-bye to his two benefactors, Jean and Robert, Doorly somewhat reluctantly accompanied the two resistance members to the station in Lourdes and they boarded the train for Toulouse. Because both Lourdes and Toulouse were in unoccupied France, there was little danger in taking the train, and the trip proved to be uneventful. This was just fine with Doorly, since he was still weak and his skin and eyes were quite yellow from his bout with jaundice. For the first time in over two months, he was with strangers whom he had to trust if he wanted to get out of France.

Any doubts that he had about the safe house in Toulouse and the escape plan were erased the moment he walked through the door, for standing there was one of his squadron mates from the RAF, Bob Smith. "My God, I thought you were dead" were the first words out of both men's mouths. Smith had also flown on the mission during which Doorly was shot down, and he, like everyone else in the squadron, thought that there was no way Doorly could have gotten out of his plane as it broke into pieces. Since he had not been reported as a prisoner of war, they all had assumed that he had gone down with his Spitfire and probably burned up in the crash. Doorly, on the other hand, had heard over German radio, while he was in Aumale, that his entire squadron, Number 133, had been shot down near Brest in late September and that there had been no survivors. He, therefore, thought that Smith had been killed.

Contrary to the German report, although five of the American pilots on the ill-fated Morlaix mission had indeed been killed, seven had survived—five as POWs, one who aborted the mission and crash-landed in England, and Bob Smith. The September 26, 1942, assignment was a routine escort mission for the twelve aircraft of Number 133 Squadron of RAF Fighter Command, one of the American Eagle Squadrons. Flying new Spitfire IX fighters, they were to escort a squadron of B-17 bombers on a routine bombing raid on the airfield at Morlaix, France. The weather briefing had been for a wind of thirty-five miles per hour from the south at 28,000 feet, with broken clouds below. When the fighters reached the assigned rendezvous altitude, the bombers were nowhere to be found and they were flying over a solid undercast of clouds. The squadron continued to fly its assigned route, assuming that the bombers had simply arrived at the point early and continued on the mission—not an unusual occurrence. If that was the case, the fighters would soon catch them. Unfortunately, the wind was not from the south, but rather nearly at one hundred miles per hour from the north, and the squadron of fighters soon found itself outside of both radio and radar range of England. Unknown to the fighter pilots, they had been blown as far south as the Bay of Biscay, much too far to be able to return to their home base before they ran out of fuel.

Eventually, they did pick up a group of bombers, but by that time the Spitfires were running low on fuel and had to turn back to their base. After flying the amount of time that should have put them back over England, the unit let down through the clouds, still in combat formation. The squadron broke out of the clouds at about 3,000 feet. Although they were over the water, they could see the coast a short distance ahead. A moment later one pilot saw a large city a few miles to the formation's right. Since they all had no more than fifteen minutes of fuel remaining, they turned toward the municipality and began searching for a place to land. But as they approached the city at about 2,500 feet, the group was caught in a terrific antiaircraft barrage. They immediately broke their formation, and it was every man for himself. "Tell those bastards to quit shooting at us!" someone yelled over the radio, assuming that the squadron was over England. But, in reality, they were over Brest, France, one of the most heavily defended ports in Europe.

Bob Smith found himself at treetop level with about ten minutes of fuel remaining. He had no idea where he was but thought it would be fatal to try to turn in the middle of the flak barrage, so, weaving wildly to the right and left, he continued east at full throttle. In less than two minutes he was out of the flak. Smith could see no other aircraft, so he continued east beneath the clouds. Although he did not know where he was, he assumed he was over France. Smith was immediately in a dilemma. He had no more than ten minutes of fuel remaining, so he either had to crash-land his Spitfire and risk injury in the landing, or bail out and take his chances. He had seen no fields suitable for a landing, so, as his fuel gauge hovered on empty, he pulled up into the clouds and bailed out.

Smith smiled to himself when the violent jerk of his parachute's opening ran through his body, telling him his bailout had been successful. He was soon out of the clouds and actually began to enjoy the sensation of the silent descent. The fields looked soft, but Smith was concerned because of the large number of trees that bordered many of the possible landing sites. His idea was to guide his chute to a place away from any people and, after landing, bury it and get out of the area as rapidly as possible. When he tried to guide the chute, however, it didn't work as he had been told it would, and as he hit the ground, pain shot through his left knee and he collapsed in the field.

A few moments later, he heard shouting and saw two men climb quickly over the fence bordering the field and come running toward him, followed by three or four others. They were wearing what he thought was typical French farmer's clothing, and since Smith had taken two years of French in high school, he knew that was the language they were speaking. For the first time, he knew for sure he was in France. In seconds they were upon him and, before he could collect his thoughts, had taken his parachute. He found himself following them as they set out at a brisk pace across the field. It was all he could do to keep up, and after about thirty minutes of hobbling through the newly harvested cornfields after his benefactors, the pain in his knee became too great and he had to stop. The Frenchmen found a large culvert by the road and told Smith to crawl inside and wait for them.

It was dusk when Smith settled in the culvert and, for the first time, was able to evaluate his situation. He had been able to evade capture when he was most vulnerable, but he was still in his RAF uniform and his knee was in bad shape. As he searched his pockets, Smith remembered that he had taken off without his small evasion kit. "I'm sure I won't need it on this routine mission," he had told his fitter as he'd climbed into the cockpit. That had been a huge mistake. The evasion kit contained a map of France, a compass, and a large number of French francs, all of which he desperately needed. He tried to make a plan in case the Frenchmen didn't return soon, but despite having no food or water and being scared to death, he fell asleep. When he again opened his eyes, it was daylight. It took him a few moments to realize where he was, but after a truck passed over his hiding place all his senses awoke at once. His knee throbbed, his mouth was parched, his stomach cried out for food, and he discovered that he had a cut on his hand. Every time he heard traffic on the road above him, his heart would skip a beat, but not knowing where he was, the desperate airman anxiously waited for the Frenchmen to return. Fortunately, the temperature was mild as he lay in the culvert all day.

It was evening when the two men returned to the culvert with three bicycles but no food or water. Smith was told to ride with them, and the three set off down the road. They had not ridden far when the chain came off Smith's bike. Forgetting where he was, he yelled "Come here, come here, stop!" to his guides. It had appeared to Smith that the two Frenchmen were very uneasy before, but they were beside themselves when he yelled at them in English. They quickly fixed his bike but suddenly seemed in a hurry to get rid of him. Within a few minutes they turned down a small lane. About a hundred yards down the road was a shed. He was instructed to go inside and wait for them to return.

Smith was able to find some straw in the shed but was absolutely desperate for food and water. He knew that he had to survive through the night, but if he did not get something to eat and drink the next day, he would have to turn himself in. A quick check of his surroundings gave him no help, and he noticed that the bike he had ridden was gone. To him that meant only one thing: the Frenchmen had abandoned him and he was on his own. Smith had never been so lonely or depressed in his entire life as he was that night. He was alone and had no idea where he was. His body was rapidly deteriorating from both pain and lack of sustenance, and it was all he could do to keep from breaking down. As he lay on his thin bed of straw, he thought of his home and family in Washington, D.C., and the lure of flying that had driven him to fly every chance he got. He smiled to himself as he remembered taking pictures of the Potomac River flood in 1935 from a biplane and his appointment to the U.S. Naval Academy in 1938. He had been heartbroken when a slight myopia was found in his right eye during his entrance physical and he was disqualified. Fortunately, he had an offer to go to the Citadel to play football. At the same time, he also wondered what had become of the rest of his squadron, and with these many thoughts jumbled in his mind, Smith fell into a fitful sleep.

When he awoke early the next morning, Smith had but one objective: he had to get help or turn himself in to the police or the Germans. With no compass or map, he got a general bearing from the sun and started to walk south across the fields. He had to take a chance and make himself known to someone, so when he saw a woman working a field, he knew the time had come. With all the courage he possessed and with a lump in his throat, the dirty, unshaven, and desperate pilot approached the lady. In his hesitant and broken French, he told the woman that he was an American RAF pilot and that he needed help. He was rewarded beyond his wildest dreams when the lady told him to follow her and took the haggard pilot to a small farmhouse. The meal of warm soup accompanied by delicious bread, cheese, wine, and, to Smith the best of all, water was the greatest meal he had ever eaten. The lady then took him to a small bedroom where she told him he would have to stay until the next day. But it was an optimistic pilot who spent the day sitting in that room, listening to the sounds of the farm and the countryside and appreciating his good fortune. Bob would never forget how a good meal can turn the world around. That evening, the meal was repeated. As Smith ate, the lady told him that her husband had been taken by the Germans and that she did not know where he was or even if he was still alive. She was ready to do anything she could to help defeat Germany, she said, although she had not helped anyone evade before. As he lay waiting for sleep to come, Smith was confident he was going to survive and evade the Germans.

Early the following morning, after a sparse breakfast, the woman took Smith to the top of a hill that was covered with thick bushes. She told him to stay there and wait for her to come for him that evening. Shortly before dark, she arrived and took him back to her house for a dinner similar to the meals of the previous day and then directed him to the barn for the night. The next morning Smith was again taken to the hilltop and given the same instructions. But at about noon he was frightened out of his wits as he heard a number of voices. Soon he was confronted by several Frenchmen and women carrying bread, cheese, wine, and cider. Most of the neighboring farmers had somehow learned about Smith and wanted to help him in whatever way they could. When his benefactress came for him that evening, he was able to provide the food for dinner from what the other farmers had given him. The same ritual was repeated for the next few days until Smith had to tell his hostess that he could not accept any more food. He knew that these poor French farmers were giving him part of the food and wine that they needed to survive.

One evening, before Smith went to the barn, a lame young man who was obviously very concerned and contrite came to the house. Smith recognized him as one of the men who had helped him in the field right after he landed. The young Frenchman had been delegated to explain to Smith why he had been abandoned in the shed a few days earlier. Fortunately, he spoke some English, so Bob could get the entire story. When the chain had come off his bike and Smith had yelled "Come here," the French farmers thought it sounded like *"Kommen Sie her"* and thought he was a German. They wanted to get out of there as soon as possible, so they'd dumped Smith at the first available place. The young man told Smith that the Frenchmen had no intention of ever coming back for him. He also said that soon they would be traveling to the small town of Hanvec, about thirty-five miles southeast of Brest, where Smith would be staying for a few days.

Late the following afternoon, the lame young man and the lady with whom Smith had been staying walked with him the few miles to the outskirts of the village. The walk was longer than it could have been, the young Frenchman explained, because they were taking the back roads to avoid coming in contact with any Germans. Fortunately, they saw none, and in the twilight they approached a modest, two-story white frame house that overlooked the main road on the edge of Hanvec. Smith was met at the door by an older man who directed him to a bedroom on the second floor and told him to remain there and stay away from the windows.

When Smith awoke late the next morning, he took a bath in a very small tub, used the razor and brush that his host had left for him, and soon felt better than he had in a number of days. He was tempted to leave the room and wander the rest of the house or to go to the window and see just where he was but, obeying his host, he simply sat in the chair next to the bed in his small room and waited for something to happen. It was nearly noon when there was a faint knock on the door and a pretty little girl, about six years old, told him to come to the kitchen with her for lunch. During the meal, Smith learned that the house was inhabited by the man he had met, his wife, and three small children: two boys about ten and eight years old and their younger sister. He also found out that this family, like the farm lady, had never aided a downed pilot before. Apparently, the family was charged with keeping Smith out of sight while the underground was contacted and a plan was devised to start moving him south to unoccupied France.

Although time hung heavily on Smith's hands as he whiled away the early days of October in Hanvec, he had company in the children. They would often come to his room, and he would try to teach them English while they helped him with his French. He spent many hours talking with the entire family about the United States and his family in Washington. But there were also times when depression hit Smith like a rock and he would consider turning himself in. He feared for the family that was aiding him and knew that, if they were caught, at least the man would probably be shot. But each time he thought about ending his evasion, something would happen—like having one of the children knock on his door or sharing a small glass of wine with his host—and his optimism would build once again.

After Smith had been at the house for about a week, a middle-aged man came and brought him a new outfit. He finally shed his RAF uniform and was given a black suit, a white shirt, and black shoes, but no hat. Although the clothes were about three sizes too large for his five-foot-eleven-inch, one-hundred-and-fifty-pound frame, they were acceptable, and with a haircut supplied by his hostess, Smith looked very much like most of the other Frenchmen he had seen. His identity was soon to be tested, for a few days later the man came again, this time to tell Smith that they were going to travel.

The plan was for Smith and his French guide to depart very early in the morning and ride bicycles nearly twenty miles to the city of Quimper. Once there, they would get the morning train that would take them to Bordeaux. Bob could find no words to thank his French hosts as he departed for Quimper. "They risked their lives and everything they had for me," he thought. "How do I adequately express my thanks for that?" Overcome with emotion, he simply said *"Merci,"* kissed each member of the family on the cheek, and rode away.

On the ride, Bob's guide told him that although they would sit in the same compartment on the train, there was no way that the Frenchman would acknowledge that he knew Smith. He explained that there would be many civilians as well as German soldiers in the car and that Smith should just pretend to sleep during the ten-hour trip. No matter what, he should not engage anyone in conversation. These words put Bob on the edge of panic. What would he do if he encountered a German? How could he ignore those in the compartment with him if they wanted to talk? What if the conductor asked a question when he collected the tickets? These and a hundred more questions were running around Smith's head when the pair approached the train station and Smith came face-to-face with his first German soldiers.

The platform was teeming with people as Smith waited for the train to come, and he soon found himself standing next to several German enlisted men. He was absolutely scared to death. His knees shook, and he was sure the Germans were all looking at him. He wanted to run and hide and forget the entire trip but there was no place to go, so he just stood there. After a few breathless moments, Smith realized that the Germans were not the least bit interested in him. Like other soldiers in a foreign country, they were busy talking to each other and ignored everyone else. But Smith's anxiety didn't cease when they boarded the train. He found himself in a compartment with his guide, and just when he thought there would be only the two of them riding together, several German soldiers entered the compartment. Smith's heart sank and the sweat poured off his skin. Following his guide's actions, he did not say anything to them, but helped them put their baggage in the overhead rack so he wouldn't look suspicious or draw any comment from the Germans. After everyone was settled, Smith, heeding the advice of his guide, was soon pretending to be asleep. In reality, he was terrified. Soon the dreaded moment came for ticket checking. When Smith gave the conductor his ticket to Bordeaux, the official gave him a rather suspicious look, but he punched the ticket and went on to another compartment. Bob again closed his eyes and retreated into his own frightened world.

As the train slowed for a stop a short time later, the Germans stood, so Smith and his guide helped them retrieve their baggage and heaved a sigh of relief when they left the compartment. No one took their place, and Bob was able to relax a little and look at the fall landscape passing by the window. "It would be easy to forget there is a war going on," he mused as he gazed at the French countryside. "And to think, a few weeks ago I was flying over this very spot on another escort mission. With any luck, I'll be able to do it again soon." Still, each time they passed through a city such as Nantes or Saintes, Smith would again find himself sweating for fear that a new person would sit in the compartment and want to talk with him or that the conductor would ask him a question. It was a relieved and emotionally exhausted airman who finally got off the train in Bordeaux.

As Smith stepped onto the platform he immediately looked around for his guide. Panic seized him as he realized that they had become separated while getting off the train. He tried his best to look inconspicuous as he waited and watched for the familiar face. Smith had not counted on the station's being crowded late in the afternoon, but in the mass of people it took him several minutes to find his guide. As soon as they made eye contact, the Frenchman set off out of the station at a brisk pace. The relieved Smith followed, staying about twenty or thirty feet behind him. Smith had been briefed that if his guide suddenly changed his pace or made any abrupt action, he was to immediately cross the street, turn the corner, or do whatever seemed appropriate at the time, since that was the signal for trouble. If that happened, his guide had made it clear that Smith was on his own. Bob was completely oblivious of the old classic buildings and the beautiful squares of the city, as well as of the activity around him; he kept his eyes glued on the man he was following. As they walked the narrow stone streets lined with stone and stucco buildings housing businesses on the ground floor and apartments above, Smith tried to figure out what he would do if there was a problem. Alone in a strange city and country, he had no idea where to go or whom to contact, so he just prayed that all would go well. His heart skipped and he felt momentary panic every time he saw a German vehicle or soldier. Fortunately, the long walk was uneventful, and it was nearly dark when they walked into a contractor's yard on the outskirts of Bordeaux.

The contractor evidently expected the two, because Smith was immediately loaded into the back of a truck among a number of bags of cement, and his guide got into the front. Smith was told to keep well hidden as the truck began its journey to the east and out of the occupied zone of France. The trip continued well into the night. At a small town outside the occupied area, the truck stopped and Smith was told to get out. Although he was elated to be away from the Germans, his guide explained that he had to watch out for the police, who would immediately turn him in if they suspected he was not French. "They are even more dangerous than the Germans," the Frenchman explained, "because they can easily identify someone who doesn't speak French correctly and they also have a knack for identifying strangers." Smith was taken to a shed where there was some straw on which he could sleep. His guide told him that someone would come for him early in the morning. With that, the hungry and thirsty airman was left alone.

It seemed that he had just closed his eyes when he awoke with a start to the squeak of the shed door. As Smith struggled to get his bearings, the young man who stood in the opening told him to hurry and follow him, again at a distance. They walked to the station, and Smith's guide bought two tickets to Vichy, the capital of unoccupied France. Bob periodically felt dizzy as they walked because he was so hungry and thirsty. He was positive that he stood out from the crowd in the teeming station, and the tendency of his guide to keep disappearing into the throng simply made matters worse. Each time that happened, Bob would tremble for fear someone would try to talk to him and immediately realize he was not French, or that he would succumb to the periodic dizziness and fall down. He was even more concerned with the number of police standing about; they would certainly question him if anything unusual happened. Fortunately, each time Smith would approach getting desperate about what he should do, his guide would reemerge. Just as they boarded the train, Smith's guide gave him a large piece of bread and immediately disappeared, leaving him on his own. "Just watch for me to signal where we will get off," were the instructions he had been given on the walk to the station. "It will be in a little over four hours." Smith's only problem was that he had no watch and certainly could not ask anyone on the train what time it was.

Unfortunately, Smith could not repeat the tactics he had used earlier. The train was so crowded that he was forced to stand during the entire trip. This time he resorted to being disagreeable, and whenever anyone said anything to him he simply grunted and looked the other way. As he swayed with the crowded car, he marveled at his situation. "Here I am on a train going to a strange city and depending on a man I don't know to tell me when to get off. I never thought I would be putting my life in the hands of complete strangers in a foreign country." His legs ached, and he thought he could stand no longer—when suddenly he saw his guide making his way through the crowded car. Although the Frenchman paid no attention to him, Smith assumed this was his signal, and so he began to work his way toward the door. Soon the train stopped and the pair alighted in a small town west of Vichy. This time his guide was more friendly as they walked to a market. Smith took a long drink from a fountain they passed on the way, and the meal of bread, cheese, a couple of pears, and a bottle of wine that they enjoyed in the late October sunshine in a nearby park made him feel like a new man. He was surprised at the amount of food available, since it had been so scarce in Hanvec. What a contrast to the area occupied by the Germans, Smith thought. Aside from the food, the people seemed happier as they gathered in small groups to talk, and there was none of the constant looking around to see if there was a German soldier nearby. Although Smith was curious about why they had come to that town, he refrained from asking his guide.

As soon as they finished eating, Smith's guide was up and moving again, back toward the railroad station. As the two neared the station, a short, balding stranger approached them. He said nothing, but as soon as he was beside Smith, his former companion disappeared. It seemed strange to Bob that they would come all that way on the train just to change guides. Although he did not know it at the time, Smith found out later that his new escort was part of the French underground. Apparently the stop in the small town near Vichy had been made to transfer him to their control.

The next destination was Lyons. As soon as Smith got off the train, his new guide took him to the small apartment of a young Frenchman. No sooner had the pair entered the flat than Smith's host, who spoke some English, turned on a record player and Smith heard the familiar sounds of Benny Goodman and American swing. His benefactor had a large stack of records, and to be polite to his host, the exhausted Smith had to sit and listen until late into the night. Finally, he was shown a bedroom, where he fell into the bed.

Smith remained with the young man for two days, never being allowed to leave the apartment or look out the windows. As Smith talked with his host during lulls in the music, it was difficult not to ask his name, what he did for a living, and why Smith was being kept in Lyons. (It was not unusual for the underground to move evaders to a number of towns or hiding places. Often they would receive word of a German search that was pending, have to hold an evader for a few days while further plans were developed, or simply keep him moving so the Germans would not get on his trail.) Still, Bob remembered his evasion training and the charge that you never asked anyone his or her name, nor did you try to find out anything about him or her. The opposite was not true, however. Smith's host was full of questions about his home and family, life in the United States, and how he happened to get into the RAF.

Smith related how he enrolled in the Civilian Pilot Training Program to get his pilot's license and then decided to leave the Citadel, even though he was playing football and wrestling, so he could pursue a career in flying. He'd returned to Washington, bought an Alliance Argo airplane, and begun to fly seriously. But as the shadows of war lengthened in 1940 and early 1941, he became convinced that the United States would soon be involved. Not wanting to fight in the infantry, and lacking the two years of college he needed to qualify for the military aviation cadet program, he searched for a way to fly in combat. In the summer of 1941, Smith heard of the Clayton Knight Committee and the opportunity to join the Royal Air Force. He jumped at the chance. After a few months of training in the United States and an unforgettable voyage across the North Atlantic, he was in England as an RAF pilot in early 1942. He had been flying the Spitfire for only a few months when the Morlaix disaster occurred.

During the course of their many conversations, the young Frenchman did tell Smith that he was staying in Lyons while further arrangements were being made to move him, but that was all. On the third day of his stay, a tall, middle-aged, mustachioed man, whom Smith had never seen before, came to the apartment and told him it was time to travel again. Smith was getting to be an old hand at railroad travel in France, and for the first time he found himself fairly relaxed as they approached the large station in Lyons. He was curious about where they

Bob Smith (*left*) and two squadron mates, Ben DeHaven and Dennis Smith, at Biggin Hill RAF base in spring 1942.   *Bob Smith*

were going next, however. When his guide bought two tickets for Marseilles, Bob was elated. He was convinced that he was in the hands of the underground and would be smuggled out of the harbor at Marseilles at night and put on a submarine for the trip to freedom. Thus, it was an excited pilot who got off the train with his guide a few hours later in the huge port city. As the pair walked through the crowded streets of Marseilles, Bob found it easy to forget about the war. There was an atmosphere of what Smith assumed was normal for a large French city in late October, as families strolled the streets, women shopped and talked cheerfully with their friends, and traffic moved briskly.

Smith and his guide walked leisurely to a neighborhood of very nice apartment houses, and Smith soon found himself in a luxurious flat talking to a man who introduced himself as Dr. Rodocanachi. As his eyes swept the rooms, Smith was impressed with the quality of the furniture, the beautiful paintings on the walls, and the oriental rugs on the floors. Madame Rodocanachi showed Smith to a very large bedroom with an attached bathroom. She instructed him, in English, to stay in the room and not go near the windows. She would take him to meals, but that was the only time he could leave his room. It was obvious from the facilities and the businesslike manner in which he was handled that the Rodocanachis had sheltered other evaders before Smith. Fortunately, there were several English-language books in a bookcase on one wall, so Smith could while away the hours reading. But no matter what he was doing, his mind continued to come back to the possible scenario of his escape from France. He thought of all sorts of ways in which he might be smuggled from the port and even wondered where he would sleep if he was put on a submarine.

After his second night at the doctor's house, however, Bob began to worry. If he was going to be taken out to a submarine or another ship, why was he staying in an apartment in the middle of the city? He should be moving toward the waterfront. And during his brief mealtime conversations with his hosts, there was no mention made of any plan of escape. In fact, when Bob brought up the topic, the only answer he got was that it was being taken care of.

On Smith's third day with the doctor and his wife, another stranger appeared at the door. The visitor was a Frenchman who identified himself as Paul Ullman. He had come to take Smith to his home in Toulouse, about two hundred miles to the west. Bob was crestfallen. None of his imagined escapes were going to take place, and he was not on the verge of freedom. Rather, he was going to a city nearly a hundred miles from the ocean, and he could see no way of moving out of France from there. The train across southern France was nearly full, and Smith and Ullman found themselves in a compartment with three other men. As the green and brown fields and forests flashed by, Smith concentrated on the beauty of the countryside lit by the autumn sunlight. Leaves were turning, most of the fields had been harvested, and workers were in the vineyards. "Smoke?" Ullman said in English to his startled companion. Smith was petrified as he waited for one of the other men in the compartment to question why Paul was using English. But when Ullman continued to use periodic English, Smith relaxed, for no one seemed the least bit interested in the two men.

The nearly forty-five-minute walk from the train station in Toulouse to Paul's house gave Smith an opportunity to see one of the most beautiful cities in France. As they walked through the old part of the town, the uniformity of the terra-cotta stucco and tile roofs made the city glow in the late afternoon sun. Eventually, Paul led the way to a modest, two-story, stucco house in a quiet residential neighborhood. Upon entering, Smith was greeted by a British soldier named Victor, who had been in France since Dunkirk, and Squadron Leader Donald Barnard, an RAF Wellington bomber pilot who had made a forced landing at night. The two told Smith that Ullman's home was an underground safe house where evaders were kept until they could be moved out of France. Smith had been in Toulouse for four days when the next evading airman, Eric Doorly, arrived.

Since Toulouse was in unoccupied France, life in the safe house was less a strain for Doorly and Smith than had been the case at their other locations. The British were supplying the resistance with all the money it needed, so the food was excellent and the underground could buy anything it wanted. Ullman's house was crowded, so Smith and Doorly had to share a room and a bed, but each could sleep without fear of being captured for the first time since he had landed in France. The only danger came from the house's being a center for sending information about German operations to England by radio, so there was always the chance that the police or some German agents might zero in on the location of the radio. "If that happens," one of the resistance fighters told Doorly, "we are all dead." The Vichy French government was responsible for keeping law and order in southern France as well as ensuring that the area did not become a center for Allied operations. It had been made clear by the Germans that failure to control such operations could result in occupation by Germany, a fate no one in the unoccupied area wanted. Therefore, the French police would react to any report of suspicious activity and turn the suspects over to the Germans. In addition, there were numerous German agents operating throughout unoccupied France, especially in the larger cities.

Because the safe house was right in Toulouse, the sixth largest city in France, and there were known to be a number of German agents in the area, the five or six evaders had to remain indoors as they waited for their escape plan to become reality. This was particularly frustrating for Doorly because he had read that the terra-cotta brick and red roof tiles that made the city an artist's dream were unforgettable in the constantly changing winter sun and that the eleventh-century part of the city was one of the most fascinating in Europe. Still, he could not risk being seen and possibly betraying the location of the safe house, so he followed directions.

As Smith had speculated when he had been moved to Marseilles, the underground's plan was to smuggle the evaders out of France by boat and then to rendezvous with a British submarine. Unfortunately, the group's wait to be delivered to the submarine proved to be in vain. During the first week of November 1942, the Allies invaded North Africa. Germany and its ally Italy immediately moved to occupy the rest of France, primarily to secure the coast and stop any support for the Allies across the Mediterranean. They also sealed the border and allowed no travel into Spain. Although the inhabitants of the Ullman house were jubilant at the news of the invasion, the radio transmission that told them that the plan for rescue by submarine was scrapped left them dejected. So during the long days of November, Smith, Doorly, who was getting stronger each day, and their companions sat around, played cards, and speculated on how they were going to get out of France. And every discussion ended with only one option: walk over the Pyrenees to Spain. Everyone had reservations about how successful that undertaking would be, given that the border had been sealed and that neutral Spain was known to be sympathetic to Germany, but there really was no other choice. The resistance, too, had major problems. It now had to change its entire operation to cope with the German occupation as well as figure out how to get the Allied airmen and refugees it had in Toulouse into Spain.

There were three major problems associated with the Pyrenees route, all not fully appreciated by any of the company, including the members of the underground. First, winter had come to the mountains and none of the evaders had adequate winter clothes. Each had shed his flying garb for whatever the French could give him, and no one had received a warm coat or boots. Further, the resistance could not provide these items without arousing suspicion. This would mean climbing over the mountains in the snow, ice, and bitter cold of winter without anything approaching adequate clothing and no survival gear of any kind. The second problem was Spain itself. Although technically neutral, Spain was not friendly to the Allies, and anyone caught trying to get from France to Spain could expect to be either sent back to France or put in jail in Spain for an unknown length of time. Directly related was the third problem. The sudden German occupation of southern France had caused thousands of refugees from all over Europe, who had taken sanctuary in Vichy France, to try to get out of that country before they were caught by the Germans. Doorly and Smith were part of that group. The result was huge numbers of illegal foreigners crossing the mountains almost every day to try to find sanctuary in Spain. This situation had caused strong protests from Germany, so the Spanish government had stepped up security along the border and stiffened the penalty for being caught trying to cross illegally. (Only about half of those who reached the Pyrenees successfully crossed into Spain. A large percentage were captured and turned over to French or German authorities, while a significant number were killed in accidents, died from exposure, or simply found the trip too difficult and turned back.)

Both Doorly and Smith had some idea of the risks, but both agreed that anything was better than staying in France. The underground decided that everyone should get moving fairly soon because the weather in the mountains would only get worse and there was no way of knowing when the resistance might have to abandon the safe house, given the increasing German presence in the city. Guides were hired by the underground to meet the evaders at a certain point, and the next great adventure began.

The plan was to take the train from Toulouse beyond the port of Perpignan to the area of Céret, which was as far as the train ran into the foothills and relatively close to the Spanish border. They would then cross near the extreme eastern end of the Pyrenees where the terrain was less rugged and the weather the most mild. The evaders were to jump from the train when it slowed for the town and start walking south. They would then meet the guides, who would take them to the Spanish border, where they would be on their own.

In early December the group set out. They did not travel together because any group naturally attracted attention, especially since there were so many refugees trying to get out of France. Eric was uneasy about the train trip from the very start. Bob, who had ridden more French trains in his evasion experience, tried to reassure him, but Doorly's concern seemed to be valid. Shortly after setting out from Toulouse, the underground escort told them to leave the train at the next stop. There they waited for several uncomfortable minutes for another train that took them back to Toulouse. Doorly and Smith speculated at length about what had gone wrong, but their inquiries to their resistance hosts brought no explanation for the change of plan.

Several days later, the group set out again. Doorly was doubly concerned this time, given his previous experience. He was also escorted by a resistance member who seemed uncertain as to what to do or exactly how to proceed. As opposed to his earlier trips, this train was crowded, so there were six other people, all Frenchmen, in Doorly's compartment. The trip was uneventful until about six miles before they were to get off, when the peaceful swaying of the car stopped as the train came to a sudden halt, and a group of uniformed French officials came on board. At the sight of the officials entering the train, Doorly's underground escort whispered "Remember the plan" and departed. Doorly was left completely on his own—and, to make matters worse, had no idea what the plan was.

The car in which Doorly was riding was typical of those found on trains all over Europe, with an aisle down one side of the car and a number of compartments that could be entered from the aisle. Since his compartment was full, there was nothing Doorly could do but sit and wait. Soon an official entered and began talking very rapidly in French. Each of the occupants produced his papers, and the official began to carefully examine each as he conversed with the person who owned the papers. The sweat was pouring down Doorly's back, and he knew every occupant of the car could feel him shaking as the official worked his way toward the hapless American. "What a way to have it all end," thought a very frightened Eric. "Here I have evaded the Germans for over three months, had several people risk their lives for me, survived a normally fatal bout with jaundice, and now I am going to get caught just a few miles from freedom."

"Vos documents, s'il vous plaît," the official said to Doorly. He dutifully produced the papers that had been given to him by the mayor in Aumale several months before. They seemed far less elaborate than the papers produced by the other occupants of the compartment. The official looked at the papers, then looked at Doorly, said *"Merci,"* and left the car. The shocked Doorly was speechless. When he had stopped shaking, he realized that the official had to have been an underground member, since there was no way his papers were adequate. As the train began to move, Eric, with new confidence in the underground, once again became optimistic that he would indeed make it to Spain.

In a few minutes, they entered the foothills, and as the train slowed for its stop at Céret, Doorly jumped from the car, rolled down the embankment, and ran some distance from the tracks. A minute later his traveling companion emerged from the shadows and instructed Doorly to follow him. They began walking south through the rapidly rising and increasingly rugged hills. Once again, there were few people on the road. Ahead Doorly could see the scrub-covered hills and beyond them the steep, rocky, snow-covered, and barren Pyrenees. His spirits soared as he anticipated that across them lay freedom.

After walking for an hour or so, Doorly and his guide were joined by their companions from Toulouse, including Smith, who'd had an uneventful trip, and another guide, who was carrying a bag of food. A short time later, seven or eight others merged with the company. It was dark, but the group continued to climb nonetheless. As they slipped and slid up the mountain, several of the hikers fell or strained muscles and soon could go no farther. Finally, they came upon a number of large boulders that formed a shelter from the wind, and there the exhausted evaders spent the rest of the night huddled against the cold.

The morning began with the discovery that the guides were gone—and with them all the food. The evaders' situation suddenly had become desperate. Still, they set out, climbing toward the south and, they hoped, Spain. As Smith looked ahead, he cringed at the sight of the high hills and the clouds that seemed to threaten a major storm. His low-quarter shoes were already coming apart, and even with the light Burberry coat he was wearing, he was already chilled to the bone. Soon the ground began to show a light dusting of snow, and temperatures dropped as the exhausted and famished group climbed until late afternoon into the foothills.

By that time, the still weak Doorly was shaking like a leaf from the cold, his legs ached with every step, and he knew he could go no farther. Several others in the group were in the same condition. Fortunately, they came upon a goat herder's shack, which provided some shelter from the bitter cold. Most, including Doorly, wanted to spend the night and make their final trek into Spain the next morning. Smith, Barnard, and two others disagreed. They believed it would be best to go as far as they could in the remaining daylight because they had no food or other supplies and the time spent resting would actually make them weaker. The ensuing discussion was intense, but in the end Doorly had no choice but to stay in the shack for the night because he simply could walk no farther. Most of the others agreed that they needed to have some rest before climbing the remainder of the way and crossing into Spain. After an emotional farewell, Doorly and Smith parted, each with his own idea of how to get to freedom.

Smith and his three companions continued their climb in the bitter cold of late afternoon. They had no map, so they had no idea where the border actually was or where they could go after getting into Spain. About an hour after setting out on their own, just at dusk, as they were following a dry creek bed through a valley, the four were seen by a pair of uniformed Spaniards. The police fired some warning shots, arrested the four, and took them a short distance to their headquarters, which, the captives realized gratefully, was heated. After a short discussion in the warm hut, the Spaniards told them, with little enthusiasm, that they had to go back to France. "I think we can bribe these guys," Smith said to Barnard. Fortunately, the underground had supplied the evaders with a considerable amount of money before they began their trek, and some of the currency, along with Barnard's watch, did the trick. The Spaniards told the four to cross the creek at a bridge farther down the mountain and then stay on the south side. The evaders assumed that this was just a ploy to lead them into more guards and more bribes, so they stayed on the north side of the creek and moved some distance into the under- growth. Sure enough, farther down the creek there was another guard station on the south side.

It wasn't long until the guards became less of a problem to the four than the weather, for it began to snow. To make matters worse, it was dark, they did not know where they were, they had not eaten for nearly two days, and they could find no shelter. The exhausted hikers finally huddled in a small grove of trees, where they spent the coldest night any of them had ever experienced. As he shivered and shook, Smith was convinced they would freeze to death before morning. Miraculously, the four were aroused from their freezing stupor by bright sun in a cloud- less sky. Although there was nothing to eat, they thought they could make good time since they were now going downhill and were confi- dent they would soon find a source of food and maybe shelter. But as the afternoon shadows lengthened, it was obvious they would have to spend yet another night in the open, still without any food. Once again, the dangerously weakened evaders lay down in the trees. Fortunately, it was not nearly as cold, but Smith still slept fitfully as he dreamed of steak and baked potatoes.

By noon the following day, the mountains were beginning to give way to foothills and farms, cattle raising, and olive groves. The desper- ate men tried eating olives off the trees, but they were so bitter that even the starving evaders couldn't eat them. They were able to buy some milk from a farmer, but it did little to counter their ever-weakening condition. Late in the day, they came to a small foothill town surrounded by olive groves. The terrain on the north fell off precipitously into a valley, so the choice was to either go through the town or cross a small stream and go around the village to the south. Two members of the group decided they would go through rather than make the difficult circle to the south. Smith and Barnard chose to go around the town and meet their comrades on the other side. The other two never arrived, and after waiting for a couple of hours, Smith and Barnard assumed that the pair had been taken prisoner by the police. They set out alone across the countryside.

Conditions soon became impossible for the pair. They were filthy and unshaven, their hair was matted, and they were starving. Too weak to continue going cross-country, they were confined to stumbling along the road. Eventually they entered the outskirts of the city of Gerona, nearly forty miles from Céret, and were able to find the British consul. Inexplicably, he offered them no aid of any kind and turned the pair back out on the road. It was only a matter of time until they would be caught by the police or have to turn themselves in.

Although they tried their best to avoid checkpoints, two days after the disappearance of their two comrades, as Smith and Barnard were walking along the road early in the morning nearly seventy miles from the Spanish border, they were apprehended by the Spanish police. The two were taken to police headquarters in the coast town of Malgrat de Mar, about forty miles from Barcelona, where they were questioned and kicked and punched around before being literally thrown into a stone and cinder-block jail cell. The twenty-by-twelve-foot cell had one cot with bare springs covered by straw mats and a barrel in the corner to serve as a toilet. Because they had no identification and neither man could speak Spanish, the jailer refused to believe, or possibly did not understand, their story about being RAF pilots, and he simply let them sit in the cell, subsisting on mush in the morning and soup and bread in the evening. "At least we have some food," Barnard remarked, trying to put a good light on their situation. A week later, the pair were transported by train to Barcelona, where they were put in a ten-by-six-foot prison cell with eight other men who had also been caught crossing the border illegally. The only consolation about being in such miserable circumstances was that Smith was warm for the first time since he had left Toulouse.

Doorly and his companions who had not elected to go with Smith and the other three spent a restless night on the ground in the bone-chilling cold. Had they not had the shelter provided by the shack, Doorly was sure they would have frozen to death. Early the next morning the starving group was hiking again, following goat tracks across the steep, rocky hills. The climb was hard, and often a member of the party would slip on the slick rocks and have to grab one of the others in the group to keep from falling. Fortunately, they were in an area of the border that was not regularly patrolled by the Spanish, and after what seemed like an eternity of climbing and reaching the top of a mountain only to find another that had to be crossed, they reached the crest of the mountains and started down. But as they were carefully picking their way along a steep, rocky ravine, their trip was suddenly interrupted by a loud shout of *"Alto!"* From the hillside, not far away, several uniformed Spanish police advanced on the group with leveled rifles. After a brief conversation with those in the group who spoke some Spanish, Doorly and his desperate companions were told to return to the French side of the border. Doorly tried to explain that he was a downed pilot, but as far as the Spanish police were concerned they were just more of the hundreds of refugees trying to get out of France and illegally enter Spain. It was obvious that the Spanish police meant business, so the evaders reluctantly turned around and began retracing their steps. In case they had second thoughts about returning, the Spaniards accompanied them. A request for some food was dismissed with a laugh from the police. "So close and yet so far," were the words that Eric repeated over and over again in his mind as he stumbled back over the hills, the tears welling in his eyes.

When they reached the border, the group was told to stay on the French side and not try to come back into Spain. The starving, depressed evaders spent the remainder of the day in the cold, taking shelter only among some trees, as they debated what to do. The discussion focused on how to get across the border without being caught, what to do if they were intercepted again, and how to find food. All agreed that they had to find another crossing point, so the exhausted evaders walked, stumbled, and slid about three miles to the east in the hope of being able to avoid being seen when they tried to cross again the next day.

The second issue of debate concerned what to do if they were caught. Doorly and his companions finally decided that if they were intercepted they would try to talk the police into letting them buy bus tickets and ride to Barcelona, where they would be turned in to the authorities. Part of the bargain would be that the group would also buy round-trip tickets for the police so they could accompany their prisoners to Barcelona and, after a few days on the town, have a free ride back to the frontier. Despite the previous rebuff, they were confident the police would give them food when they saw the condition of the group.

After spending their third night in the cold, Doorly's starving group prepared to cross the border once again. Although they had thought about trying to cross at night, they did not know the way and the mountains were steep, so wisdom prevailed and they waited until the sun came up. Initially, all went well, and they succeeded in walking far enough to be sure they were again well into Spain. But as they approached a small village on the rocky slopes, they were once again halted by the police. A long and involved discussion followed, impeded by an inability of any of the group, or the police, to speak the other's language with any fluency. Fortunately, the evaders spoke enough Spanish to explain their idea. Evidently, the thought of spending a few days on the town in Barcelona won over the police, and they agreed to the plan. The refugees were given some food and took a much-needed rest on the floor of the crude, but warm, police building before the ancient vehicle that would take them to Barcelona arrived.

During the four-hour ride to Barcelona, through farmland, olive groves, hills, and the cities of Figueres and Gerona, Doorly and his companions speculated on their fate. They found they could talk very freely since no one on the bus seemed to understand English, nor were any of the passengers at all interested in the ragged, filthy foreigners. The small band of travelers concluded that they might be put in some kind of jail for a few days but that the British would certainly get them out in short order. Thus, their spirits were high as they entered the beautiful city of Barcelona with its colorful streets lined with stately buildings. On every side was the hustle and bustle of a country not at war, and it was initially strange to see no Germans, given their preoccupation with them every minute for the preceding four months. Doorly even hoped to spend a day sight-seeing after the British embassy got him set free.

Any euphoria was rapidly dispelled as the group was deposited in the city jail on charges of entering the country illegally, bringing foreign currency into the country, and bribing police officers at the border. Each was given the opportunity to contact the appropriate embassy, but it did little good. Since he was an RAF pilot, Doorly talked to the British embassy, but the call gave him no comfort. Not only would there be no sight-seeing, but the only assurance he received was that the embassy would report his whereabouts to England and the RAF and would try to get him some food, clothing, and blankets. "Beyond that," he was told, "we will work to get you released but be patient; it may take quite a while." With these less than comforting assurances, Doorly and his companions were put in jail. Although he did not know it, a few days later Bob Smith would also be brought to the same facility.

Eric was convinced he was having a nightmare as he was rudely pushed into the twelve-foot-square cell with nineteen other men. There was not enough room to sleep, no place to sit and eat, and the bathroom was one toilet in the corner of the room; he soon discovered that the toilet was simply a seat over a hole that got stopped up with great regularity and appeared to never have been cleaned. There was no furniture in the room, just a concrete floor on which to sit, lie, stand, eat, and sleep, and the stench of the men's bodies and the toilet was almost unbearable. Because it was so crowded, Eric initially thought he might be in the wrong cell, maybe one reserved for hardened criminals. But he soon found that, because of the huge number of illegal refugees entering Spain, every cell in every jail was equally full. The Spanish were simply overwhelmed by the influx. And it seemed to Eric that every man in his cell was a refugee. He was the only American among the group, which included Arabs, Englishmen, Frenchmen, Danes, and several men of unknown nationalities.

In order to sleep, each man had to lie on his side; there wasn't enough room for them even to lie out flat. The six or eight blankets also had to be shared, although it was never very cold because of all the body heat in the building. If one was unfortunate enough to have to go to the toilet during the night, it was like traversing a human sea. When the time came for Doorly's first meal in jail, several loaves of bread and a big bucket of watery soup were put in the room by the guard—and then it was every man for himself. And although no one starved, everyone was hungry all the time. This same meal pattern was repeated day after day, the only change being occasional cans of corned beef, which the British embassy would deliver to the jail along with a few blankets and the admonition "Keep your chin up." Exercise was impossible since there was no facility to handle the prisoners outside their cells.

Within a week of his arrival at the Barcelona jail, Doorly discovered two ailments that made life even less bearable. The first was scabies, little parasites that got under the skin and itched like crazy. The other was fleas, which infested everyone in the close quarters of the jail and also kept the entire population scratching. Fortunately, there was a doctor available for the inmates, and Doorly was given a crude but effective treatment for scabies. First, the skin of the infected area was rubbed with sand to expose the parasites, after which they were dusted with sulfur, which killed them. While the first treatment was painful, the discomfort got worse when the area began to heal and had to be sanded again to keep the critters exposed. If anyone got really sick, he was taken from the cell—but no one knew just where such people went. In any case, the crowding continued, for it seemed that when one person left, whether he was sick or moved to another jail, someone else was there to take his place.

About a month after the evaders arrived in Spain, they stood trial on the charges and, despite the efforts of the British, were pronounced guilty. The sentence was confinement in the Spanish prison camp at Miranda de Ebro for an undetermined length of time. The only consolation for Doorly was that he was again assured by the British embassy's personnel that they were doing all they could to get him released. (Conditions for those who crossed the Pyrenees rapidly improved after mid-1943. As German fortunes worsened, Spain realized that she had to establish better relations with both the United States and Great Britain. By early 1944, evaders were no longer put in jail but were housed in hotels or similar facilities, at their government's expense, and were turned over to their own embassy representatives soon after arrival in Spain. Thus, if Doorly and Smith had crossed the border a year or so later, they would have avoided both the jail in Barcelona and, for Doorly, the camp at Miranda de Ebro.)

Smith's experience was quite different from Doorly's. Shortly after being put in the Barcelona prison, he was taken from his cell and questioned extensively, with periodic kicks and punches, about who he was and where he had come from. Since every person who was captured had a different story, the Spanish had apparently decided to believe none of them. But Smith and Barnard were fortunate. They had talked a lot to a young Belgian who was in the same cell and had convinced him that their stories were true. When the Belgian was interrogated, the authorities believed his story, and a few days later he was released to the custody of the Belgian consul. Smith was able to scribble a message about his situation that the young man hid in his sock. After hearing of the plight of Smith and Barnard and reading the note, the Belgian consul contacted his American and British counterparts. On Christmas Eve 1942, the two officials arrived at the prison with food and chocolate, clean clothes, blankets, and the assurance that they would soon return.

The day after Christmas, Smith and Barnard were released to the custody of a friendly Spanish air force major who took them by car the two hundred miles to the headquarters of the Spanish air force at Zaragoza. They stopped along the way for a delicious Spanish meal, and when they arrived at their destination they were given rooms in a very nice hotel. Smith celebrated his good fortune by soaking in the bathtub for an hour. The following day, Smith awoke in better spirits than he had been in since he'd abandoned his Spitfire three months earlier. Both he and Barnard were soon taken to an interrogation session, where they were asked about their aircraft, combat tactics, and the like, but the two assumed that the Spanish were gathering this information for the Germans and so they divulged nothing of value.

After three days of eating, sleeping, getting new clothes, and beginning to feel like healthy people again, Smith and Barnard were put on a bus to Madrid. They were met there by Bob Gilliland, the representative of a British chemical company, and taken to his luxurious apartment. Although they were allowed to move freely about the city, Smith and Barnard stayed at the apartment most of the time. Gilliland had told them that the arrangement with the Spanish government allowing them to go free was quite fragile and that any unusual activity on their part could jeopardize the chances that future evaders would also gain their freedom. Gilliland took them to dinner, even to a couple of parties, and showed them much of Madrid.

All was not well with Barnard, however. When he and Smith were in Zaragoza, he had lost control of himself and, in a yelling frenzy, threatened to kill Smith for no apparent reason. Smith was eventually able to calm him down, but a few days after arriving in Madrid, Barnard again became uncontrollable. Gilliland called the British embassy and Barnard was shortly taken away by a British air vice marshal. Smith never saw him again.

Early in January, nearly a week after arriving in Madrid, Smith was given a bus ticket for the nearly five-hundred-mile trip to Gibraltar. It was strange to be alone and completely free for the first time in nearly four months. And although the bus trip was long, Smith had never enjoyed a journey as much. He took the opportunity to sample diverse Spanish food and stroll through the small towns in which the bus stopped. He was also fascinated by the countryside as it changed from olive groves to rather barren hills, the most extensive orange groves he would ever see, and finally the Mediterranean seacoast.

Smith could not conceal his emotion when he crossed into Gibraltar nearly two days later. The ordeal was finally over and he was a free man. It was only then that the significance of what he had done began to sink in. He had evaded capture by the Germans, traveled the length of France, crossed the Pyrenees, been thrown into jails that were hellholes, gone without food, and endured numbing cold, but as he looked around him at the British flags and Allied soldiers, he knew it had been worth every hardship. And he could hardly contain his emotions as he thought of all the Frenchmen who had risked their lives so he might make it to this moment. After three or four days of eating and drinking with anyone and everyone and sleeping until noon, during which time he also got a new uniform, Smith boarded an American B-17 bomber for the flight back to England. When he reported to the Fourth Fighter Group, he found out that, aside from the one pilot who had turned back because of engine trouble, he was the only one who flew the Morlaix debacle and had not been taken prisoner or killed.

In the meantime, Doorly had never, in his wildest dreams, thought he would be sent to a prison camp. But a day after the sentence was pronounced, he and his fellow "criminals" were herded into boxcars for the long, cold, two-day trip to the foothills of the Pyrenees and the city of Miranda de Ebro. Eric wondered if he could survive the ordeal. He was already weak and malnourished from being in jail, and a flare-up of the jaundice that had almost killed him before would surely be fatal during the journey. He really feared he might die as the train lumbered across northern Spain. The temperature continued to drop, and he sat huddled in the corner of the boxcar, shaking like a leaf. The unventilated car full of men reeked with the smells of unwashed bodies and the bucket used as a toilet. No one looked forward to the fate that awaited them at Miranda de Ebro, but it would certainly be better than life on the train. Stops were frequent, but at most the door of the boxcar was simply left shut. And the few meals they got were just like those in jail: a bucket of soup and a few loaves of bread.

Arrival at the camp plunged the normally optimistic Doorly into absolute despair. Thousands of men and women, some of whom were political prisoners from the Spanish Civil War and had been in the camp for six years, were in the approximately ten acres of space. Many were desperate to get away, and ill-prepared escape attempts were common. Rather than using Spanish soldiers or police to guard the camp, the government used inmates who were serving sentences for siding with the Communists in the Spanish Civil War. If they shot an escaping prisoner, they got a certain number of days taken off their sentences. And although Doorly never lost confidence that he would be released, seeing the countless souls who had been there for so long tested his faith to the utmost.

The camp consisted of a number of permanent buildings and a conglomeration of shacks and other makeshift structures haphazardly strewn across the bare ground. The prisoners were not assigned to any particular shelter. They were simply taken from the train and through the gate—then it was every man for himself. The mainstay of the prisoners' diet was bread, which was augmented once a day by some kind of stew cooked by the inmates themselves from the ingredients supplied by the Spanish, including on occasion such items as a donkey's head—hair, teeth, and all. Doorly was fortunate because the British got a good supply of canned beef to him that helped keep him better fed than some of the other prisoners. Toilet facilities were a number of holes in a concrete slab with no running water or any effort at maintaining sanitary conditions. But although everything was dirty, there was a shower formation once each week, and even a few seconds in the cold water got at least the worst of the dirt off. Not that this really mattered, for most of the inmates, like Doorly, had but one set of lice-infested clothes. Since these were never washed, a fairly clean body was quickly contaminated by the filthy garments. Doorly was still wearing the gray suit that had been given to him by the old woman after he'd bailed out some five months before.

Shortly after Doorly arrived at the camp, he got to know a young English-speaking Greek seaman named Manos, who had been in the facility for over two years. His offense was leaving his ship for a few hours and being picked up by the Spanish authorities for not having the proper papers. He was nearly six and a half feet tall and weighed over two hundred pounds. Doorly shared a shack, which resembled something a group of kids back home would build in their backyard, and the food he got from the British with the young man. In return, the big Greek gave Doorly some very welcome protection from the less desirable elements in his primitive surroundings. It was not unusual for a prisoner to be stabbed to death during the required morning accountability formation for some transgression the day before. Although men and women were technically segregated, prostitution was also rampant, and spurning the advances of one of the ladies could also lead to becoming a morning statistic. But Doorly's friend was one of the biggest men in the camp, and so Doorly was left alone.

Doorly soon found that the camp was actually a complete city unto itself. There were all types of small businesses, including a shop that made rings out of coins, one of which Doorly bought, a thriving black market that dealt in about anything a prisoner wanted, a loose but often effective inmate government system, and, of course, a tremendous amount of crime. Theft, prostitution, murder, and gang fights were a part of everyday life. And since the Spanish did not have the necessary resources to control the situation, they simply turned their backs unless things really got out of hand. Fortunately, the British periodically sent a representative from the embassy to do what he could for the British prisoners. This enabled Doorly to take advantage of the camp environment, because the British gave him, in addition to some food and a few blankets, some of his back RAF pay. This put him in a situation where he could get whatever he and his friend needed to at least survive.

Money was small consolation, however, as time hung heavy on everyone's hands, and Doorly was no exception. There was no organized work to be done and there were no facilities for recreation. Although the British were able to do little to get Doorly out of the camp, the embassy was able to provide him with a number of books and periodicals. Since there was no electricity in the camp, he had to read during the day. In order to get some exercise, as well as maintain their sanity, most prisoners walked around the perimeter of the camp for several hours each day. Eric found that the walk not only provided exercise, but it also gave him an opportunity to talk with other inmates. But during the evening and late at night time dragged, and he found himself thinking about his situation and the events that had led up to his being shot down.

From his first day in the squadron, Eric had been concerned with how little instruction he had received about gunnery and combat. He had never really learned how to get into position to shoot at another plane, how much to lead it with your gun sight, or how to get away from an enemy if he was after you. The RAF philosophy was to learn by doing, and that is exactly what he had done. He often thought of his first encounter with the Luftwaffe, during which he was so anxious to get after the Germans and so confident in his ability that he'd peeled off after four FW-190s. Luckily, they kept on going and didn't turn around to fight. He had taken a couple of shots at them but was too far away. Such actions were commonplace because everyone wanted to get into battle. But Doorly learned, as did his squadron mates, and by mid-1942 he had been a very proficient fighter pilot and an element leader in his squadron.

As he reminisced, an old Englishman who had befriended him often came to mind. The old man owned a brewery, and Doorly could almost taste the beer he'd often drunk with his friend. He thought, too, of London and what a great town it had been before so many Americans arrived there. Being in the RAF meant that everyone opened their doors to you and really couldn't do enough for you. The girls would fall all over you, and if you spent the night alone in London, you had no one to blame but yourself. And the pubs were so quaint and friendly. It was hard to turn down another beer, especially if one of the old gents from the neighboring village was buying.

Eric couldn't resist telling his Greek friend Manos about the day he and his flight commander had had a few too many at the pub and flew to another base, at treetop height and not more than five feet apart, to see a mutual friend. After having five or six beers with their friend, the pair climbed into their Spitfires and flew back, this time about four feet apart. Every time he thought of the adventure he marveled that they had not crashed.

So it went almost every night as the pilot and his sailor friend shared stories of flying and of the sea, talked about their hopes and dreams, and planned how to get through another day. And Eric soon learned that the secret was to take one day at a time, concentrate on surviving the challenges of that day, and never give up hope.

By mid-February 1943, the entire camp was speculating on the prospect of a German invasion of Spain in order to stop the exodus from France and to give Hitler virtual control of the Mediterranean. This was a matter of grave concern since a significant number of the prisoners were refugees who had fled the Germans, and no matter how bad conditions were in the camp, everyone agreed they were better than being captured by the Germans.

As the weeks of winter dragged on, Doorly met several other airmen who had, in one way or another, managed to evade the Germans and walk over the mountains, only to be put in jail and then be sent to the prison camp by the Spanish. But he was unable to find another RAF pilot. So although the British embassy did all it could for its people, the wheels of government turned slowly and no one was released. Still, the group remained optimistic that the periodic assurances of the embassy staff were sincere.

Unbeknownst to Doorly, there was considerable pressure being put on the government in London on his behalf. When he'd arrived in Barcelona, the British embassy had notified the RAF that he was safe. The RAF, in turn, had informed Doorly's family, who had promptly written their relatives in England asking for help in getting Doorly released and back to duty in Britain. Whether the intervention of his relatives had any impact or not, in late March, Doorly and a group of nine or ten other British military personnel were told that they were about to be released. Once again, he had to say good-bye to someone who had helped him survive and whom he could not repay.

The first step in leaving the Miranda de Ebro camp was having your head shaved. The departing inmates also hoped for a bath and clean clothes, but that was not on the initial agenda. The now-bald prisoners were taken to the front gate, and there they waited for what seemed like hours before a small bus arrived. Surprisingly, once they got outside the gate of the camp, there was no guard. Rather, a young Spanish army lieutenant got them together and gave them a number of instructions in Spanish that Doorly only partially understood. Fortunately, a few members of the group spoke enough Spanish to facilitate communication.

The lieutenant informed the group that he was in charge and that the group would be going to a holding area in southern Spain for an unknown period of time, after which they would be taken to Gibraltar and turned over to the British.

The mood on the bus was jovial as the group began the long trek. It wasn't long before some liquor appeared and everyone, including the Spanish lieutenant, was celebrating the end of their long incarceration. After a few hours on the road, one of the Spanish-speaking inmates suggested to the lieutenant that the group would be much easier to handle if they stopped at a house of prostitution. "After all," he told the officer, "some of us have been in prison or evading the Germans for nearly a year." Again, Doorly understood little of the conversation, but the bus soon pulled over and the ripe-smelling group, along with the lieutenant and the bus driver, got out and proceeded to take advantage of the services offered. Although Doorly was not particularly impressed with the caliber of the establishment, he was sure that the girls thought even less of the way this group of bald-headed prisoners smelled.

Other stops were made at small restaurants as the bus slowly made its way southeast. It seemed to Doorly that the stops for food were always timed so that there were few patrons about. "I can certainly understand why they are stopping when they do," he told the British soldier next to him. "I can't imagine anything less appetizing than having to eat with this bunch of smelly men."

Eric was very conscious of the countryside as they passed from the foothills of the Pyrenees onto the plains of central Spain. He was amazed to see small donkeys being led down the roads carrying loads of sticks, and wagons, filled with all sorts of things from tires to bottles of wine, being drawn by a horse or two, miles from any visible habitation. He had never seen a cork tree, and he learned that the bark was cut from the trees every five years and was made into corks that were sent all over the world. Olive groves, too, fascinated him, especially when someone in the group said that such trees produced olives for centuries. It was in one such barren area that the group spent its first night. The bus simply pulled over shortly after dark and the lieutenant announced that they would sleep on the bus. Certainly it was a golden opportunity to escape, but since no one wanted to risk getting sent back to jail, and nobody had anywhere to go anyway, all was quiet.

Late the next day, as the rocky hillsides and arid fields began to gave way to the narrow coastal plain, the driver pulled into what appeared to be a resort and the group disembarked. They were met by another military officer and a civilian who explained that this would be their home for the next few days, or possibly weeks, until the British were ready to take them at Gibraltar. The group had the run of the resort, but they were not to leave the grounds because they were still prisoners—and any infraction of the rules would mean a return trip to Miranda de Ebro.

The first order for everyone was a bath, the first in months. This was followed by a thorough clothes washing and, for some, even new items. Doorly was able to get a clean shirt, but the item he needed most, a pair of shoes, was not to be found. His size-twelve feet had been an insurmountable obstacle since he'd bailed out, and he was still wearing his fur-lined flying boots, with the soles now held on by pieces of string. And although he was not very familiar with some of the seafood they were served, he appreciated the three good meals a day and the clean plates, and he even grew to like squid and octopus. With no planned activity or work to do, the group put together games and started trying to get back into some kind of physical condition by taking long walks. They also fell back into the standard fliers' pastime, playing cards.

After about a week, they were again assembled, put on another bus with another Spanish army lieutenant, and began the day-long trip to Gibraltar. As luck would have it, the trip took them through wine country. The new officer seemed as amenable to a good time as his predecessor had, so they stopped at countless wineries along the way and sampled the wares, using a ladle to dip wine from the barrels. Their arrival at Gibraltar must have been something—heads nearly bald, clothes in various states of disrepair and fit, and all at least partially drunk. But despite his slightly inebriated condition, Eric had tears in his eyes when he saw the Union Jack and heard the Spanish officer turn the group over to a British flight lieutenant. Doorly stepped once again onto British soil, a free man for the first time in months.

The first hours in Gibraltar were spent ensuring the identity of each of the former Spanish prisoners. It was not uncommon for refugees to try to pose as British soldiers in an effort to get out of the Spanish prisons, so this step often took some considerable time. Once his identity was established, Doorly got some new clothes—and, finally, new shoes. A good British meal, clean sheets, a night's rest on a proper bed, and Doorly was ready to begin trying to get back to England.

But as he lay in his bed that night in Gibraltar, Eric could not help but think back at how fortunate he had been. He was sure he would have been captured that first night if he had not stumbled into the ditch and been able to hide under the leaves. And who could have thought that Jean, the young man he'd contacted at the bridge during that first terrifying day in France, when he was really desperate for some help, would take him home, keep him there, and even travel to southern France with him. The fact that a doctor had been staying at the place where he came down with jaundice was beyond luck. Without him, Eric would have died in Lourdes, miracle water or not. And then there was Manos, his big friend in the prison camp. Who knows what might have happened without his protection? Eric owed so much to each one of those people, and so many more. He fell asleep hoping that in some way he would be able to repay them.

Gibraltar was crowded with people who wanted to get to England. After spending nearly a week trying to get a flight, Doorly found a friendly flight crew at a pub and hitched a ride on their RAF transport. On April 15, 1943, three months after Bob Smith, Doorly arrived back in London and reported to the Air Ministry. He had been gone from England for a little over seven months. The next few days were filled with debriefings by both British and American intelligence personnel. He was outfitted in a new RAF uniform and then promptly changed it for the uniform of the U.S. Army Air Forces. He also learned that Bob Smith had successfully made it back to England but that his wingman on the day he was shot down, Dick Gudmundsen, had been shot down on the same mission and was killed.

Doorly's ill-fated flight in his new Spit IX turned out to be his last in the Spitfire. It was U.S. Army policy that returned evaders could not fly combat again, at least for a number of months, because of possible knowledge of how the underground system worked, the location of safe houses, and the like. Because of this, Doorly was allowed a week on the town in London, a short visit back to his old unit, the Fourth Fighter Group, and then was returned to the United States. After a few weeks of leave, he joined the 371st Fighter Group of the Ninth Air Force. Ironically, his squadron was commanded by Dale Taylor, another former RAF squadron mate, who had been wounded and sent back to the United States to recuperate.

Smith also fell victim to the army policy of not allowing evaders to fly combat immediately. After arriving in London, he went out for three days on the town. Unfortunately, he had not been authorized to do so, since he had not completed his interrogation by the intelligence officers. He was therefore listed as AWOL (absent without leave) and had the military police looking for him. When he returned to his squadron after his celebration of freedom and survival, Smith was awarded an Air Medal by General Spaatz and was told that he could not fly combat with his squadron because of his evasion experience. He chose to return to the United States for leave, then retrain in another aircraft and return to England.

Returned to duty in England, Eric Doorly (*center*) is flanked by Don Ross (*left*) and Edwin Taylor (*right*) in fall 1944.   *Donna Livingston*

After a month's leave in Washington, D.C., Smith was assigned to tour Army Air Forces combat training bases to talk with air crews about the reality of escape and evasion. In preparing for these talks, he learned that Dr. and Madame Rodocanachi, the couple who had housed him in Marseilles, had been executed for helping a number of Allied airmen escape from France. He also found out that the British agent who had the radio in Toulouse had been tortured and executed by the Germans. Contrary to the agreement he had made when he left England, when he completed his lecture circuit he was not sent back to combat but rather was assigned to fly P-39 Airacobras at Hamilton Field and P-38s at Santa Rosa in California until the end of the war.

In the spring of 1944, Doorly returned to England. Within a few days, he was again looking down on France, this time from his P-47 Thunderbolt, as he escorted B-17s on bombing raids into Germany. He could never fly over the area around Aumale without wondering about the fate of the Ransons and all the other people who had helped him evade and survive and about whether he would ever meet them again to thank them for their help.

Doorly and Smith were both discharged from the Army Air Forces shortly after the end of World War II. During the conflict, Doorly had shot down three enemy aircraft and was awarded five Air Medals and the Distinguished Flying Cross. He went back to college to earn his engineering degree, and after graduation he went to work for General Electric as an engineer. A number of years later, he moved to the solar and gas turbine division of International Harvester, where he remained until he retired. He was also a scratch golfer, and in later years, that sport really became his first love. He had four children and four grandchildren. He never returned to France to meet again with those who had helped him evade, but he did maintain occasional correspondence with Jean and Robert Ranson for several years. Doorly lived the last years of his life in San Diego, where he died in 1994.

When Bob Smith left the Army Air Forces, he had been awarded the Distinguished Flying Cross, the Bronze Star, five Air Medals, and the Purple Heart. He initially went to work for American Telephone and Telegraph at night while he worked on a plan to build an airline in Ecuador. When the Ecuadorian officials with whom he was working fell out of favor, the idea of the airline died, and Smith went to work full-time for the telephone company. He had remained active in the Air Force Reserve, flying several different aircraft, including the F-84, and was recalled to active duty during the Korean War, in which he flew the P-51

Mustang. On a strafing run at about fifty feet, he was wounded in the head by rifle fire. He recovered and completed a total of one hundred and seventeen missions in Korea. At the end of that conflict, Smith stayed in the Air Force and retired in 1970 as a lieutenant colonel. In the meantime, he had earned his B.S. degree from Colorado College and his M.S. from Georgia Tech. He then worked for twelve years for Mitre Corporation, where he was involved in the automation of the air traffic control system. His last position was president of a mortgage lending corporation from which he retired in 1993. He and his wife, Denice, have three children and presently live in Norfolk, Virginia.

· F O U R ·

"Find the Amerikanischer Flieger"

Don Willis, better known to his friends as D.K., had never been one to let others do something for him. Whenever the quiet young man had an idea, he wanted to see for himself how it worked out. It was that spirit that had led him to travel from the headquarters of the 67th Fighter Wing, where he was the tactics evaluation officer, to Kingscliffe Airfield in East Anglia, England, on April 9, 1944. A year earlier, Willis had made a radical proposal to Brigadier General Frank Hunter to put bombs on the wings of the P-38 Lightning and use it as a fighter-bomber rather than only as an escort fighter. Part of his proposal was to modify several P-38s so a bombardier could fit in the nose of the center fuselage with a Norden bombsight. The modifications included lowering the front of the nose section slightly to make room for the bombardier, as well as putting a Plexiglas panel in the lower front so he could use the bombsight. The P-38s would fly to their target in tight formation, the bombardier in the lead Lightning would acquire the target, and on his command, all the aircraft would drop their bombs. As soon as the bombs were dropped, all but the lead P-38 would assume their traditional role of fighters and strafe any target they might be assigned, such as airfields, locomotives, truck convoys, and the like. Although Willis's suggestion was turned down in 1943, it had been accepted for evaluation in 1944 because the P-38 was being rapidly supplanted as an escort fighter by the faster, longer-range, and more maneuverable P-51

Mustang. One aircraft was modified to make room for the required bombardier, and the first evaluation mission of the "droopsnoot" P-38 was to be flown at Kingscliffe on April 10. Willis wanted to be there.

The weather over the Continent was not particularly good that day, and the first two missions were not able to attack their targets. The bombs were duly salvoed (dropped) into the English Channel. The third mission, in which Willis was flying his first combat misson and only his second operational mission in the P-38, took off at about 1400 hours (two P.M.). Its target was an airfield at Gütersloh, Germany. This time the weather cooperated and the target could be clearly seen. On the command of the bombardier, all the aircraft, including Willis's, released their bombs, but they did not drop down to strafe the facility since it appeared to be heavily damaged.[1]

As the formation turned for home, however, Willis had some second thoughts. He decided he had better see for himself just how much damage had really been done, since he was scheduled to go back to headquarters the next day and report on the effectiveness of the new tactics. He was fairly confident that he had proved his point, but he had to be sure. Fortunately, the formation had encountered no enemy fighters and very little flak on the way into Germany, and D.K. expected none as he turned back to the target. He began a fairly rapid descent so he could see better, but no sooner had he leveled off than the antiaircraft guns, which had been silent during the first bomb run, opened up. Willis was hit almost immediately. He made a gut-wrenching turn back to the west and pushed both his throttles to full power. In less than a minute, he was out of the flak area and could assess the damage to his aircraft. He immediately saw a hole in the floor of the cockpit and the shredded toe of his flying boot. After closer examination, he decided that the shell had just grazed his toe. He checked all his controls and found no problem, but a much more serious situation greeted him as he looked at the engine gauges. He saw that the fuel pressure was fluctuating on both engines and realized that a fuel tank or a fuel line had been hit. He quickly switched to his auxiliary fuel tanks, which seemed to solve the pressure problem, but the quantity of fuel in the main tank continued to decrease. Obviously a fuel line had been cut.

Willis decided he would try to make it back to England on the remaining fuel by flying with reduced power and accepting the resulting low speed. But by the time he crossed the coast of Holland and could see nothing ahead but the icy water of the North Sea, his confidence had disappeared. A quick check of the distance to England and the fuel remaining told him that there was no way he could make it back, and a landing in the water of the North Sea was probably suicide. He would freeze or drown long before any rescue craft could pick him up. With a lump in his throat, D.K. called the squadron leader and reported his situation. He had fallen miles behind the formation and feared he would have to crash-land in Holland. He was not sure where he was, since the formation had been following the navigation of the lead aircraft, so he could not make any sure position report. The squadron leader responded that he would send some aircraft back to guide Willis along, but the pilot declined the offer, knowing they would not be able to find him. He briefly thought about bailing out but decided he would have a much better chance if he could control where he landed, especially since both his engines were still running. That decision made, he busied himself with the preparations for a crash landing.

D.K. had very few options. He wanted to land in Holland, as far from the German border and as close to Belgium as possible, in order to have the best chance of evading capture. As the fuel gauges continued their relentless march toward empty, D.K. realized that he had to act fast. But what he saw as he looked for a place to land was not encouraging. Everywhere, it seemed, there was a dike, canal, drainage ditch, fence, or house that would make a successful crash landing all but impossible. The only promising area he saw was a good-sized open area adjacent to a soccer field where a large number of people were gathered. As Willis got lower, he saw that there was a game in progress. Knowing how much Germans liked soccer, he was sure there would be a few at the game and that he would be captured as soon as his plane stopped moving. However, by this time he was too low to find another field and his fuel gauges were on empty, so he took off his oxygen mask, disconnected his radio cable, jettisoned his canopy, and began his approach to the field.

D.K.'s confidence that he had picked a good landing area remained as he turned his plane onto its final approach. There were a couple of low dikes he hadn't seen, but he was sure the spot he'd picked to touch down in would avoid them. No sooner had he congratulated himself on his choice of fields, however, than his engines began to cut out and he knew the end had come. He needed another thirty seconds of power to make the field. Miraculously, his engines caught again as they desperately sucked the last drops of fuel, refusing to die. The procedure for a crash landing was to shut off the fuel and electrical power prior to impact to minimize the possibility of fire, but Willis did not have to worry about that because the mighty V-12 engines gave their final death gasp and quit about five seconds before he was ready to turn everything off.

Fortunately, Willis had planned to land near the middle of the field, so despite the loss of his engines, he was able to just skim across a road, forcing two bicyclists to dive for cover in a ditch. He braced himself as his fighter settled, plowing into the mud and throwing a great spray of dirt and water everywhere. He couldn't see a thing, so he just held on and waited for his wild ride to end, which it did with a mighty thud as one wing hit a small dike and the craft spun around. D.K. had expected the worst, but the muddy ground had cushioned his landing and he was able to ride out the slide without being injured. As soon as his plane came to a stop, Willis released his lap belt and shoulder harness, struggled out of his parachute, climbed from the aircraft, and without pausing to assess his situation, began to run.

The low approach of the P-38 had brought the soccer game to a standstill as players and spectators alike watched and wondered what was going to happen. When the plane crash-landed everyone began to run toward the spot, and almost before the plane came to a complete stop, the first Dutchmen had arrived. Fortunately for Willis, there was more interest in his plane than in him. He quickly made his way through the crowd and up a short embankment to the road, where most of the spectators had left their bicycles. He snatched a red raincoat from one of the first bikes he saw and put it on over his flying jacket. It was a long coat, so it covered his green uniform pants as well. He then grabbed a nearby bicycle and began to ride toward the little town of Oud-Gastel. He had no idea what he was going to do, but he knew that if he was going to successfully evade the Germans, the first requirement was for him to get away from his aircraft.

There were several people on the road, and Willis began pedaling at a leisurely pace, keeping his head bent slightly forward to avoid any eye contact and fit into the scene. Soon, he was overtaken by a young woman who slowed down to ride next to him. She said nothing, but kept looking at Willis out of the corner of her eye. She then indicated to him that he had an outline of his oxygen mask around his nose and mouth. It was obvious from this gesture that she knew he was the pilot, but she said nothing. Not more than a minute later, the two approached several German soldiers running from their gun emplacement toward the crash site. The woman put her finger to her lips and kept riding alongside Willis as though they were a couple. The Germans paid no attention to the two riders, but any confidence that Willis had in the situation was severely tested again, moments later, when they were met by a German truck and staff car speeding toward the crash site. Intent upon getting to their objective before the pilot could escape, the Germans ignored the man and woman leisurely riding their bikes toward town. The remaining few minutes of the ride into Oud-Gastel were uneventful since all the attention was focused on the crash. Just as Willis entered the town, the young lady turned down a side street. Since she had not indicated anything else to him, he did not think he was to follow her, so he continued riding through the village. As he rode, his mind raced with the options of what he should do. He knew that he needed to move out of the area as soon as possible, but he also had to find a way to hide until the initial search for him was over. He rode around Oud-Gastel for a few minutes, but unable to think of anything else to do, he stopped in front of the large village church and sat down on an outside stone bench to collect his thoughts.

The Germans were rapidly organizing to deal with the situation. They had initially formed a cordon around Willis's airplane, assuming that the pilot would try to hide in the crowd. When they discovered that he wasn't there, they began a systematic search of the surrounding area. Oud-Gastel was a small village with only one main street, but it had a very large cathedral that dominated the area. Since the church was the central point of the village, it was only logical for it to be chosen as the assembly point for the search team. D.K. was still trying to figure out a way to escape from the town when his thoughts were interrupted by the roar of a truck engine. A terrified Willis watched in horror as a truck loaded with German soldiers stopped in the square in front of the church and the soldiers jumped out of the back, boots ringing on the cobblestone street. The troops formed two lines facing straight toward him, not more than thirty feet away. Willis was beside himself with fright. Sweat pouring from his brow and his stomach in knots, he waited. Fortunately, the officer in charge, who was much closer, had his back to Willis. Several of the Germans had binoculars around their necks and some were holding the leashes of German shepherds. A chill ran down D.K.'s spine from just looking at the unfriendly animals. He dared not look up, or even move, for fear that someone might notice the marks on his face or see his shiny shoes, so he just sat there, draped in his red raincoat, shaking from head to toe. As the soldiers were given their directions by the officer in charge, D.K. could not help but think, despite his petrifying fear, that this was indeed an amazing scene: he was watching the Germans get their final instructions about how and where to look for him! He even heard and understood some of the words. When the officer forcefully said *"amerikanischer Flieger,"* he knew it could only mean him.

The Germans took this photograph of D. K. Willis's P-38 shortly after he crash-landed near Oud-Gastel, Holland. *Pat Willis*

Since any action on his part might raise suspicion, D.K. decided that he would simply sit on the bench and watch the search as it got under way. The Germans realized that the pilot of the aircraft could not have gone far, and they concentrated their search with that idea in mind. They first went into the fields surrounding the village. One soldier would stand on the bank of a dike while another soldier, with a dog, would crisscross the field in an effort to flush out anyone who might be hiding there. If there was any movement, the observer would see it from the bank and the dog could immediately be let loose to chase down the evader. As D.K. watched the search's progress, he became more calm and confident, and suddenly he had an idea of how to get away. He would just wait until a field and the adjoining farm had been searched. When the soldiers moved to another area, he would find a place to hide at the already searched farm. The only problem was keeping track of just where the search parties were located. Willis solved this problem by nonchalantly strolling around the little village, positioning himself so he could watch the Germans' progress.

After about half an hour, D.K. thought it safe to move to the out-skirts of Oud-Gastel, where he had seen the soldiers searching a barn sometime before. But as fate would have it, just as he entered the barn, intent on hiding in the hay, a woman hurried out of the adjacent house to quietly tell him he could not stay there. Fortunately, Willis spoke some Norwegian, and since that language is similar to Dutch, he could communicate with her. She was too frightened of what the Germans would do if she sheltered him, she told him, but she agreed not to tell anyone she had seen him. He then made his way into an adjacent field, where he hid in a culvert to wait for darkness.

But the lady in the house was not the only person who had seen Willis go to the barn and then into the field. It took the village shoe-maker, Jan Kuppens, only a moment to figure out that the man in the raincoat was probably the pilot of the crashed American airplane. He also realized that the man needed help. After finding an old coat, which he put on over his own coat so he wouldn't look suspicious, Kuppens walked toward the same house that Willis had just visited. Just before getting to the house, Kuppens detoured into the field, acting like he was looking for a lost animal. He went only a few yards and then he heard a rustle in the undergrowth and found himself staring into the muzzle of a Browning automatic and looking into the steely gaze of a pair of bright blue eyes. Kuppens had found Willis!

Through a combination of Norwegian from Willis and Dutch from Kuppens, Willis was able to determine that the shoemaker wanted to help. Kuppens warned Willis that the search he had seen was only the beginning and that the Germans would no doubt do a house-to-house search of the village in the next few hours. He gave Willis the coat, told him to put mud on his shoes and the bottoms of his pants legs, and to wait for him to return. With that, he left. After following Kuppens's instructions about his shoes and pants, Willis got farther into the shelter of the culvert to wait for his new benefactor to return.

True to Kuppens's word, after failing to find Willis in the fields and the farms, the Germans launched a search of the entire village. By this time the search force numbered over twenty soldiers, and every house in the village was searched from top to bottom as the residents were bombarded with questions about the crash and the disappearing pilot. Kuppens, too, was questioned intensely as the occupying force ransacked his home. After they departed, the shoemaker waited for several minutes and then he, and one of his three sons, Sjef, departed to get Willis and bring him back to their house. Fortunately, the German troops were so intent on searching houses that they paid little attention to people walking on the street, and after taking several detours, Mr. Kuppens and Sjef found Willis.

For D.K. the wait had seemed like forever. Because of his inherent nature of trusting people, he was sure that Kuppens would return, but as the hours dragged by, he had begun to think that maybe the man's plan had gone awry and he would not be able to help. While he was hiding, Willis had opened his escape kit and used the compass to sight to the southwest, the direction of Belgium. His plan was to wait until dark and then begin the journey that would get him across the border, where, in some unknown way, he would contact the Belgian underground and make his way, with its help, to France and across the Pyrenees to Spain and freedom—a distance of nearly eight hundred miles. The arrival of Kuppens and his son brought the promise of welcome relief from the culvert, but Willis had no idea what lay in store for him.

The plan devised by Kuppens and his son was to take Willis to the shoemaker's house and keep him there until it appeared safe for him to begin his trek toward Belgium. Both Kuppens and Sjef were afraid that the Germans might launch a second search of the countryside, with even more men and dogs, once they failed to find Willis in the town. If Willis were still in the field, he would surely be found. To get to his house, Mr. Kuppens walked about a hundred feet ahead of Willis and Sjef brought up the rear, about a hundred feet behind. If Kuppens saw a problem, he would cross the street and Willis would then be on his own to deal with the situation as it developed. The son would help in any way he could.

The Kuppens family in October 1944. From left are Sjef, his father Jan, Bert, and Marinus.

Fortunately, there were no problems on the walk to the shoemaker's house, and Willis was soon inside the warm kitchen, where Mrs. Kuppens was expecting him. She quickly gave him a sandwich and some warm milk. Mr. Kuppens then hid him in a pile of wood shavings under the workbench where he made wooden shoes, in the unlikely chance that the Germans might come back.

As soon as he was sure that the Germans had abandoned their search for the night, Kuppens retrieved Willis from the shavings. He gave him a shirt, a pair of pants, and a coat that belonged to his son. D.K. was careful to keep his U.S. Army Air Forces identification card so he could prove that he was an American airman if he was captured. He also transferred the contents of his escape kit to his new outfit. They then buried Willis's clothes behind the house. Mr. Kuppens explained to Willis that his son would go a short distance with him to ensure that he got started in the right direction. He then produced a rough map he had drawn showing the way to Belgium as well as two German military installations D.K. had to avoid. He also gave Willis a little Dutch money, since there were only Belgian francs in his escape kit. Mrs. Kuppens supplied him with a couple of sandwiches, a few apples, and, because the Germans had confiscated all the tea and coffee in Holland, a flask of a locally made coffee substitute. His supplies in hand, Willis and his guide left the security of the Kuppens house to begin his trek to Belgium. Because the Germans had laid a curfew on the town forbidding anyone to be out after dark, the walk to the outskirts of town was quick, and after pointing the way to Belgium, about ten miles away, Sjef left Willis on his own.

As D.K. looked at the black sky and felt the chill of the April night descend, he was suddenly very lonely. He was confident that he could survive and evade, but the realization that he was a hunted man in a strange country where he knew no one gave him a momentary feeling of desperation. Mr. Kuppens had told him that it was dangerous to travel at night because of the curfew, but D.K. realized that he had to quickly get as far from the crash site as possible. He set off toward Belgium. Any idea that he could make rapid progress was rapidly dismissed from his mind as he ran into fences, ditches, and dikes that caused him to constantly detour. He often fell, tripping on the unseen obstacles, and as he picked himself up, his frustration with his slow progress increased. Although he was able to keep heading generally southwest, there wasn't enough light to read his compass, so he had to make his best guess as to the direction in which to walk. This was further complicated by Mr. Kuppens's admonition that he stay clear of the town of Roosendaal at all costs since it was the site of a large German military garrison.

After walking for several hours, Willis suddenly came upon a barbed wire entanglement. His first thought was that he had reached the border and his night's trek was a success. But his elation was short-lived when he heard German voices and desperately dove for cover. Not more than ten feet away, three German sentries passed in the darkness. Willis lay still for several minutes waiting for his heartbeat to return to normal. When he again got up the nerve to move, he realized that he was not at the border but rather had almost stumbled into a German gun emplacement. The experience was enough to convince him that he had better forget walking any farther and find a place to sleep. Carefully retracing his steps, in a short while he found a haystack. After eating a sandwich and taking a drink from his flask, he dug into the hay and fell into an exhausted sleep.

It seemed like only moments later that the warmth of the sun awoke D.K. After eating his last sandwich and drinking the rest of the contents of his flask, Willis carefully made his way from the haystack and, using his compass to sight the southwest, was again on his way. He had not walked for more than five minutes when he was confronted by a young Dutch couple who wanted to know what he was doing on their farm. After some difficulty communicating with the pair, he convinced them that he was an American pilot by using some of his Norwegian and a little English. The young man indicated to Willis that he should return to the haystack and wait.

After about an hour of increasing doubt that he had done the right thing, D.K. was ready to set out again on his own when the young man returned. He brought another welcome sandwich and some wine, and indicated that Willis was going in the wrong direction to get to Belgium. In fact, he was headed directly for the major German air base Jan Kuppens had told him he must avoid. The young man pointed out the correct direction to Willis and then began to walk with him, apparently confident that the pair would not arouse suspicion. After guiding the pilot around the problem air base and past the village of Roosendaal, Willis's new friend left him at a railroad junction. He told Willis to follow the track to the Belgian border, about three miles away, but to watch for frequent German patrols. His spirits buoyed and his confidence renewed, Willis set off down the edges of the fields that paralleled the track. Fortunately, he blended well into the morning scene as he trudged along because all of the farmers were in the fields doing spring plowing and planting. As he walked, he thought about what he should do next. He decided that he had to get to Brussels, where, he was confident, he could blend into the populace enough to keep from getting caught and surely would be able to make contact with the underground.

About noon, Willis approached the northern edge of the town of Essen, just across the border in Belgium. He had anticipated that the border would be heavily guarded, and he was right. Not only was the railroad blocked, but it also appeared that all the roads were also guarded. He had been thinking about how to get across the border as he had been walking and decided that he was going to have to take a chance and ask someone how to make the crossing. His good fortune with the Dutch thus far made him confident that he could find help. Soon he passed an older woman in a field. Drumming up all his courage, he approached her and asked if she spoke English. She shook her head so Willis tried his Norwegian, but he met with little more success. Still, the woman seemed friendly, so using all the ways he could think of, including drawing in the dirt, Willis indicated to her that he wanted to get across the border and that he had to avoid the various official crossings. The woman pointed him in the direction of a road that went into a forest. He understood that he would soon see a number of workers in a field. The field was in Belgium, and if he could join the workers in some way, he could get into Essen and Belgium without any trouble. Confident after having again received the help he needed, Willis set off down the deserted road.

After walking for about half an hour, Willis came to a clearing in the forest. Just as the lady had indicated, there were a number of men working in a large field. Staying in the cover of the forest, Willis decided that it would be pushing his luck too far if he tried to join the group while they were working. He would just have to wait until they finished to make any move. The afternoon dragged on slowly for Willis as he sat under the trees watching the workers. He ate the sandwich that the young man had brought him earlier that morning and washed it down with some wine from the goatskin container. Despite his most valiant efforts, he was unable to keep from dozing off several times.

Being alone in strange places was not new to the soft-spoken, blond-haired, thirty-two-year-old Willis. He had run away from home for a year when he was a junior in high school and worked on a freighter plying the waters between the West Coast and Japan. His parents, both college professors, had urged him to continue his education, but school didn't appeal to the adventure-prone D.K. So after graduating from high school and dropping out of college, he had returned to the sea, working as the purser on a freighter that made runs to various ports in South America.

It had been the adventure of the sea that had turned D.K. to the air. He loved the freedom that he found on the ocean, and after his first flight, he felt that same spirit in an airplane. Flying and adventure ran in his family; his mother was a relative of aviator Jimmy Doolittle, although Willis never met his famous kinsman. He took a shot at the business world in the mid-1930s, when he managed his grandfather's furniture business, but never really got attached to the world of manu-facturing. In the back of his mind, he always wanted to fly full-time. On a furniture-selling trip to New York he met a violin-playing Finn in a bar. When the drinks stopped flowing and Willis woke up, he found that he and his new red Chrysler automobile were on a freighter headed for Helsinki. Thus it was that he had joined the Finnish air force.

The sun was getting very low on the horizon when the workers began to gather up their coats and lunch pails and move toward another small back road that led into the town of Essen. Willis had decided that he should not try to become part of the group, so he hung back a short distance and simply followed the road. Once they were in the town, all of the men turned off on the same small street, and as Don made the turn he momentarily panicked to see a guard post a block away to his left. The route used by the workers was obviously one that bypassed the border patrol. Willis had successfully made it to Belgium. He assumed that the curfew that had been in place in Holland was probably the rule in Belgium as well and that he had better get out of the town before it became dark. The last thing he needed was to be stopped by anyone since he neither spoke French nor had any official papers.

It did not take long for Willis to walk through Essen, and soon he was paralleling the railroad tracks that led south toward his next desti-nation, Antwerp. His experience with the German gun emplacement the night before had eliminated any desire to try to travel at night. So when it got dark, Willis found a large pile of straw about half a mile from the railroad track, ate his last small apple, and dug in for the night.

He awoke with the sun, rested but famished. He returned to the vicinity of the railroad track and again began his trek southward. His big problem was food. He ate some of the chocolate from his survival kit, but knew that it wouldn't keep him going very long. He did not want to take the chance of stopping at a farmhouse, so he just kept walking. Fortunately, the day was cool and overcast, which made it easier to walk without food or water, but by late in the morning he knew that he had to at least find something to drink. A solution to the problem soon be-came apparent. The Belgian farmers often brought goatskins of wine and left them in various locations as they went into the fields to work. Survival overcame honesty for D.K. as he happened on a skin of wine, so he refilled the skin he had emptied long before. Although it wasn't water, the wine helped Willis continue to walk. Twice during the morning he was forced to make a panic dive for the cover of a ditch when he nearly ran into Germans who were out in the fields bird hunting, but he was relieved that he saw no organized search parties or formations of soldiers.

About midafternoon, Willis saw that the railroad tracks were leading him to a large town. From where he was walking he could not see any road signs, but the city seemed far too small to be Antwerp, which Willis had seen many times from the air. Fortunately, most of the town, which Willis later found out was Kalmthout, was built on the east side of the tracks, and since he had been walking on the right side of the right-of-way he was able to stay away from it. Still, he was uneasy when he found himself having to move farther and farther away from the railroad in order to stay out of Kalmthout. He soon lost sight of the tracks altogether. He thought he could continue in a southerly direction and intersect the tracks as he left the city behind. After walking for another hour, however, it began to get dark and he had not yet found the railroad. On top of that, he felt sick from having no food and too much wine during the day. For the first time since he had left Sjef Kuppens, he had an overwhelming feeling of loneliness and even felt a twinge of panic. Willis had always seemed to be in charge of his circumstances, but this was something new—what if he couldn't find the tracks, where would he get something to eat, how far was Brussels? If only he had someone to talk with. The more he thought, the more frightened and uncertain he became. He decided that he had better find a place to spend the night; he could address his problems in the morning. Fortunately, he came upon a deserted shack in a field, and there he curled up and fell into an exhausted sleep.

Willis was up again at sunrise, still feeling exhausted and desperate to find something to eat. As he walked, he again saw the farmers coming out into the fields, many carrying their lunches with them. D.K. sat down in a clump of tall grass and waited for the men to become immersed in their work. After a short time, he cautiously approached the place where he had seen a farmer place his water bottle and lunch. In a matter of seconds, the airman had found his breakfast and the farmer had lost his lunch.

Eating the sandwich and piece of cheese that he'd found soon gave D.K. a new sense of hope. It wasn't long before the railroad again came into view and his confidence soared. Walking at a brisk pace, the wandering flier reached the outskirts of Antwerp early in the afternoon. But although he was elated at having arrived at another milestone, he was also confronted with the dilemma of how to get around the city. He could not follow the railroad tracks any longer, and not having a map, he had no idea of the layout of the city. He wished he had paid more attention during the countless times he had flown over it. He decided to detour to his right and make it at least partway around Antwerp before it got dark. His stomach also told him that food and water were again becoming a big problem. For the first time since he had crashed, lady luck was not on Willis's side, however. After walking for over an hour, he found himself confronted by a large river that was impossible for him to cross. He decided he would have to retrace his steps and look for another way around the city.

Unfortunately, it was beginning to get dark and he hadn't paid a great deal of attention to his route. He decided to follow a small lane that went in a general northeasterly direction: the way he figured he had to go to get around Antwerp on the other side. Willis had not walked for more than fifteen minutes when his entire world came crashing down. As he rounded a sharp corner, he came face-to-face with a German sentry. Beyond the soldier, he saw a huge gun, its barrel pointed toward the sky. He had stumbled into a German antiaircraft battery! His heart seemed to stop, and filled with absolute terror, he seemed to be frozen on the spot. He had no Belgian identification, could not speak French, and still had his American identification card in his pocket. D.K. was sure his evasion experience was over. But lady luck was not done with him yet. The German sentry simply motioned Willis to go away, a command with which he complied at a very brisk pace.

It took D.K. half an hour to regain his composure. One close call was enough, so he decided that he had better find some food and a place to spend the night. He didn't know what to do about the food, but it didn't take long to find a small haystack. Still, sleep did not come easily to the hungry airman. The temperature began to drop, and it seemed that he couldn't burrow deep enough into the hay to get warm. As he huddled in his cold surroundings, he remembered what it was to be really cold. When he arrived in Finland in the summer of 1939, he had been impressed by the beautiful countryside and the vast forests. He could never seem to get enough of flying over this lovely landscape. But all that had changed as winter approached. By then, Willis had been sent into combat against the Russians. It was bad enough to be flying in an open-cockpit biplane, the British-built Bristol Bulldog, against the modern Russian planes, but the cold was almost unbearable. He had to fly with a leather mask to protect his face and so many layers of clothes he could barely walk. He wished he had some of those clothes now.

By the middle of that winter, things had looked hopeless for Finland, and D.K. had decided that he had better make his escape from the Finnish army if he was going to leave. With a companion, he left Finland for Norway in early March 1940. He arrived later that month and was able to begin flying for the Norwegian navy. He had been with the Norwegians for only a few weeks when Germany launched its attack against that Scandinavian nation and Willis was again forced to flee. This time he stole a two-engine German Heinkel 115 light bomber that was equipped with floats. He flew under British radar to the Shetland Islands, where, since he was piloting a German plane, he surrendered to a British naval officer. After his identity was confirmed, he was taken to London and assigned to a Norwegian navy contingent. In August 1941, he joined the RAF, making England the third country he had served in World War II. Despite his flying experience, he was sent to RAF pilot training, which he completed in March 1942. After being assigned to advanced training in an RAF operational training unit, he finally joined an RAF combat squadron, Number 121 Squadron of Fighter Command, one of the famed Eagle Squadrons, in June 1942. But throughout all of this varied duty, he had never felt as cold and alone as he did now.

D.K. had slept little, and before daylight he decided that he had to get something to eat and drink if he was to have any hope of surviving, much less being able to travel. As the first rays of light streaked the eastern sky, he made his move. A short distance from the haystack he saw a small farmhouse. He approached cautiously, scarcely daring to breathe. Fortunately, there was no dog in the vicinity to alert everyone of his presence. Had he been thinking more clearly, D.K. would have realized that he was getting off to a bad start because he was probably going to get the farmer out of bed. But he was so desperate for food and water that he summoned up all his courage and knocked on the door. After a short time, a short, stocky man dressed in a nightshirt came to the door and told the scraggly, dirty, unshaven American to go away. Willis pleaded with the farmer in English, but to no avail; he slammed the door in Willis's face. Willis had noticed that there was no telephone line going to the house, so he was sure that the farmer could probably not notify anyone of his presence. He decided to wait until it was obvious that the family was up and then try again.

Willis spent one of the longest hours of his life trying to stay warm in the haystack as he waited for any sign of life from the farmhouse. Finally, he saw some smoke issue from the chimney and again steeled

D.K. Willis with a British Spitfire early in the war.   *Pat Willis*

himself to approach the house and knock. This time the farmer apparently realized that Willis was indeed in trouble and so brought him a large piece of bread and a bottle of beer and told him to leave. The bread was a godsend to the famished aviator, and once again he could concentrate on the next problem, how to get around Antwerp. As he weighed his options, he realized that it would take him a day or two to walk around the large city. He was sure that he would be unable to stay out of sight of the Germans or the Belgian police during such a trek unless he stayed well away from the populated areas. Since obtaining food had become a major problem and he was having little luck solving it in the countryside, he decided to take a huge gamble, go into the city, and ask someone for help. That decision made, he set out.

As is the case with most old European cities, the streets of Antwerp form a crazy crisscross pattern in all directions. In order to keep from getting hopelessly lost, Willis used the huge cathedral as his aiming point as he wandered the ancient streets. His confidence soared when he realized that no one paid any attention to him, but he was not making any progress in his quest for help. Not far from the center of the old town, Willis walked past a store where a man was standing in the doorway. No sooner had he passed than the man said, "American?" D.K. was speechless. He nodded his head, and the man took him inside the store. The man explained in English that it was safe to ride the trolley through the city and gave Willis directions on where to get the correct car. He then opened his wallet and handed Willis three hundred Belgian francs—it would take one franc to ride the trolley, he explained—wished him good luck, and sent him on his way.

Willis was still dumbfounded as he followed the directions to the trolley stop. "How did that man know I was an American?" was all he could think. A few blocks later the ability of the Belgians to identify Willis as an evader was again demonstrated. As he walked to the trolley stop, a young woman walked up beside him, put her arm in his, and said, in English, "I'm a prostitute, but I'm not asking you for business. I have V.D. and so I only do business with the Germans. That's the way I fight the war." With that she let go of his arm and walked away. Willis could only look after her in amazement.

True to the stranger's word, the trolley ride was uneventful, and Willis soon found himself on the south side of Antwerp. His main concern was again something to eat and drink. He had walked only a short distance when he saw a roadside café. Confident in his good fortune and having some money in his pocket, he decided to try to buy some food. As the filthy evader took a seat at a sidewalk table, he saw a prominent sign advertising Bock beer. It looked irresistible to D.K., so when the proprietor came to take his order, he put down a one-franc note and said, "Bock." There were several patrons enjoying the spring day at the outside table, but no one paid any attention to Willis. The proprietor was not so easily deceived, however. After Willis had finished his beer, the owner motioned for Willis to come into the café. D.K. was confronted there with a table set with bread, fried eggs, and beer. Although the proprietor didn't speak any English, he had guessed his customer's identity and cooked up a feast while Willis blithely drank his beer. When Willis finished eating, his new benefactor took him to a bathroom where he could wash and shave for the first time since he had left England. The final touch came just as a refreshed Willis was leaving. The man reached up, brushed off some straw that was clinging to the back of Willis's coat, smiled, and bade him good-bye. Again, Willis could only walk away amazed at the Belgians' ability to identify him and forever grateful for their help.

Once again Willis started his familiar routine of following the railroad tracks, but it was now a greater challenge since there were a number of tracks leaving Antwerp. After walking beside a track for a couple of hours, he noticed that his shadow had changed position and, glancing at the sun, realized that the track he was following had apparently been turning slightly and he was now headed southeast, a heading that would soon take him farther from his destination of Brussels rather than closer to it. He began to feel increasingly desperate about his situation. Still, everything had worked out for him in Antwerp so why not try again? Before long he came to a village railroad station. Since he had plenty of money, he approached the ticket agent and tried to buy a ticket to Brussels. The ticket agent explained in broken English that this particular railroad did not go to Brussels. He then astounded Willis by asking if he had parachuted from an airplane. When Willis nodded that he had, the agent motioned Willis to follow him to a place where there was an English-speaking person who might be able to help him. After a few minutes' walk, they entered a house and were greeted by a Belgian who spoke fluent English. Upon meeting him, D.K. felt a huge sense of relief. He could now find out just where he was and how to get to Brussels. Possibly he could even determine how to make contact with the underground.

But Willis's good fortune was not to last forever. Just as he was sitting down to another meal and talking with his host, a man barged in and said that the police had somehow been informed of Willis's presence and were on their way to arrest him. The panicked flier was out the back door in a flash and on his way out of the town as fast as he could walk. Fortunately, one of the first things his English-speaking host had told him during their abbreviated conversation was that he should take the tram to Boom, which was nearly a third of the way between Antwerp and Brussels. Within an hour, Willis came to another small town and was able to find the tram station with little trouble. Since he could simply board the car without buying a ticket or talking to anyone else, he thought the process would go smoothly. He waited until a trolley was approaching the stop and then walked toward the tracks. He was less than ten feet from his destination when a German soldier walked up and asked him a question. D.K.'s heart stopped and his breath stuck in his throat. This was it! But from out of nowhere a small elderly lady stepped up and answered the question for the soldier, who thanked her and left. The lady smiled at Willis and walked away. When he was again able to breathe, Willis entered the trolley; by midafternoon, he found himself in the town of Boom.

In a day filled with emotional ups and downs, Willis was about to take another dive. As before, he departed Boom walking in the fields that paralleled the railroad. But he had gone only a few hundred yards when his way was blocked by the very large Rupel River. A quick re- connoiter of the area showed him that there was only one road and one railroad bridge across the river and that both of these were controlled by checkpoints manned by both German sentries and Belgian police. As he watched from a grove of trees near the bridge, Willis saw, to his horror, that everyone who crossed had to show their papers to one and some- times both of the men manning the checkpoint. Further, a small train soon appeared and everyone had to get out, show their papers, and walk across the bridge before resuming their journey. Willis spent the last couple of hours of daylight searching for another place to cross the river, but to no avail. As darkness fell, he made his usual bed in a haystack. The adventures of the day took their toll almost immediately, and Willis was soon fast asleep, oblivious to the cold.

A hungry D.K. awoke just as the sun was breaking over the horizon. Rather than immediately get on his way, he lay in the warm hay and tried to piece together some plan for getting across the large river he had faced the preceding evening. He was sure that there had to be another, more remote crossing and decided that he would look for it. Even if there was no crossing, he was confident that there would be a boat somewhere along the shore that he could take. Willis walked along the bank of the nearly deserted river for over an hour but found neither a crossing nor a boat. Discouraged and hungry, he sat down by a tree. He saw no way to get across the river, and for the first time since he'd crashed, he began to doubt that he would be able to get to Brussels and the help he was confident he could find there. That turned his thoughts to his fiancée, Pat, back in England. Did one of his squadron mates tell her what had happened? D.K. had told her that if he was shot down he would survive and make it back to her, but would she really believe him? As he brooded, he instinctively reached into his pocket for a cigar and found the stub of one that he had apparently put there when he had changed clothes back at the Kuppens house. In his squadron, the five-foot-four, one-hundred-forty-pound Willis was known as "the little guy on the end of a cigar," and just being able to chew on the old stub made him feel better. Unfortunately, it did nothing for his hunger, but the river was his biggest problem.

After a few minutes, D.K. decided that his only realistic option was to return to the main crossing and see what materialized. There was still the hope that he might see a boat. The walk back produced nothing, but as the discouraged Willis approached the bridge outside of Boom, a new option suddenly opened. A number of men were moving a stack of large wooden poles from his side of the river across the bridge. After watching for a few minutes, he noticed that the guards apparently paid no attention to the laborers as they went back and forth. Presently, a young woman stopped to talk to the guards, and as they chatted, Willis saw his chance. He quickly joined one of the groups of laborers and grabbed one end of a pole. The workers looked at him, but no one said a word. Since they were carrying the poles on their shoulders, the laborers' faces were hidden as they crossed the bridge.

Willis helped carry his pole into the woods on the other side and discovered that they were evidently being used to build some sort of fortification. The work was being supervised by a German guard with a Schmeisser machine gun. There was no way to escape, so he had to walk back across the bridge, help pick up another pole, and repeat the trip. Just as his group was putting down their pole from the second crossing, a young girl pedaled an ice cream cart onto the end of the bridge. Several of the workers asked the guard if they could go buy an ice cream, and a famished Willis joined the group. When he got to the cart he put down a five-franc note, took his change and his ice cream, and wandered back to the building site. At about that time a small commotion broke out as the guard tried to get the workers to hurry and get back to the job. With the German momentarily distracted, Willis dove into the woods and began to run, gulping his ice cream on the way. After a short distance, he stopped but heard nothing to indicate that he was being followed, so he again walked to where he was in sight of the railroad track and continued south.

Fortunately for Willis, there were no other large cities in his path as he continued on toward Brussels. He spent the next two days walking through the countryside, buying food at cafés in small towns when it appeared safe, stealing from farmers, or just staying hungry. As he had all along the way, each night he went to his hotel in a haystack. Late in the morning of April 18, eight days after he had been shot down, Willis entered the outskirts of Brussels. And although that city had been his objective, he had no idea what he would do now that he was there. As he had in Antwerp, he decided that he would simply walk into the huge city and see what happened. Had he looked in a mirror he would have been frightened by the filthy, bearded, bedraggled soul that he saw.

Early in the afternoon he entered the Brussels suburb of Schaerbeek and stopped at a small café for a glass of beer and a sandwich. After he paid the check—with almost the last of his Belgian money—and started to walk again toward the city, the hair rose on the back of his neck as he realized he was being followed. Had someone recognized him as an evader and called the police? he wondered. Suppressing the desire to run, Willis continued to walk into a residential area. As he walked, he realized that the man following him was probably not a police agent, otherwise he would have simply taken Willis into custody at the café. His shadow must have some other idea, so Willis began to walk more slowly. Soon the man was only a step or two behind him. "This is it," thought D.K., the sweat running down his dirty back. From behind him came a voice asking in English if he was a pilot. Still amazed at the Belgians' ability to identify him, D.K. nodded yes. The man then came up beside him and asked if he was an American. D.K. again acknowledged that he was. The stranger then told Willis to follow him, and the pair continued through the streets of Schaerbeek. After walking only a few blocks, Willis's guide turned in at a modest row house, opened the door, and motioned that Willis should come in. Although D.K. didn't realize it, he had been found by the underground.

The first order of business was for Willis to identify himself. Fortunately, he had his U.S. Army Air Forces identification card, which seemed to satisfy his host for the time being. The next essential item was to get cleaned up, and he took his first bath in nine days. He had never seen dirtier water in his life than the water in the tub when he was finished. A cleaned and shaved Willis then sat down to a modest—but for him gourmet—meal of ham, potatoes, bread, cheese, and beer. He wanted badly to find out who his host was and, most important, if he was really in the hands of the underground. He had been told time and again during his survival training lectures not to ask questions of those who helped him, so he continued to be silently curious. After supper, his host explained the rules of the house, such as staying away from windows, not going outside, going to his room if anyone came to the door, and staying quiet if there were visitors. He then talked briefly with Willis about his evasion experience and showed him to the bedroom. As

Willis lay down in the first bed he had seen since leaving England nine days earlier, he marveled at his amazingly good fortune and, in the process, fell asleep. What Willis did not know was that the underground had probably been watching him for some time, possibly since he had left Boom, to determine if he was really an evader or a German imposter. Apparently they had decided he was genuine, so the decision had been made to pick him up in Schaerbeek.

D.K. was surprised when another man came to the house the following morning. Along with his host, this man began asking him a number of questions about his activities since being shot down. As Willis recounted his adventures, his stories seemed to be treated with skepticism. Evidently his hosts found it hard to believe that he had been able to journey all the way from Holland without papers and without any help from the resistance. They further questioned some of his sources of help in Antwerp. D.K. soon realized that the two men were trying to positively establish his identity and ensure that he was not some sort of infiltrator. Willis dutifully answered questions that only an American pilot would be able to field, questions ranging from aviation slang to training locations in England. They then asked him a number of personal questions. Although D.K. was initially reluctant to answer any of the questions, he realized that these men had a great deal at stake in identifying him and so he had better cooperate.

Willis stayed in the house in Schaerbeek for nearly another week as the underground checked his story with its sources in England via shortwave radio. During that time the initial wall created by mutual suspicion was gradually broken, and Willis learned that his host's name was Gaston Matthys, although he was never able to determine what Matthys did for a living. He also found out that the other man's name was Henry Maca and that he was in charge of verifying Willis's identity. It was obvious to D.K. that they were members of the underground, but they would not talk about the resistance at all.

Finally, Willis's identity was verified to the satisfaction of Matthys and Maca. He then saw an immediate change in their relationship with him. They confided that they were members of the Patriotic Militia, an organ of the underground, but unfortunately they were not part of the Comète, the organization that moved evaders to Spain. However, Willis's spirits were lifted sky-high when they told him that the Comète would be taking him to Spain when the time was right. In the meantime, he was to be patient and follow the instructions they gave him.[2] After his ordeal in the countryside, these were easy instructions for D.K. After all, he was getting three meals a day without having to beg or steal and was sleeping in a warm bed. "It's funny," he thought to himself one night as he lay in his bed, "how much the things you just take for granted, like food and a bed, can mean when you don't have them."

About ten days after he was picked up on the street by Matthys, Willis was told he was going to be moved to Brussels. He felt strangely vulnerable as he left the security of the house in Schaerbeek and boarded the trolley for the large city. The week of inactivity had taken the edge off the survival instincts he had developed in the countryside. Fortunately, what he found when he arrived in Brussels was hustle and bustle, thousands of people, and little concern on the part of the occasional German patrol on the street for who they met. After walking for about half an hour, exercise that was welcome to D.K., his guide led him down a small side street. They turned in at a two-story building, climbed a flight of stairs that led to a flat above a garage, and knocked on the door. They were greeted by an attractive young Belgian lady who introduced herself as Monique.

Yvonne Bienfait, known to the evaders only as Monique, was one of the bravest members of the Comète. She regularly housed from one to four evaders in her four-room apartment. Not only did she risk betrayal and probably death every day, but she also had to face the challenge of getting food for several people and still maintaining the pretense that she was living alone. Her primary means of getting food was to smuggle it from the hospital, where she was a nurse, since that was one of the few places in Brussels that had sufficient supplies. Early in her experience of housing evaders, Monique was photographed walking down the street with an American she was helping. Fortunately, she had been able to get both the print and the negative of the picture, but the incident had convinced her that anyone she was hiding had to stay in the apartment day and night.

When Willis arrived at Monique's he met another American, Colonel Thomas Hubbard, who had parachuted into Holland in November 1943 and had been at Monique's apartment for a number of days. As Willis surveyed the tiny flat, he could not see how three people were going to stay there for any time. The stairway to the second-floor entrance was outside. The door opened into a living room furnished with a table and four chairs, two larger easy chairs and a china cabinet. Almost opposite the main entrance was Monique's bedroom, next to that a small bathroom, and finally a small room with one double bed that was shared by the evaders. The entire flat contained less than five hundred square feet. As soon as Willis's guide departed, Monique told him the rules of the house. Neither airman was to ever leave under any

Yvonne "Monique" Bienfait and an American evader, George Vogel, on a Brussels street during the war.
Pat Willis

circumstances unless he was accompanied by her. They were not to look out the front windows and had to be quiet since there were neighbors in the adjacent houses. Difficult for Willis was the prohibition against smoking, since that would surely give them away. Finally, Willis was shown the arrangement of plants growing in pots in the windows of both Monique's bedroom and the room where he was to sleep. "If the Germans visit or anything unusual happens that would make it unsafe for me to come home," she said, "change the location of one of the plants in either room. That will be my signal, and I will immediately go to a friend's house. In that case, you will be on your own."

Time passed slowly for the two airmen cooped up in the tiny apartment. They played cards until they could not stand the games any longer. Both read Monique's few English-language books, and they slept a lot. D.K. had never been interested in drawing, working mathematics problems, or writing, so those avenues, often used by other evaders to pass the time, were not of use to him. Still, there were some moments of excitement, one of which occurred a few days after his arrival at Monique's. He was watching an American air raid on the suburbs of Brussels from the back window when he saw one of the B-17s catch fire and leave the formation. A few seconds later, several parachutes opened above the city. One seemed to be coming down in his section of town. Sure enough, the airman landed in the walled-in garden of the house next door. Just as the airman touched the ground, a German motorcyclist, who had been following the parachute, stopped in front of the house. He quickly ran around to the back of the house and started to climb the fence. At the same time, Willis watched the American shed his chute and go into the house through the back door. Just when the German got into the garden, the American burst through the front door, jumped on the German motorcycle, and sped away. As he rode down the street, a number of Belgians who had seen the parachute come down cheered him and waved their handkerchiefs. Willis was never able to find out who the American was or how he fared.

Evenings were more social times, and the three inhabitants of the flat spent many hours in the evening talking. D.K. told Monique about his experiences flying combat in the British Spitfire. He recounted that in September 1942, he had transferred to the Fourth Fighter Group of the American Eighth Air Force, where he continued to fly the Spitfire with American markings. On March 22, 1943, he'd made his first flight in the P-47 Thunderbolt, and in May he'd been transferred to the headquarters of the 67th Fighter Wing, from which he'd made his ill-fated flight of April 10, 1944.

Willis also learned a lot about surviving in German-occupied Brussels from Monique. Aside from describing the problem of getting food and her concern over being suspected of having too many visitors in her house, she confided to her guests that her biggest concern was being turned in by her own countrymen. "There are so many collaborators," she told them one night, "that one doesn't know who can be trusted and who can't. The only way to really be safe is to not even confide in your friends. That is why we watch evaders for so long. The Germans have been successful in infiltrating our operation on several occasions, and each time that happens a large number of our countrymen are killed or sent away to prison and forced labor." She also told them of the terrible damage and loss of life that occurred in Brussels as a result of Allied air raids. (Brussels had a large railroad marshaling yard, was a critical road hub, and was used by the Germans as both a headquarters and a billeting area for large numbers of troops. Although the Allies tried to bomb only strategic targets, stray bombs or those that were dropped on the wrong targets would often land in residential areas or other places with large civilian populations.) One evening, she took Willis and Hubbard out to see the damage one such raid had caused. And even though the two airmen knew that this was the nature of war, they were surprised that these people would continue to help them under those circumstances.

As if conditions were not crowded enough, a week after Willis's arrival at Monique's flat, two British fliers also arrived, Ron Emeny, a Lancaster pilot, and Alfred Bonds, another crew member. They were to remain there for a few days until the connections with the Comète Line were complete and a way opened to get the four into Spain. Willis thought that just getting enough food for the four men would tax Monique beyond her resources, but amazingly enough, she still brought home enough food that no one went hungry. Even more extraordinary was Monique's ability to get Willis a new suit of clothes, except shoes, so he would look more like he lived in the city.

On May 28, 1944, the four were told that they would begin their journey the following day. For each, it was a bittersweet occasion. Although Willis and the two Englishmen were anxious to get back to Britain, they felt sorry to have to leave Monique, who had done so much for them. Hubbard, on the other hand, did not want to leave Belgium and hazard the trip through France. His solution was to wait for the Americans to come to him. The Belgians had other ideas, however, and Hubbard reluctantly joined the other three as they made their way, with two guides, to the Brussels station and the train that would take them to Paris.

The usual route taken by the Comète Line evaders to Spain was from Brussels through Lille and Beauvais to Paris. From there, when the time was right, they would be moved by one of several routes the length of France to the foothills of the Pyrenees. The Comète Line had been formed in Belgium in 1940. It had been instrumental in moving many British, and later American, fliers into Spain during the early years of the war. It was infiltrated by the Germans in 1943, and a number of Belgians were either killed or sent to concentration camps as a result. The operation was restored in a few months, however, and continued to move Allied fliers into Spain. The pressure of the occupation and of running the operation was clearly voiced by Comtesse Andrée de Jungh, the founder of the Comète Line, in 1941, shortly before she was arrested by the Germans.

We lost all kinds of liberty and freedom [under the Germans]. Our own laws counted for nothing—there was only one law, the German's law, and that could change each day. The death penalty was always there, written on posters in cities and villages, for helping any former allies. You could be searched at any time—they could do what they wanted and steal what they wanted. German soldiers were parading in the streets, arresting and killing people in front of you and ill treating others for nothing at all.[3]

Willis was strangely unconcerned as they bought their tickets to Paris and boarded the crowded train. Each member of the group had been given official-looking identification papers while they were at Monique's house. They had been instructed to give the papers to any official who might ask for them but not to engage the official in conversation, look at him, smile, or do anything else that might stimulate more than a cursory and passing interest. The trip to Paris was uneventful, but the four evaders were completely unprepared for what they found as they stepped from Gare du Nord. The beauty of May in Paris could not be camouflaged by the war, and everywhere there was activity. Willis had to pinch himself to be convinced that this was war and that he was evading the Germans. As had been the case in Brussels, the Germans on the street seemed far more concerned with enjoying themselves and soaking up the ambience of the city than with looking for suspicious people on the street.

They were met at the station by another young lady, Madelaine Boutreloupt, who led them through a combination of walks and rides on streetcars to a rather large house owned by Philippe and Virginia d'Albert-Lake. When the four arrived they discovered that there were about fifteen other Allied airmen staying with Philippe and Virginia, all of them awaiting arrangements to get out of France. Virginia was an American, which made her an instant favorite of Willis and Hubbard, since they could talk with her so easily. The number of evaders waiting at the house discouraged Willis, since Monique had told him that there were only three or four in any group going into Spain. He could imagine that he and Hubbard would have to wait for weeks before their turn came.

Thus, it was a surprised D.K. who was told on June 2, just two days after his arrival, that he, Hubbard, Emeny, and two other fliers, Jack Cornett and Len Barnes, were going to leave the next day for southern France. D.K. and Hubbard speculated that because they were pilots they were picked to move ahead of most of the others in the house, but they were never able to find out for sure. Within a few hours they were provided with French identification cards and French workers' clothes. Their other clothes went into the stock that would be used for other evaders coming through Paris. That night, for the first time, Willis began to think about the Pyrenees and what lay ahead. He had talked to several British and American pilots who had successfully made the trip, including both Eric Doorly and Oscar Coen. They had impressed on him the difficulty of the terrain and that the unexpected was the rule. Further, Eric Doorly had told D.K. of his terrible ordeal after arriving in Spain, just the thought of which sent shivers up D.K.'s back. Still, it was a confident Willis who was awakened before daylight the morning of June 3, 1944, to catch the express train for Bordeaux.

The trip to Bordeaux was uneventful for the five fliers, and in the early afternoon they transferred to the train for Bayonne. That trip went smoothly until Cornett, finding himself in the middle of a group of German soldiers, panicked and jumped from the train as it slowed for its approach to Bayonne. Surprisingly, the soldiers paid little attention, and the rest of the group disembarked in the picturesque old port city without incident. A short time later, as they were preparing to leave Bayonne, they bumped into Cornett on the street. For Willis this was just another sign that everything was going to work out well.

Shortly before dark, the group set out on their first dangerous trek: nearly six miles, past stately stone mansions and across green fields, to their first night's destination, a small restaurant and inn. It was in the hamlet of Sutar, near the town of Anglet, on the Bay of Biscay, not far from the resort city of Biarritz. The inn had been used as a way station by the Comète travelers for a long time, and the Germans, who often frequented the tavern and restaurant, were never aware of the illegal activity.[4] To get to their destination, however, the small group of evaders had to pass as near as one hundred yards to the German patrols and often stop and wait for them to pass by. The evaders had been told by their guide that any sort of movement would certainly alert the patrols and that there would be no way to escape capture.

After their slow, quiet, exhausting trek, Willis and his cohorts were taken aback as they were led in the front door of the inn, through the tavern, past several German customers, to a back stairway and up to the second floor. They were greeted there with a warm meal and comfortable beds. Despite the noise from the activity in the bar below, D.K. was soon asleep.

The morning of June 4 dawned clear and bright. Everyone was in high spirits, anticipating their freedom. After a hearty breakfast, the five were provided with bicycles and rode for about six miles into a dense forest. They were instructed to wait there until the guide who would take them across the Pyrenees appeared. The group was cautioned that they might have to wait all day and that they had to remain silent and make no unnecessary movement since the area was heavily patrolled by the Germans. They were also warned that the Germans were very frightened of the Basque people in the region because of their tough, warlike nature, and would probably shoot anyone on sight. For Willis and his four companions, this was sufficient motivation to remain still and quiet.

It was nearly dark when a short, muscular Basque man arrived to start the group on what they assumed would be their final trek to freedom. He brought some bread, cheese, and milk for the hungry travelers. Since the guide spoke very little English, Willis, who had become fairly fluent in Spanish during his days of sailing to South America, became the translator. "Do not speak, always stay close behind me," the guide began.

> When I stand still, do the same and don't move a muscle. Only when I give you a sign do you move again. Do not smoke, under any circumstances, for a cigarette can be seen and smelled at a far distance. Danger lurks everywhere. There are Germans everywhere. They patrol the area, at least in pairs, often accompanied by a dog. They will shoot immediately because they are afraid. Continue walking and stay tough. It will be a long journey

and you will be dead tired, but we have to hurry. Darkness is our only protection. When it gets light, we will hide. We will rest when we are across the border and out of reach from the police. If we are caught, we will be delivered to the Germans. That means jail for you and death for me![5]

With that admonition, their guide set out.

D.K. thought he had some idea of what to expect, but he was in no way prepared for what lay ahead. For the evaders, who had been kept in relative inactivity for over two weeks, the pace set by their Basque guide was impossible. It seemed to make no difference if he was going up or down a hill, his pace remained the same. The problem was compounded by the darkness and the terrain. It seemed that one moment they would be crossing a sloped field and the next be in a nearly impenetrable forest on a steep, rocky slope. If one of the party got more than a few feet from the person in front of him, he could become lost in the darkness. It was only when the evaders were gasping for breath and nearly unable to move on their aching legs that their guide would stop for a few moments. After the most torturous five hours of their lives, the completely exhausted group arrived at a river, which, their guide told them, was the boundary between France and Spain. Rather than stop, their guide simply plunged into the ice-cold water and began to wade across. In a matter of seconds, his followers were slipping and stumbling on slick rocks and trying vainly to keep their numb feet under them in the wet blackness. Any euphoria they might have felt upon their arrival in Spain was quelled by their miserable condition.

(It was not until after the war that Willis learned that his group was the last to be taken across the Pyrenees by the Comète Line. The combination of the Allied invasion of France and German infiltration of the Comète organization brought the operation to a close after four years of returning hundreds of Allied airmen to fight another day.)

Although Willis and his companions thought they had reached safety, the march continued. Finally, at about four o'clock in the morning, Willis told the guide that they could not continue. They had to rest. It seemed to the evaders that they had scarcely taken a drink from a nearby mountain stream and sat down than they were up again, stumbling through the night on aching legs. Shortly after daybreak, they were led to an old sheep barn and bruskly told to stay there until that night, when their guide would return. Without food or water, and having no idea where they were, the exhausted survivors fell into a fitful sleep.

It was nearly dark when the guide returned to the famished and still exhausted group. Soon he had the men back on the trail at the same impossible pace. To make matters worse, he had not brought them any food. The objective, he told Willis, was to get far enough into Spain by daybreak to eliminate any chance of being sent back to France if they were caught by the Spanish police. So the starving fugitives stumbled through the night. Hubbard had blisters so severe that every step was agony. Willis finally gave him the one shot of morphine that remained from his survival kit so his friend could continue. Just as they reached the point where they knew they could go no farther, the evaders were met by two men. After a few words, which Willis did not understand, their guide departed into the darkness. The men motioned for the group to follow them, and within a few minutes they'd arrived at an isolated farmhouse, where they were greeted with bread and milk, their first food in two days. The five were then taken to the barn, and they again fell into an exhausted sleep.

They were awakened shortly after daybreak by a young girl frantically saying something in Spanish. Willis could hardly believe his ears. She was saying that her mother had sent her to warn them that one of the men had gone to get the police so he could collect the reward for turning the group in so they could be sent back to France. In a matter of minutes, the five fugitives were again on the move, only this time they had no guide and no map. Fortunately, Willis still had the compass from his escape kit, and so they were able to continue going south. They soon came to a road they decided to parallel.[6] If they could just keep going for a few more days, the men believed, they would be so far into Spain that they would surely be safe. But fatigue continued to take its toll, and after two more days of existing on a few berries and water from streams, the airmen decided that they had to have help.

Late one morning, as they emerged into the gently rolling Spanish foothills near Oricain, they saw a solitary farmhouse and decided to try to buy some food with their French money. Since Willis was the only member of the party who spoke any Spanish, he knocked on the door. It is hard to imagine the surprise and fear the farmer must have felt when confronted by a group of five haggard, bearded, filthy men asking if they could buy food. Willis quickly explained who they were and that they were desperate for help. The farmer was unable to give them anything to eat, but he pointed the way to Pamplona, the capital of Navarre and the most important city in the Pyrenees, a few miles farther down the road. He told them that they should contact the police and that he was sure they would be helped. After a short conference, the desperate evaders decided that they had reached the end of their rope and that they would turn themselves in, hoping they were far enough into Spain to be safe.

Early in the afternoon of June 8, they approached the old Roman city, site of the annual festival of the running of the bulls and known to many from Ernest Hemingway's novel *The Sun Also Rises*. The group had traveled nearly sixty miles through the mountains in five days. They paid little attention to the beautiful squares, fountains, arcades, and classic Spanish houses as they stumbled along the old streets. They collapsed in a small park. Their only hope, they decided, was for Willis to try to find the post office, where, they were sure, there would be a telephone he could use to call the English or American consulate in San Sebastian. Fortunately for Willis, the walk was not far, and after convincing the skeptical clerk that, despite his ragged and filthy appearance, his situation was an emergency, Willis was able to establish contact with the British consul. The consul, after assuring Willis that help would be coming for them, told him that the police had probably been alerted by the telephone operator and that they would soon be arrested. As Willis walked out of the post office, he came face-to-face with the chief of police and two other officers. The starving airman knew he was far too weak to even try to escape or resist, so he told the officers where they could find his comrades and accompanied his new hosts to the police station.

At the police station, the five expected the worst. They were flabbergasted when they were accorded a friendly welcome, given a chance to clean up as best they could, and taken to a nearby restaurant for the most welcome meal any of them had ever had. Willis spotted a newspaper that announced the Allied invasion of France and realized that the Spanish knew their old friends, the Germans, were not going to win the war. But, unbeknownst to Willis, that was not the primary reason for their reception. In 1943, an agreement had been reached with the British, and later with the United States, that British and American fugitives who came across the mountains from France would be held at the expense of their respective governments until they could be moved out of Spain. This meant that a long stint in jail awaiting trial and confinement at Miranda de Ebro, the fate suffered by Eric Doorly, was a thing of the past.

After a day of rest, three good meals, and a bath, the five were taken, under guard, by bus to the coastal city of San Sebastian and then by train the short distance to Irún, where they were given rooms in a local hotel. The amazing thing to Willis was that Irún was only a mile from the French border and less than twenty miles from Sutar, where they had begun their trek. After a two-day rest, during which they were given fresh clothes by an English family, the group parted company. The three Americans—Willis, Hubbard, and Cornett—were picked up by a representative of the American consulate and taken to Madrid. Near the end of June, the trio was put on a train for Gibraltar. On June 28, 1944, Willis and Hubbard caught an airplane to England. Cornett followed two days later.

Arrival in England did not mean the end of the ordeal for Willis. He was immediately taken to the Dorchester Hotel in London and put under what amounted to house arrest. He was not allowed to contact anyone or leave his room until the American intelligence authorities finished with him. The first step was to determine if he was really D. K. Willis. A few hours after he checked in at the Dorchester, one of his old squadron mates arrived and spent several hours with him to ensure his identity. Willis then spent an entire day being debriefed by intelligence officers. It was only after that, on July 1, 1944, that Willis, resplendent in a new uniform, was able to contact the outside world.

His first call was to his English fiancée, Patricia Gilis, a nurse at a hospital north of London. During the time he had been evading, she had been moved to another hospital, and Willis eventually had to call his old commanding officer, General Anderson, to find out where Pat was. She had known that he was missing, but she did not know he had successfully evaded until she heard the familiar voice on the phone saying "I'm back." Willis was then returned to his home base of Debden, and on July 3 he was again in the sky checking out in the P-47. Willis remained at Debden until the end of the war. By that time he had destroyed one German aircraft and been awarded two Air Medals.

After the war, Willis remained in the Army Air Forces and was part of the occupation force in Germany. He and Pat were married, and he returned to the United States in 1946. His first assignment was to Williams Air Force Base, Arizona. He was later transferred to Wright Patterson Air Force Base, Ohio, and left the Air Force in November 1953. He subsequently worked in the insurance industry, then took a position with Global Van Lines, and finally went back to sea as the quartermaster on one of the first supertankers. The Willises had two children and one grandchild at the time of D.K.'s death in 1977.

In 1982, Pat Willis, who now lives in Florida, returned to the site of her husband's crash landing in Holland. She was able to visit with Mrs. Kuppens and view the area where Willis landed. During that meeting she learned that Willis was the only Allied airman to crash in the area of

Oud-Gastel and the only one the Kuppenses had aided. When Pat asked the elderly lady why she and her late husband had helped D.K., Mrs. Kuppens replied, "He was someone's son and he needed our help. I only wish we could have done more." Pat Willis also went to Brussels, where she visited with Monique in the apartment where her husband had been housed during his evasion.

Notes

1. Hans Onderwater, *Reis Naar De Horizon* (*Journey to the Horizon*) (Uitgave, Hollandia BV: Uitgeverij, Hollandia, 1984), pp. 107–9.

2. Onderwater, pp. 119–22.

3. Alan W. Cooper, *Free to Fight Again* (William Kimber and Co. Limited: Wellingborough, Northamptonshire, England, 1988), p. 136.

4. Onderwater, pp. 156–61.

5. Onderwater, p. 164.

6. Onderwater, p. 167.

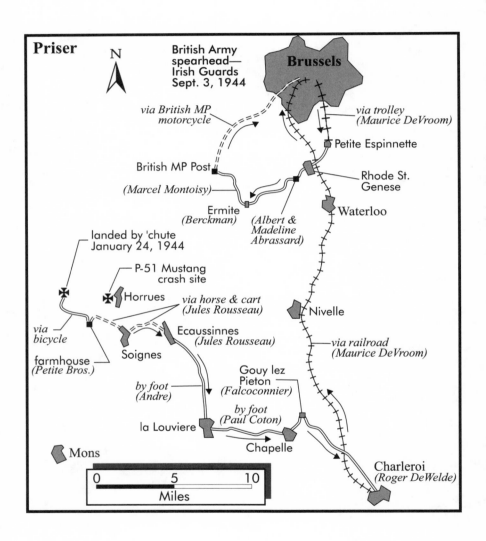

Priser

N

British Army
spearhead—
Irish Guards
Sept. 3, 1944

Brussels

*via British MP
motorcycle*

*via trolley
(Maurice DeVroom)*

British MP Post

Petite Espinnette

(Marcel Montoisy)

Rhode St.
Genese

Ermite
(Berckman)

*(Albert &
Madeline
Abrassard)*

Waterloo

landed by 'chute
January 24, 1944

P-51 Mustang
crash site

Horrues

*via horse & cart
(Jules Rousseau)*

*via
bicycle*

Ecaussinnes
(Jules Rousseau)

Nivelle

Soignes

farmhouse
(Petite Bros.)

*via railroad
(Maurice DeVroom)*

*by foot
(Andre)*

Gouy lez
Pieton
(Falcoconnier)

*by foot
(Paul Coton)*

la Louviere

Chapelle

Charleroi
(Roger DeWelde)

Mons

0   5   10

Miles

• F I V E •

"Please, God, Help Me Get Out of This!"

"**T**he target for today is Frankfurt," Squadron Commander Bob Priser told the assembled P-51 Mustang pilots of the 353rd Fighter Squadron as they drank their morning coffee in the briefing room at Boxted Air Base in England on Monday, January 24, 1944. "We will be escorting B-17s and we can expect the usual flak and possibly some fighters. There should be no weather problems over the Continent and the target should be clear, but it could be a little dicey landing back here. You might want to be prepared to go to an alternate field, because Boxted could get pretty well socked in while we're gone. We'll pick up the bombers just after they cross into Germany and take the place of a group of P-47 Thunderbolts when their fuel gets too low for them to continue the escort. It should be a good mission. Any questions?" And with that, what would be Priser's last briefing to his pilots ended.

He had been thrilled a month earlier when he had finally been given a squadron, and he enjoyed being in command. He had worked long and hard to get the job, starting when he arrived in England in December 1941. He had flown the best single-engine fighters in the world, beginning with the Spitfire, then the huge, radial-engined P-47, and finally the long-awaited P-51. Priser especially liked the Mustang because, with its Rolls Royce V-12 engine, it flew very much like the Spitfire, and at five feet six and one hundred thirty-five pounds, he was comfortable in the small cockpit. Bob was one of the old-timers, having flown for the

RAF as a member of one of the famed Eagle Squadrons, Number 133, even before the American fighter pilots had begun to arrive. This was what he had always wanted to do, and he had never had any misgivings about his decision to volunteer to fly fighters, even in the thick of the many air battles in which he had flown.

Robert Priser atop a P-47 at Debden in 1943.   *Robert Priser*

After the usual small talk, joking around, and review of the previous night's activities at the pubs in the area, plus a few accounts of the men's exploits while on three-day passes in London—conversations in which the quiet, introverted Priser seldom participated—the pilots reluctantly left the warmth of their briefing room to brave the cold winter breeze that blew across the ramp. This was always the hardest part of the flight. Everything was cold, from the concrete ramp to the controls in the cockpit. Ever since his college days in Arizona, Bob had never liked the weather in his native Ohio, and he was unable to get used to the damp cold of England that seemed to blow right through anything you had on and just chilled you to the bone. But it did make you want to get that big Rolls Royce V-12 fired up, the cockpit heater turned on, and most of all, get up above the overcast and let the bright morning sun beat in through the Plexiglas hood and really warm you up. Priser had to spend a little more time in the cold than usual that morning because he had a colonel flying his wing who had just arrived in England and who had never flown in combat. It was common practice for a pilot without any combat time to fly on the wing of one of the more experienced squadron members in order to get checked out in combat flying. But soon the entire squadron was airborne and flying in the welcome sun over the English Channel.

A short time later, the coast of southern Belgium passed beneath the formation, and as he always did, Priser noted how calm and peaceful everything appeared thousands of feet below. There were never any signs of war visible from over 20,000 feet. Right on schedule, the bombers appeared ahead and below, lumbering along with their full bomb loads, and Priser watched the P-47s peel off and turn back toward England. He put his squadron above and behind the bombers, since the Germans liked to attack the tail ends of the formations, and settled down for what should be several hours of weaving back and forth while constantly scanning the sky for German fighters. Just before noon, as the group crossed the German frontier, radio silence was broken by a recall order from Ninth Air Force. The bombers and their escorts were to return to England because the weather was deteriorating and, if they flew the full mission, there could well be no place to land on their return. The formation began its slow turn toward home, and Priser's squadron continued to zig and zag while bringing up the rear. About the time the turn was completed, Priser looked to his right and saw four fighters, led by a P-47 with a white ring around the cowling, approaching the formation. Priser thought it strange that a P-47 would still be in the area, since his unit had relieved the Thunderbolts earlier, but he didn't have time to give the matter a second thought as he went back to the business of checking on the bombers, the placement of his squadron, and the continual search for enemy aircraft. Moments later, Priser again looked at the incoming fighters and was startled to see black smoke coming from the wings of the lead aircraft.

"My God, that guy is shooting at me! It's not a P-47—it's an FW-190," he said out loud. But before he could take any evasive action or warn his squadron, Priser's aircraft shuddered as it was hit in the right wing by several twenty-millimeter cannon shells. He couldn't believe he'd made such a stupid mistake after briefing his squadron time and again on the deceptive tactics used by the Germans, including making an FW-190 look like a P-47. The adrenaline was beginning to flow as he searched the sky for another enemy aircraft since the German who'd shot him appeared to be nearly a mile away and flying ninety degrees to Priser. Seeing no other Germans, Priser had to give his adversary credit for making a nearly impossible shot, but fortunately it initially appeared that it had caused little damage. "He'll pay for this," Bob thought as he dropped his wing tanks, turned hard right and then left, and got behind the enemy formation. He started to shoot at one of the German FW-190s. He realized suddenly that the aircraft leading the formation was indeed a P-47, obviously one that the Germans had captured. Since he had lots of combat experience in the Thunderbolt, Priser knew he could beat a P-47 with his P-51 in a dogfight, so he attacked the flight leader. "I'll show you!" he yelled as he fired a three-second burst at the German. He could see where his bullets were hitting the aircraft, and he closed in for the kill. Just then his engine backfired and began to run roughly. Priser pulled off to the right and let the Germans go as he concentrated on his own problems. It appeared that white smoke was coming from the wing of his Mustang, but closer inspection showed it to be fuel vaporizing as it hit the air flowing over his wing. Even closer inspection revealed a big hole where the wing joined the fuselage. Chills ran down Priser's spine as he saw that the inside of the wing was blazing brightly. There were also a couple of more holes where cannon shells had gone through the wing but not exploded. With this damage and a rough-running engine, Priser knew he had been hit a lot worse than he'd initially thought and was in real trouble. It was time to head for home.

No sooner had he established a course for England than the fire got worse. With the fuel and hydraulic fluid burning in the wing, his wounded Mustang was not going to fly much longer. It was time to get out. He had gone through the bailout procedure countless times in his mind, so everything was pretty automatic. With his heart in his throat and clammy hands, he jettisoned his canopy, disconnected his oxygen and radio, unfastened his seat belt, and pushed the stick forward, a movement that should have thrown him out of the cockpit and clear of the tail of his plane. However, the procedure did not work as advertised, and Priser found himself with his feet stuck in the cockpit and his body laid out along the fuselage behind it. To make matters worse, his aircraft had begun a spiral and was building up speed. "I really screwed this up," the panicked pilot thought to himself. "I'm going to go in with the plane, so no one will ever know what happened and be able to tell my family." There was nothing he could do but squirm and kick harder than he ever had before. Suddenly he was free of the cockpit, but with a huge thud he hit the horizontal stabilizer. The impact, right above his waist, sent pain shooting through his body, and Priser knew it was the end of the road. He was in the situation every fighter pilot feared: pinned to the tail of his plane, with his upper body across the top of the stabilizer and his feet underneath. The tremendous force of air, as the speed of his plane continued to build in its death spiral toward the ground, made escape almost impossible. The terrified Priser kicked, shoved, and clawed but was unable to get free. "Please, God," he prayed, "help me get out of this!" About that time, he lost consciousness.

When Priser came to, it was dark, quiet, and cold. He realized that he was not dead but rather was descending in his parachute, but he couldn't see. He had no idea how he had gotten off the tail of his plane, but he assumed that the airflow had eventually just torn his parachute open and it had pulled him off. But how high was he and where was he going to land? There was no way of knowing in his black world. He was surprisingly calm as he tucked his cold hands under his Mae West inflatable life vest and waited for the inevitable impact. Suddenly, the black turned to a gray haze that rapidly lifted and Priser could see again. He found himself about three hundred feet above a pasture bordered by a narrow dirt road on which a man and two little children, all with bicycles, were watching him descend. A few moments later, Priser hit the soft ground and rolled with the impact. He struggled to his feet, took off his parachute harness, and ignoring the searing pain in his side, began to run from the area. After stumbling along for a short distance in his big fur-lined flying boots, he realized they were not made for fast travel and stopped to take them off. He heard someone shout and noticed the man on the bicycle pointing to a farmhouse a short distance to his right. Priser remembered being told in his evasion briefings that you initially went away from your objective so you would leave a false trail for those who might be looking for you. He continued running away from the farmhouse, and when he was out of breath, he stopped to get his escape kit out of his flying suit. His heart sank when he found the kit gone; apparently it had dropped out of his pocket when he bailed out. He took off his flying suit and made a halfhearted effort to conceal it, along with his leather flying helmet, thinking that might help confuse any pursuers, and then doubled back to the farmhouse, which was about two hundred yards away across the pasture.

By the time Priser got to the house, the man he had seen by the field had already arrived, but the children were nowhere in sight. The farmer took Priser into the house, where an older lady, who reminded him of his grandmother, gave him a basin of water so he could clean up. It was then that he realized he not only ached from head to toe but had blood on his hands from numerous scratches, probably sustained when he was hung up on the tail of his aircraft. The lady also gave him a mirror, and he was startled to see all the small scratches on his face. That was not as great a shock as were the whites of his normally very blue eyes. They were bright red from the impact of the opening parachute, which had temporarily blinded him. After his quick washup, the lady gave him a civilian suit coat and a beret, for which he exchanged his leather flying jacket. She then bade him good-bye. The man accompanied Priser outside and took him to a bicycle that was leaning against the side of the building. He indicated, through using his hands and with a little English, that Priser should follow him on the bicycle, staying a good distance behind. Priser took a minute to smear mud on his brown army shoes and on the cuffs of his olive drab wool trousers, and then, gritting his teeth against the pain, he mounted the bike, hoping that his outfit would keep him from standing out from the other people who might be on the road.

As he began his trek down the little lane, trying hard to keep the proper distance behind his guide, Bob thought about a book he had read on his voyage to England, *The Thirty-nine Steps*. It was a mystery in which the main character had to assume several disguises and play the appropriate roles to go with his new identities to keep from being killed. The lesson from the book that continued to run over and over in Bob's mind was to always act as if you belonged where you were. Priser never thought that he might have to use some of these ideas. But he'd always prided himself on being prepared for this eventuality whenever he flew, so he believed there was a good chance that things would work out okay.

The pair had ridden only a short distance along the one-lane road when they topped a small hill. Priser's blood ran cold. Coming from the other direction was a column of German soldiers, evidently going to the site where his aircraft had crashed. Priser had received no instruction from his Belgian guide about what to do, nor had any of his survival training addressed this kind of situation. Scarcely able to breathe from fright, he followed his guide and pedaled right past the Germans, focusing on the road ahead so they wouldn't see his red eyes.

About a mile farther on, the lane intersected with a cobblestone road. At the corner was a small stone farmhouse. Priser's guide stopped, they put their bicycles behind the house, and they went inside. Beyond the doorway was a steep, low, narrow stairway, which they descended; it was so steep that Priser banged his head against the header board. They entered a small kitchen, and Priser's guide told him to sit down while he made some coffee. One of the instructions Priser had received in his training was to give your watch to the person who initially helped you evade as a token of appreciation. Bob thought this would be a good occasion, so, while they waited for the coffee to brew, he took off his watch and offered it to the Belgian. With a sly chuckle, his guide accepted the watch, then pulled up the sleeve of his coat and displayed several watches, ample evidence that Priser was in experienced hands. Priser didn't know it at the time, but the Belgian underground had been successfully infiltrated by the Germans several months earlier, which had resulted in hundreds of arrests and the closure of the escape route through France to Spain. Still, underground observers were posted throughout the countryside every time there was an Allied air raid to watch for Allied airmen who were forced to abandon their aircraft. Apparently, the man who had watched Priser land was one such observer, and he had helped several airmen evade initial capture by the Germans. Further, the places where Priser was initially taken were evidently prepared for the arrival of Allied airmen, several of whom had preceded Priser along that route.

As soon as Priser finished his cup of coffee, his guide took him out the back door of the house to a barn and showed him a place in a hayloft where he was to stay. As Bob lay down in the warm hay, he realized even more graphically that his injuries were a lot more serious than just a few scratches. It was obvious that his ride on the stabilizer of his P-51 had done more damage to him than he'd originally thought, since both his chest and his abdominal area were throbbing with pain and he found it almost impossible to get comfortable. Still, the combination of his harrowing experience getting out of his aircraft, his injuries, and the stress of the initial evasion experience—and probably a mild case of shock—took their toll. He fell asleep, even though it was still early afternoon.

After a couple of hours, Priser was awakened by his guide. He found it almost impossible to move, but he took a deep breath and followed the Belgian to the rear of the house, where they retrieved their bicycles. The two started off down the cobblestone road. Riding a bicycle on cobblestones was not easy, and Priser had a difficult time keeping his balance, much less staying up with his guide. His several aches and pains didn't help matters, but he kept on pedaling. A few miles down the road, he followed his guide to the back of another farmhouse, where they again parked the bikes and went inside. There Priser was greeted by several people, both men and women. He was introduced all around as an American pilot and then joined the group in drinking glasses of beer. Although he did not understand anything they were saying, it seemed to him that they were celebrating having rescued another Allied airman and really had little concern about being interrupted by the Germans. But Priser was getting more tired and weak by the minute. Much to his relief, his guide soon led him back to the bicycles and they were on their way again.

As Priser pedaled after his guide, he hoped that the next stop would bring something to eat and a place to stay for the night, but that was not to be. After riding a short distance, the pair stopped at another farmhouse and the entire ritual of introductions, a drink, and conversation was repeated. After the fourth stop, Bob realized that, despite his injuries and being unable to move without pain, he was going to spend the rest of the day riding, greeting, and drinking. On top of it all, he was already starting to feel a bit drunk. Apparently, his hosts were just taking up time while someone in the organization looked for a place in which to hide him for a longer period.

Late in the afternoon, Priser's guide finally took him to a small farmhouse, near the village of Braine, that had large barns attached to either side forming a U-shaped building. Two men were waiting there. They were obviously farmers, short and chunky, looked to be in their sixties, and each had a large mustache. This was different from the other stops because there were no other men or women around. He was led into the house, through the warmth of the kitchen, and beyond the living room into a bedroom, where the farmers indicated he could go to bed. Bob had never been so glad to lie down in his life, and after a short prayer thanking God for his survival, he was soon asleep. When he awoke the next day he ached from head to toe, and his ribs hurt whenever he moved or breathed. His entire abdomen was one big mass of bruises, and it felt like he had several broken ribs. Aside from getting up for meals and trips to the bathroom, Priser stayed in bed for nearly a week. But he mended rapidly, and by the end of the week he was able to get up, walk about the house, and sit in his room. He would have liked to have gone outside, but his hosts made it clear that it would be too dangerous, although he never saw any indication that Germans were in the area. He was not able to converse with the two farmers to any degree, since they spoke no English and Priser couldn't speak French, so he spent most of his time sitting in his room and daydreaming.

Dominating his mind were thoughts of his wife, Jill. They had been married in England just a month earlier, on Christmas Day, 1943. They had not had a real honeymoon since Bob had gone AWOL to get married. He hadn't been too concerned about it—the squadron commander had gone along to witness the wedding and the day after Christmas, Priser had been back in his squadron. A few days later the squadron commander had been transferred and Priser was named to succeed him. The couple had not even had the chance to find an apartment before Priser was shot down. As he lay in the Belgian farmhouse, he wondered what she had been told about his crash, whether she knew he was alive, where she was living, and a hundred more questions. He wished there was some way he could tell his hosts about his wife, but he had to just think about her in silence.

But Bob also thought about other things. He recalled his first flight in an OX-5 Waco when he was just eight years old, and building model airplanes in his spare time as his interest in flying continued to grow. And he could never forget going through ROTC at the University of Arizona and wearing wool uniforms for parades in the hundred-degree heat.

As he lay in his strange bed, Bob's thoughts were often interrupted by the sounds of airplanes, and he would try to get to a window to see whose they were. Each time he was disappointed to see only planes of the Luftwaffe, probably going out to intercept an Allied bomber formation. The sounds of their engines invariably caused his mind to wander back to his early flying days. His dream of becoming a pilot had been realized when he'd enrolled in the Civilian Pilot Training Program while he was at the University of Arizona. And the feeling of freedom and wonder that came to him on his first solo flight had never left him. Convinced that flying was his future, he'd dropped out of the University of Arizona after two years and gone back to his home in Ohio to get a job with Waco aircraft as a mechanic. He was able to get enough time off to take advanced flying training through the University of Dayton, and in the summer of 1941 he heard about the chance to join the RAF. He was convinced that this was the only way he was ever going to get to fly really first-line planes, so he moved to San Diego in July 1941

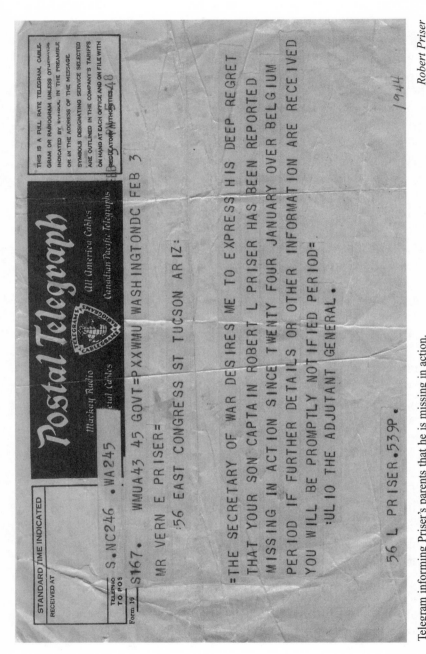

Telegram informing Priser's parents that he is missing in action.

Robert Priser

and volunteered. He was sent to Glendale, California, for three months of intense advanced flying training and was still there on December 7, 1941. He smiled as he thought of the efforts he and his friends had made on December 8 to become Marine pilots. When the group was told they would have to go through boot camp first, they decided to stay with the RAF. So, after a brief leave at home, it was off to Canada and then, along with about two hundred other new pilots, the fifteen-day voyage across the North Atlantic. But it was not until he saw the bomb damage and destruction on his arrival in Liverpool that the reality of war began to soak in.

When Bob was able to wander around the small Belgian farmhouse more easily, it became obvious that the two men had sent their wives away to make room for him, because he clearly was occupying one couple's room. The general lack of concern about his presence and the established routine of the two farmers led Priser to assume that he was not the first Allied airman to be accommodated by them. But all three men found out how much the women were missed one evening when the farmers indicated that they would be cooking a special meal of chicken. What emerged from the oven was burned on one side and raw on the other.

As Bob began to feel better, he also started to wonder if there was any plan for getting him to Spain and freedom. Because he couldn't communicate well with his hosts, he wasn't able to get much information from them. He finally learned that he was in Belgium a few miles from the French border. But he remembered the instruction from his evasion lectures not to try to pry information out of those who were helping him, so that was about all he learned. However, the underground was watching him more closely than he realized. About the time he really began to feel like he could travel, a tall stranger, who introduced himself as Jules Rousseau, appeared at the farmhouse one morning carrying a top coat and a hat. He spoke some English and was able to tell Priser that he was leaving immediately to continue his trek. He handed Priser the coat, stuffed some paper in the hat so it wouldn't fall down around Priser's ears, and motioned for him to follow. After bussing the two farmers on both cheeks, in typical French fashion, and thanking them for their hospitality, Priser climbed up beside Jules in a horse-drawn two-wheeled buggy, and off they went, the two farmers waving as they left.

Bob's stomach was tied in knots as the cart rumbled slowly down the cobblestone road. Who was this man and where were they going? Occasionally they met other Belgians, some of whom spoke to Jules. They were also passed by a few German soldiers who didn't seem the least bit interested in the stranger Jules was carrying in his wagon. As Priser's confidence in Jules grew, he began to relax and enjoy the slow tour through the countryside. He even found himself momentarily forgetting that he was in an occupied country.

A few miles down the narrow road they entered the village of Soignies, through which they had to pass to get to Jules's home in the hamlet of Ecaussinnes. Priser was jolted back to reality as they approached the most formidable building in town, identified by a sign as the College of Soignies. It was now a German headquarters, and Priser was shaking in his shoes as they passed near the entrance and the German sentry. But despite the fact that he was in civilian clothes and had no identity card, he acted as if he belonged, buoyed up by Jules's optimism, and they rode uneventfully past the German. (Priser knew that being dressed in civilian clothes and having no identification to prove he was an American airman meant that he would not be subject to the rules of the Geneva Convention if he was captured. All the American airmen had been briefed on this eventuality, but they were told that the only concern would be if they were captured by the German SS.) No sooner had they passed the vicinity of the German headquarters than they came up behind a formation of German infantry marching down the road. Jules kept the wagon behind the formation, but Priser breathed much easier when the soldiers turned off the street and went into a church.

Along the way, Bob learned that Jules was a miller. His mill was their destination and the first step on what Bob thought was to be his trek into Spain. As they entered Ecaussinnes, Jules turned on a side street and approached a large fenced compound. Two long single-story buildings, which came right to the edge of the street, formed the front of the compound, so there was no front yard. A gate led to a courtyard that separated the two structures. Behind them were fields and farms. As they approached, Jules pointed out that the building on the left was the mill and that his house was the one on the right. Jules drove the wagon through the gate, behind the house, and getting out of the cart, took Priser into the house with him.

Priser found himself in another kitchen where the fire glowed in the stove and a pot of coffee bubbled away. Jules introduced Priser to his wife, Jane, who led him through the dining room to a bedroom where he was to stay. After he surveyed his living area, Priser joined Jules and his wife in the kitchen for a cup of coffee. Jules explained the rules of the house. Priser was particularly interested in Jules's warning that there were Belgians in the town who were more dangerous than the Germans and, for that reason, Priser was not to go near the windows or outside the house alone. Apparently, some townspeople routinely announced the presence of strangers to the police, which meant an investigation and possible capture for both the evader and his protectors. Jules explained that all young men had to be able to prove they were employed in the area or they would be sent to Germany as laborers, so Priser had to be careful. The American was also questioned to prove that he was not a German infiltrator. But since he had left his dog tags on the night stand in the hotel in Colchester where he was staying with his wife, and because air crews were no longer allowed to carry identification cards or other personal identification when they flew combat missions, he had no way of proving who he was. The longer they talked, however, the more convinced Jules evidently became that Priser was who he said he was.

Priser's confidence was buoyed a few days after his arrival at the mill when a photographer arrived and took his picture for new identification papers. Shortly thereafter, he was provided with Belgian identification, a work permit, and all the other papers that any Belgian would carry with him, each properly signed and stamped. His new name was Robert Wosswinkel, and he was a mining technician in a coal mine near the town of Charleroi. While these all eased his concern, Jules still maintained that Priser had to be extra cautious, for if he was taken in for questioning, it would be apparent in a few seconds that he was not a Belgian worker at all. Priser found out later that the police chief of Soignies was a member of the underground and was able to provide all the papers needed by any evader who happened into the area.

Priser had the run of Jules's house, but time still hung heavily on his hands. He occasionally looked through a crack in the door at the farmers who came and went from the mill and could often see townspeople as they stopped to chat or have a cup of coffee in the kitchen. Jane served most of the delicious meals she made in the dining room, and these meals were the high points of his day. Because Jules was a miller and money was scarce, most of the farmers paid him for milling their grain with various farm products. As a result, he had access to more food than many Belgians, so meals generally included a vegetable, some meat, plenty of bread, maybe some cheese, and an occasional glass of wine, but there was never any fruit. Priser rarely even went into the kitchen. When he was allowed to sit in the kitchen and drink coffee or talk to Jules, on the rare occasions when the miller was not busy, he had to go back to his room whenever someone came to the house or the mill. Although he did have paper and pencil and spent a lot of time drawing the scenes around the house or his ideas for new airplanes, with little to

Jules and Jane Rousseau.　　　　　　　　*Robert Priser*

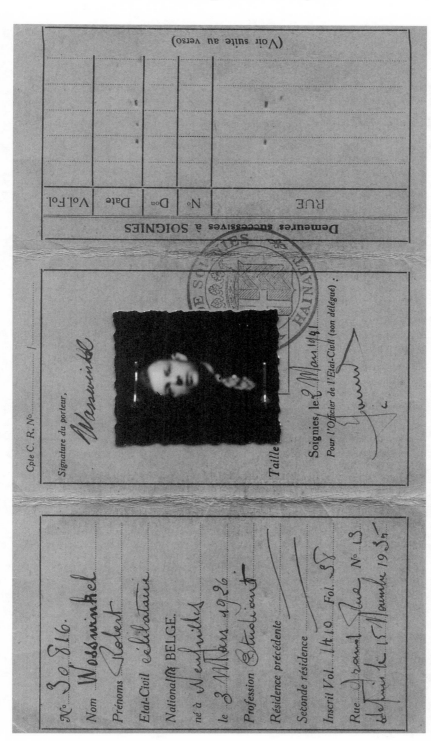

Priser's false identification papers supplied by the Belgian underground name him as Robert Wosswinkel.

Robert Priser

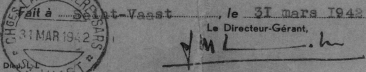

CERTIFICAT

La Société Anonyme des Charbonnages de La Louvière et Sars-Longchamps, à Saint-Vaast, *certifie que*

Monsieur ⎯WOSSWINKEL⎯⎯⎯⎯Robert.⎯⎯⎯⎯⎯⎯⎯⎯⎯⎯⎯⎯⎯⎯⎯⎯⎯⎯⎯⎯⎯⎯⎯

Carte d'identité ⎯⎯30.816⎯⎯⎯, *demeurant à* ⎯⎯Soignies⎯⎯⎯
Rue ⎯Grand' Rue⎯⎯⎯⎯⎯⎯, N 13⎯⎯, *est occupé à son service*

en qualité de ⎯⎯⎯⎯Technicien.⎯⎯⎯⎯⎯⎯⎯⎯⎯⎯⎯⎯⎯⎯⎯⎯⎯⎯⎯
Il y travaille régulièrement 48 heures par semaine.

En cas de départ définitif de la Société, l'intéressé devra restituer **immédiatement** le présent certificat au service qui le lui a délivré. Dans la négative, la Société se réserve le droit d'exercer des poursuites judiciaires contre lui pour cette infraction.

Fait à ⎯⎯⎯Saint-Vaast⎯⎯⎯⎯, le 31 mars 1942

Le Directeur-Gérant,

En. Diou. S.I.

BESCHEINIGUNG

Die A. Gesellschaft der Steinkohlen-berwerken des **Charbonnages de La Louvière et Sars-Longchamps, à Saint-Vaast,** bescheinigt

dass Herr ⎯⎯⎯WOSSWINKEL⎯⎯ROBERT⎯⎯⎯⎯⎯⎯⎯⎯
Kennkarte Nr ⎯⎯30816⎯⎯⎯ wohnhaft in ⎯⎯Soignies.⎯⎯
Strasse ⎯Grand'Rue⎯⎯⎯⎯⎯ Nr 13⎯⎯ bei ihr als technischer

beschäftigt ist. — Er arbeitet regelmässig 48 Stunden die Woche.

Bei entgültigem Verlassen der Gesellschaft, hat der betreffende Herr diese Bescheinigung SOFORT dem Dienste wieder abzugeben, der ihm sie ausgehändigt hat, andernfalls die Gesellschaft sich vorbehält, ihn wegen dieser Übertretung gerichtlich zu verfolgen.

Ausgestellt in ⎯⎯Saint Vaast⎯⎯⎯ am 31 Mars 1942

Der General-Direcktor,

False work papers identify Robert Wosswinkel as a technician.   *Robert Priser* read and no one to talk to, he again found himself spending hours daydreaming.

Bob's thoughts were still dominated by his wife, but he also found himself thinking fondly of his early days in England while he was training to become a fighter pilot. Getting to know the country and the people had been fun, although it took some time for him to get used to the food and the shortages caused by rationing. He had attended tea dances while he was at the personnel processing center in Bournemouth, and he never tired of walking around that old English resort town. Of course, it hadn't hurt that he'd met a very nice young lady, with whom he spent a lot of time, that first week in England. After a week, he and the other half dozen Americans in his group were sent to officer training at Uxbridge for six weeks and then to operational training in fighters. It was not until August 1942 that he finally flew his Spitfire in combat for the first time, in support of the ill-fated British and Canadian landing at Dieppe. Two months later, he transferred to the American Army Air Forces.

In Priser's conversations with Jules's family, he learned that the plan was for him to continue south into France, then cross the Pyrenees to Spain. Jules could not give him any idea of when he might begin that journey or how it would be accomplished. This did not surprise Priser, for he knew that the members of the underground did not know many others and plans were not disclosed until the last minute in order to keep them from being compromised if anyone was betrayed to the Germans. So Priser's questions of how he would be moved across France were met with a shrug of Jules's broad shoulders.

Jules confided in Priser that one of his ways of dealing with the Germans was to act as if he were a little crazy. Whenever he was in contact with the Germans—or Belgians whom he considered collaborators— Jules would often make no sense in conversation or talk to his horse and ramble on about irrelevant topics. On one occasion, the Germans confiscated Jules's horse. This meant he could no longer get grain or deliver flour. He promptly went down to the corral where the Germans had the animal, walked in right past the sentry, and took the horse home, talking to it all the way.

One evening, Jules told Priser that he should be ready to travel the next day. "That's easy," Priser replied, "since I don't have anything to take with me but the clothes on my back." He was apprehensive and had a difficult time sleeping that night. He imagined himself going to a train station and being whisked to Paris and on to Spain or again riding a bicycle to the border, where he would be turned over to the French

Priser in disguise as the Belgian technician, Robert Wosswinkel.   *Robert Priser*

underground. He spent a good portion of the night thinking up other scenarios of what might happen.

The next morning he was completely taken aback when a fat priest appeared at Jules's door and indicated that Priser should follow him. Priser's good-bye to Jules and Jane was particularly difficult. Not only had they risked their lives for him, but he had become quite attached to the couple.

The priest spoke almost no English but was able to communicate to Priser that he should follow about one hundred feet behind as they walked through the countryside. Priser was very concerned and apprehensive as they set out down the road. The situation was complicated for him because Jules had given him a pistol and a pair of brass knuckles the night before. He had no idea what he would do with them, but Jules had told him that since he had no American identification he would be in real trouble if he was caught. His best defense, according to Jules, would be to shoot any German who stopped him and then run. As Priser slowly trudged along at a pace dictated by the priest's bulk, he decided that Jules's suggestion was not practical. Better to be an American evader without identification than a fugitive who had killed a German soldier.

After walking for what seemed like three or four hours, the pair entered the outskirts of a town the priest identified as La Louvière. They had encountered no Germans in the countryside, but they saw several as they went farther into the town. Bob was encouraged when, just before they entered the town, the priest motioned for Priser to walk beside him. If they were stopped, Bob was sure that the priest would know what to do and say. He quickly observed that the way to keep from arousing suspicion was to stay out of the Germans' way so they would have no reason to stop you. Whenever they met any German soldiers on the sidewalk, the priest would simply greet them, step off into the street to let them pass, and continue walking. The procedure worked well, and the two were never stopped or questioned. Nonetheless, Bob was sweating in the February cold as they continued through the streets to their destination. He assumed that they were going to a church, so it didn't help matters when the priest walked into a photo shop where two Germans were getting film. Rather than make any pretext of being a customer, the priest led Priser through the store and into a back room. From there he went through a short, narrow hall and up the stairs to the second floor, which was the home of a policeman.

As had been the case at Priser's previous lodgings, he was shown to a bedroom and was cautioned to stay away from the windows, but otherwise he was given the run of the house. After a dinner of potatoes, chicken, bread, and a little wine, the policeman told Priser, in halting English, that he would be there for only one night. After coffee, bread, and cheese the following morning, the policeman walked with Priser a few blocks to the home of a schoolteacher. The teacher's wife showed Priser to a small room on the second floor where he was to stay. It was apparently a guest bedroom, and Priser wondered if other evading airmen had been there before him. Once again, he was instructed to stay away from the windows and to go immediately to his room and remain quiet if anyone came to the house. The family also had a small child, and Priser would occasionally watch him when his mother had to hang out clothes or do other work around the house. The teacher spoke better English than many of his hosts and explained that his main fear was not the Germans but, like Jules had said, other Belgians who might betray him to the authorities.

During conversations with his host, Bob began to get the feeling that the plan to move him out of Belgium was not working out and that he was being kept in various hiding places while the underground tried to figure out what to do. His host had casually mentioned the possibility that Priser would get out by submarine, which didn't seem practical. Priser also began to wonder about the other evading Allied airmen in Belgium. The more he thought about the situation, the more he began to realize the size of the problem that the underground faced.

After June 1944, the Comète Line was unable to move any evaders out of Belgium, much less across the Pyrenees to Spain, because of German infiltration. Thus, the load of hiding evaders fell to individual Belgians and small groups of underground members. This situation was complicated by the increasing number of airmen landing in Belgium during the first six months of 1944, as the bombing was accelerated prior to the June 6 Allied landing in Normandy. In January 1944, at the time Priser was shot down, there were already over one hundred Americans all over Belgium in hiding and waiting to be moved. It was a continual strain on these heroic Belgians to find food, clothing, and places to hide the evaders.

In June 1944, Anne Brusselmans was responsible for taking care of thirty-four men hiding in Brussels alone. Mrs. Brusselmans wrote about the problem in her diary:

> The Nazis are getting furious and are deporting masses of people every week. Still, as one goes away, there are ten to replace him or her. This is the beginning of the end and we are all determined to help as much as possible, even if it means losing your life. When we think of the men who have left their homes, and have come from so far to help us, we owe them all the help we can give them. It is difficult to find houses to shelter men. Houses near aerodromes and railways must be avoided. It is risky to hide them where there are children, for they might talk at school, people without children don't like to be bothered with

a third person. Then one has the jealous husband, the old maid
who thinks too much of her reputation, the young girls who do
not think enough of theirs—so it leaves us with very little
choice.[1]

When the Allies liberated Brussels, Mrs. Brusselmans had over sixty
Allied airmen hidden in the city.

About a week after his arrival in La Louvière, Priser was again told
he was going to move. By this time, he had become quite confident in
the underground and the methods it used, so he really was not concerned
with where he would be going. Right after lunch, another policeman arrived at the teacher's house and bade Priser to follow him as they walked
out of La Louvière and into the Belgian countryside. Because he had
been kept indoors all the time and had had little opportunity to look out
of windows, Bob was surprised at how the trees were starting to bud and
the air of freshness everywhere. The farmers were busy in their fields,
turning the rich, black soil behind their teams of horses, and others were
close behind, planting for the coming season. The sunshine and the
freshness of the scene were so welcome that Bob hoped the peaceful
walk would last all day. He was not disappointed, and it was not until
shortly before dinner that the pair approached a typical, two-story farmhouse near the village of Gouy le Pieton.

After a warm meal, Priser was shown to the guest room on the
second floor, where he was to stay. He was told he could go anywhere
in the house, but despite the fact that they were in the country, this
farmer again cautioned him to stay away from the windows and not to
go outside—a particularly difficult assignment given the beautiful
weather. Fortunately, there was a small courtyard in back of the house
that was bordered with flower beds and roses, and Priser was occasionally allowed to go there in the evening or after dark. Priser had also
been told that he was to hide if any visitors came, once again because
of the fear of being betrayed to the local officials. This proved to be a
challenge, for during the week and a half he was there, it seemed to him
that visitors came and went with unusual frequency. At first he was suspicious, but he finally concluded that this was just the way of Belgian
farmers. On occasion, he was asked by the farmer's wife to stay in the
kitchen and was introduced to the visitors as "our American pilot," an
occurrence that always made him uneasy. Most of the time he had to remain hidden. When no visitors were present, Bob would occasionally sit
in the comfortable living room, which was just off the kitchen, and listen to the radio. Although listening to the BBC (British Broadcasting

Company) had been declared illegal by the Germans, it was the favorite station of most Belgians. Listening to the news each evening helped Bob feel in touch with the war to some degree. The most entertaining stations, however, were German, and he was never able to keep a straight face when a German singer would perform an American cowboy song.

One morning, while he was having coffee in the kitchen with the farmer and his wife, the usual conversation was broken by the sound of an airplane in a dive. As the engine noise continued to evolve into a scream, Bob realized that the plane was going to crash very close to the house. There was nothing they could do but wait. The entire house shuddered when the aircraft hit the ground, and everyone's first reaction was to run out and see what had happened. No sooner had he started for the door than Bob realized he could not go outside, so he told his host to see what kind of plane it was and also if the pilot had bailed out. Bob was not only concerned for the welfare of the pilot, but also he knew that if it was an Allied airplane and the pilot had bailed out, the Germans would soon mount a search for him. That would put Bob in danger because he was being hidden so near to the crash site. After what seemed like hours of waiting, the farmer returned with a piece of the airplane and some papers from the body of the pilot. He indicated that the plane had hit about a quarter of a mile from the farmhouse and had pretty well disintegrated on impact. Priser identified the piece as the cockpit door handle from a P-51. The pilot was Lieutenant Ben Bennick, but Priser didn't know him. Priser's host said that he would be given a proper funeral and be buried in the local cemetery. Although he wanted badly to attend the memorial for his fallen comrade, Priser had to remain at the farmhouse. He was impressed when his host told him that most of the residents of the nearby village had attended, along with a Luftwaffe representative.

After about ten days, Priser was again on the move, this time to the small town of Le Chappel. His hosts there were a fairly wealthy Belgian doctor and his wife. Their two-story house was nicely furnished and considerably larger than the farmhouses in which Priser had been staying. Not only were the rooms larger, but there was a rather formal dining room and three bedrooms in addition to the usual kitchen and living room. They also had a maid. Priser was given the guest room, which was furnished with a very comfortable bed covered with a down comforter, an oak nightstand and dresser, and lace curtains on the window, next to which was a very comfortable rocking chair where he would spend much of his time reading the few books in English that the family owned. The couple had a ten-year-old boy and a twelve-year-old girl.

As soon as he met the children, Bob was uneasy, for both Jules and the schoolteacher had told him that he must be careful about letting children know who he was. The teacher told him that the Germans had informers in the schools and that more than one evader had been captured because children had talked about his presence with their friends. When Bob was introduced as an American pilot, he really got concerned. Still, it did not seem to matter to the doctor and his wife that the children knew who he was, so after a few days, Priser got comfortable with the situation. Once again he had the freedom to roam the house, but he received the usual cautions about the windows and being seen by visitors. The food was cooked by the maid, and Priser had his meals in the dining room with the family. They ate well, considering the circumstances of the war, and every evening meal featured some meat, a vegetable or two, usually potatoes, and bread. Coffee was always served with the cheese at the conclusion of the meal. One of the family's favorite activities around the dinner table, as well as sitting in the living room during the evening, was practicing English. Although all the families with whom Bob had stayed knew at least a little English and seemed anxious to learn more, the doctor's family seemed the most eager to improve their ability in the language. Bob enjoyed this activity—and it helped him learn more French as well.

But the move to the doctor's house had about convinced Priser that the underground had no plan to get him out of the country and to Spain, so he decided that he would start to formulate his own scheme for returning to England. His concern that he was going to have to stay in Belgium until the end of the war was reinforced when he was visited by a tailor who fit him with some older clothes so he would look more like a Belgian worker. He was also given a haircut in the kitchen. He decided that the old clothes, plus the reasonable amount of Spanish that he remembered from high school and college, might enable him to pass as a Spanish worker if he decided to try to get to Spain on his own. He had been able to copy a map of southern France while he was in Gouy le Pieton, and while he was staying with the doctor he spent several hours covering the map with wax to make it waterproof, as well as memorizing as much of it as he could. He debated discussing his plan with the doctor, but before he had a chance he was moved again.

The doctor had told Priser to be ready to go in the morning but that he did not know his destination. Priser spent a restless morning waiting for something to happen. When the maid produced lunch, he decided that there must be some snag in the underground's plan. And although he did not mind staying at the doctor's house, he still had some hope that this might be the move to take him to France.

About midafternoon there was a knock on the door and a large man entered. He identified himself as Maurice DeVroom, a plainclothes detective for the Brussels police, and said he was there to take Priser to Brussels for questioning about a crime that someone who fit his description had committed. He gave no indication that he was connected with the underground. It was obvious that the doctor did not know the man and could be of no help. Priser was terrified. He knew he had done nothing wrong, but he also knew that as soon as he was questioned and his real identity was known, he would be turned over to the Germans to spend the rest of the war in a POW camp. He considered trying to escape from the detective but realized he would have no chance. With his stomach tied in knots and sweating profusely, Bob said good-bye to the doctor and his family and left with the detective on what, he was sure, was the first part of his trip to prison. He accompanied the detective to the train station and stood helplessly in line with him to buy the tickets to Brussels. There were several Germans in the station as well, but none paid any attention to either Priser or his companion. "I'll be seeing more of these guys in the near future, I'm afraid," Priser said to himself as he watched two German officers who were standing nearby.

In a short time the train pulled into the station and Bob was shocked again. Along the sides of the engine and around the engineer's cab were great slabs of inch-thick steel armor plate, obviously for defense against strafing attacks by the Allies. "On top of everything else, all we need is to be strafed," Bob thought as the train began the relatively short trip to Brussels. Fortunately, the two were able to get a compartment to themselves. By that time, it was obvious that Bob had had about all the uncertainty he could take, so his guide revealed that he was a member of the underground, as well as a detective, and the ruse was necessary to get Priser safely to Brussels. The American had never felt so relieved in his life, and tears of emotion came to his eyes as his spirits soared.

The pair arrived in Brussels in the early evening, which frustrated Bob because he had flown over the city so many times and heard so much about it that he really wanted to sightsee. DeVroom hurried Priser out of the station, which was packed with Germans waiting for trains to various destinations, and on to the dark and fairly quiet streets. Despite their hurried pace, Priser noticed the many beautiful old buildings that lined the streets. There was also a more subdued air than in London, which was always festive in the evening despite the blackouts. He had really not walked through any city since his days in the RAF, and the experience brought back memories of his early time in England and walking around London wide-eyed as he looked at the historic buildings.

Maurice DeVroom and Priser in Rode St. Genese in 1944. *Robert Priser*

After he transferred to the U.S. Army Air Forces, and received the huge pay raise that went with the move, he generally took a taxi when he was in London.

After about half an hour, DeVroom turned down a residential street, lined on both sides by narrow, several-storied town houses. He approached the door of one and talked briefly to the lady who answered his knock. He then wished Priser well and left as the lady asked Priser to come in. He found himself in the living room of a twenty-foot-wide, multistoried town house with a stairway along the left wall. As he later found out, each floor had just one room, accessed by that stairway. The living room was very nicely furnished, including rugs on the floors, lace curtains in the windows, and what Bob perceived to be very expensive furniture. The woman took him into a rather small kitchen, located in the basement, where she had prepared a dinner for him of bread, a slice of ham, and a few slices of cheese, all to be washed down with hot coffee. The woman spoke some English, and as Priser talked with her over dinner, he found out that she was the housekeeper and that the town house belonged to the king's physician. "The folks back home aren't going to believe this," was his thought when he found out the identity of his host. The lady further told him that he would be there only one night but she did not know where he was to go next. After being shown his room, a spacious, well-furnished bedroom on the fourth floor, and given the usual caution of staying away from the windows, Priser was left alone. The bathroom was down a short hall. Upon entry, Priser was confronted by a device next to the toilet that he had never seen before: a bidet. He was unsure of its purpose, but decided it was to wash your feet in. Rather than test it out, he took a leisurely, hot bath and went to bed.

Because of the excitement of the day and the strange surroundings, as well as the sounds of the city, Bob lay in bed for a long time before finally falling asleep. As he lay there in the dark, he let his mind wander over the past months and how difficult it must be for the underground to keep finding places for him to stay. He had been in so many different locations, from small farmhouses, where the people were obviously struggling to make a living and yet were ready to sacrifice to help him, to elaborate homes such as the one where he now was in Brussels. He marveled at the willingness of these brave Belgians, from every walk of life, to risk their lives and the lives of their families to keep him from being captured by the Germans. He wondered, too, who was masterminding all of his movements, and about the countless other Allied airmen who must be hiding throughout Belgium—and all over western Europe, for that matter. He would never forget these people and what they were doing for him.

He also began to doubt that his plan to try to get to Spain on his own would work. It would be nearly impossible to avoid a confrontation with either the authorities or the Germans at some point, and he knew nothing about France. He realized that there was no way he could walk or ride a bicycle all the way to Spain, so he would have to ride the trains. But he had no money and knew nothing about the railroad routes or schedules. It had also become obvious to Bob that help was essential in obtaining food and shelter, and that meant taking a chance every time he tried to make a contact with someone. Unless something unusual happens, he decided, I'll just stay here, put my faith in the Belgians, and hope that the war will soon be over.

Early the next afternoon, DeVroom returned to the town house to take Priser to his next destination, which was identified as Petite Espinette, a tiny village in the country south of Brussels. As they walked through the narrow lanes to the stop where DeVroom said they would get the trolley for the trip to the country, Priser was able to look at the city. The old buildings, the narrow streets, the little shops below the four- or five-story houses, and the clean streets resembled the sights of London. What was missing was any air of excitement or happiness, but the German staff cars, military trucks, and motorcycles all served as vivid reminders of why this was the case.

After a short wait, the trolley arrived, but Bob didn't like what he saw: it was packed with German soldiers and he was going to have to elbow his way in among them. His Dutch guide was on the car in a flash, and Priser squeezed in beside him. The ride to Petite Espinette should have been another chance for him to do some sight-seeing, but because of all the Germans on the streetcar, he was so uncomfortable during the entire trip that he spent little time enjoying the scenery. Still, he was able to look at the flowers that were beginning to bloom, the new leaves on the trees, and the general beauty of Brussels in the late spring. It took nearly an hour to get to their stop. Fortunately, the detective did not have to use the story about taking Priser in for questioning, for no one seemed to pay any attention to the two.

Petite Espinette was actually just a trolley stop on the main road from Brussels to Waterloo. It consisted of a few houses and a bistro about a quarter of a mile south of the trolley stop. As they left the hamlet, Priser assumed DeVroom was taking him to another farm. However, it quickly became obvious as they walked away from the tram line and the highway, down a country lane, that they were not in a typical farming area. Rather, the road was lined with rather large houses built on various size plots, which Priser estimated to be from one to five acres. Aside from a few animals grazing in the fenced meadows, there was no sign of traditional farming. After walking a few hundred feet from the trolley line and passing a dwelling with several German staff cars parked in front, they approached the second house. It was a large, two-story, brick affair surrounded by a huge lawn that sloped down to a very large garden behind the house.

"What a beautiful home," Priser remarked to the detective.

"That's where we're going," was the reply. "It is the summer home of the king's physician."

Priser was dumbfounded. It was enough for an evader to stay in the beautiful town house in Brussels, but how did he rate this kind of accommodation in the country?

DeVroom's knock on the front door was answered by a rather tall, very distinguished-looking, middle-aged man who identified himself as Robert, the physician's valet. He talked for a moment with the detective, who then wished Priser well and departed. Robert took Priser into the house and began to show him around. There was a spacious living room, a dining room, a sitting room, and one bedroom on the main floor. As had been the case in the town house, the kitchen was in the basement. Priser's large bedroom was on the second floor, along with two other bedrooms and two bathrooms. The bathrooms had the same strange appliances next to the toilets that Priser had found in the town house in Brussels. When he inquired, Robert told him that they were bidets and explained their purpose. Priser did not tell the valet his theory as to the use of the fixtures. The furnishings throughout the house were the same quality as those in the town house in Brussels, but there were no pictures on the walls, nor were any of the expected articles of glass and silver about. Priser later found out that these had been hidden to keep them from being taken by the Germans. Robert and his wife were in charge of the house, the only other resident being an older, bedridden lady who lived in a room off the kitchen and whose identity Priser never learned.

Robert then laid out the usual rules for the house. For the first time, there was no caution about staying away from the windows, but Robert did tell Priser to be careful about being seen. He pointed out that the house next door was the headquarters for the German staff that controlled the war in most of northwestern Europe and that several other houses were being used as barracks. He reassured Priser that the presence of the Germans was not a matter of any concern because so many people came and went from the Petite Espinette area that the Germans paid little attention to strangers. Still, he urged Priser to use good sense in what he did.

Priser was often left alone with the older woman because Robert and his wife went into Brussels almost every other day to get food. Bob always knew when they were going to town, for Robert dressed out in his finery. He wore his dark suit, a white shirt, and a beautiful bowler hat that he always brushed just before donning it and going out the door. Robert had said that there would be no visitors, so Bob got to feel quite comfortable after a few days. One day, he was completely taken aback when Robert asked him if he would like to go down to the bistro for a beer. When he'd walked past the establishment the first time, he'd noticed the large number of Germans sitting outside, drinking beer, and enjoying the sun, so he was not anxious to go into the midst of that group. Still, Robert gave him a little instruction on how to order and off they went. Even though Priser found it impossible to relax and really enjoy his beer, the excursion went off smoothly, and the next week the pair went again. Bob soon became confident enough that he began to occasionally take the quarter-mile trip down a side street to the bistro by himself. The Germans ignored him; the most attention he received was when the occasional German stopped to ask him in broken French for a match. And although he was frightened the first few times this happened, he soon learned that the key was an unlit cigarette in the German's mouth—he could get the jump on him if he offered a match before it was asked for.

Shortly after his arrival at Petite Espinette, the BBC announced that the Allies had landed at Normandy. Bob was euphoric, as were his Belgian hosts, and they all thought it would only be a matter of weeks before Belgium was liberated. But as time went by and they continued to listen to the BBC, it became obvious that the liberation of Belgium was going to take a lot longer to accomplish. Despite his relatively luxurious surroundings, the days still passed slowly for Bob. He had been in Belgium for over six months and, with the announcement of the invasion, had abandoned any thought of getting back to England before the Allies liberated the country.

One of Priser's favorite rooms in the summerhouse was the sunroom that had been added to the main floor. It was glass on three sides and had a beautiful view of the countryside. He often sat there and enjoyed the summer sun while he made sketches of the surrounding area or read one of the many English-language books he found neatly cataloged in the living-room cases. It was not unusual for him to just let his mind wander as he looked at the summer sky.

It was in that sky, over Belgium, that he had flown his first mission in his "American" Spitfire. Because the Army Air Forces had no American-built fighters available, Priser's squadron had taken their Spitfires with them when they transferred from the RAF, so the planes sported the insignia of the U.S. Army Air Forces. After nearly six months the entire Fourth Fighter Group completed transition into the new P-47 Thunderbolt and the Spitfires were returned to the RAF. The P-47 was a huge plane to Priser, twice as heavy as the Spitfire and swinging a propeller twelve feet in diameter at the front of the 2,500-horsepower radial engine. It was a brute all right, and Priser had spent nearly a year flying it in combat when the call went out for experienced fighter pilots to transfer from the Eighth to the Ninth Air Force and fly the P-51 Mustang. For Priser that was the siren's call. He had never really liked the Thunderbolt, affectionately called the Jug, because it was so heavy, didn't climb nearly as well as the Spitfire, and wasn't as maneuverable. He always thought you flew in the Thunderbolt whereas you became part of the Spitfire. So he jumped at the chance to go to the Mustang, especially since it had a liquid-cooled Rolls-Royce engine, just like the Spitfire.

The sky often became the focus of attention for everyone in Petite Espinette as well, when the huge American bomber formations came over on their way to targets in Germany. All activity would cease at the bistro as the German soldiers watched in silence and whatever people lived in the houses would go outside to gaze at the awesome spectacle of hundreds of planes being attacked by antiaircraft fire and German fighters. If the bombers and their escorts were high enough, they left contrails that made the entire sky look like one mass of jumbled sky-writing. When they were at lower altitudes, the noise of the engines was almost earthshaking and the sounds of the exploding antiaircraft shells and the machine gun fire would often drift down to the onlookers. Priser also watched, and on one occasion saw a B-24 blow up in flight almost over the little hamlet. He counted ten parachutes, one for each crewman, but did not see any of them land. This was always difficult for him. Here he was looking at the action as a spectator even though some of those contrails belonged to his friends. "If only I were with them rather than here watching," he wistfully thought.

One afternoon, a few weeks after he arrived in Petite Espinette, complacency got the better of Bob. Robert had always cautioned him to be alert when he was sitting in the sunroom, but on this occasion he'd evidently dozed off, because he looked up with a start and found himself gazing directly into the face of a man who was walking around the outside of the house. Bob was petrified! Who was this stranger and what did he want? Bob had no idea. His only consolation was that the man was wearing civilian clothes instead of a uniform. Still, what to do? Bob got out of his chair and tried to act nonchalant as he wandered back into the main part of the house. The man kept on walking around the house and disappeared, but Bob was convinced that he was a German agent and that he was going to have to leave. He remained in his room, on pins and needles, until Robert arrived home and he could tell the whole story. Robert was quite concerned also, because he could not figure out who the individual might be but decided that they would just wait and see what happened. As the days went by, nothing came of the encounter, but Bob was never again able to completely relax in the sunroom.

A couple of weeks later, in early July, Bob was given the biggest jolt of his stay. When the valet and his wife were gone, it would be his responsibility to take care of the lady who lived by the kitchen. She spoke no English and was unable to prepare her own meals, so he cooked for her. One afternoon, as he was standing near the high window of the kitchen by the sink peeling potatoes, he looked up and saw several German officers. Fortunately, they were looking up at the first floor rather than down into the basement. His heart stopped! "They know I'm here and they've come for me," was all he could think as he rapidly hid the pan of potatoes under the sink and carefully made his way up to his room. No sooner had he gotten to the second floor than the dreaded knock came at the door. Priser stayed in his room despite the fact that the knocking grew more persistent. Finally, when there was no answer, the knocking ceased and Priser took a peek out of his bedroom window. He counted seven officers making their way back toward the headquarters next door. Since he had not been told what he should do if the Germans came to the house, he decided to stay in his room the rest of the day.

When Robert arrived home, both Priser and the older lady resident of the house told him about the experience. Robert immediately went over to the German headquarters to see what they wanted. "What courage Robert has to go over to see the Germans," Bob thought. "If they really do know I'm here they will arrest Robert on the spot and probably shoot him." Fortunately, Bob's fears proved to be unfounded. On his return, Robert reported that the Germans had to expand their headquarters and would be taking over the physician's house in two days. Priser would have to move quickly.

About noon the following day, Priser saw a familiar figure walking down the lane from the trolley stop. It was the detective Maurice DeVroom. After a warm greeting, DeVroom asked Priser if he was ready to travel. After saying good-bye to Robert, away they went. The pair turned down the lane in the opposite direction of the German headquarters, walked for about fifteen minutes, and entered a small road. After walking about two more hours, DeVroom pointed out a very small farmhouse on the edge of the forest of Soigne and told Bob this was where he was to stay. The place was identified by the detective as Rode St. Genese. Priser was greeted at the door by the English-speaking owner, Albert Abrassard, and was introduced to his wife, Madeleine. The house consisted of a combination kitchen and living room and one bedroom. Off the kitchen, at the back of the house, another very small room had been built, and that was where Priser was to stay. Despite being small, the place was cozy, and Madeleine soon had a simple but hearty dinner of stew and bread on the table.

During the conversation following dinner, Priser learned that Albert had been an efficiency expert prior to the war. He would be hired to go into a business that was failing and get it back on its feet. In return, he would get part ownership of the business. When the war started, he and

Albert Abrassard.   *Robert Priser*

his wife moved to the small house at Rode St. Genese so they would not attract the attention of the Germans. He had buried all of his stocks in containers around the small house and taken the guise of a farmer. His real job was working full-time with the underground.

Although the surroundings were quite different from those at Petite Espinette, Priser enjoyed Albert and Madeleine, for they treated him like a son, and he was quite comfortable in their house. He particularly liked living near the forest because he was able to spend most of the time outside, walking through the trees and enjoying the summer. It was on one such walk that he met Marcel Montoisey, the son of the supervisor of the forest. Marcel, along with thousands of other Belgian boys, had been impressed as forced labor in Germany. He escaped and returned to Belgium, only to be caught, terribly beaten, and returned to Germany. He had escaped a second time and was hiding in the forest for fear that the Germans might pick him up again and, this time, kill him. Priser spent many hours with him, and, in the process, Marcel showed him a large cave that he had dug among the roots of a huge tree. Marcel used it as a hiding place, and in days to come, the cave would prove to be a lifesaver for Priser.

Bob actually did not think he would be at Albert and Madeleine's house very long. They all thought that certainly by the end of August the British would be in Brussels and they would all be free. Although the news from the BBC was not that encouraging, Albert had told Priser that he believed the Allies were well ahead of where the radio was reporting them to be, since accurate news would simply help the Germans. The Belgians were convinced enough of rapid Allied progress that they began to dig up all sorts of guns that they had hidden so they would not be confiscated by the Germans. Priser spent several hours each day while he was at Albert's house cleaning and oiling these weapons so they would be available to use against the Germans when the time came. Everyone's optimism was also fueled by the almost round-the-clock presence of Allied bombers over the area of Brussels. Every night, it seemed, Priser would be awakened by antiaircraft and rocket fire from the battery about a mile from Albert's house, and he would go outside and watch the flak bursting as the Germans attempted to stop the Allied bombers. And far too often, both during the day and at night, Priser would see a bomber get hit and explode or dive to its doom on fire. It was particularly disheartening to see the German night fighters as they intercepted the bombers and to watch a plane slowly catch fire and finally fall like a torch, the fate of its gallant crew unknown. Often, after watching the spectacle, Priser would find it impossible to sleep just thinking about what he had witnessed and feeling heart-wrenching pity for the crew members.

The increasing number of Allied airmen landing in Belgium was rapidly making it more difficult for Priser and most of the other evaders. He was, after all, no different from any of those who were presently bailing out of their crippled planes. If the Germans launched a house-to-house search for Allied airmen, Priser could well be caught. The answer to his problem was Marcel and the cave. Whenever there was a big bomber raid, or Albert heard that there might be a German search in the area, Bob would take some food and a blanket and go to Marcel's cave. He also made sure he took his map and pistol, since he never knew when he would have to take off on a dead run to get away from the Germans. He would sometimes stay in the cave as long as three days, thankful that it was not winter, venturing down to Albert's house only to get some food before retreating to his hideout again. On one such visit to Albert's, Priser got still another shock.

He was sitting in the kitchen talking to Albert when an old Chevrolet pulled up and Albert told Bob they had some work for him to do. Bob got into the car and was driven back into the woods, where he confronted a dark-complected airman, about his size at five feet six and 130 pounds. The underground wanted Priser to interrogate the man and determine if he was really the American B-24 gunner he claimed to be. The Belgians were concerned that he might be a German trying to infiltrate their organization. Priser listened as the airman told his story in heavily accented English, and the more he heard the more absurd it sounded. The man claimed his parents had immigrated to Hawaii from India before the war. He had been drafted, trained as a gunner, and placed on an all-Indian American B-24 crew flying out of England. They had been hit over Belgium and the entire crew had bailed out. He had no idea where the other crewmen were. Bob talked with him about the United States, bases in England, and where he trained in the United States. Priser finally concluded that the Germans could not have concocted such a wild tale so the man must be who he said he was. The Belgians took the downed airman back to the car and drove off. "It is a good thing you decided he was an American airman," Albert commented. "If you would have said he was not, we would have shot him right on the spot and buried him right here." Bob was deeply bothered by the comment, for he didn't like the idea of being judge and jury in that situation. Several days later the same scenario was repeated, only this time with two airmen. As Bob talked to them, one pulled out some tobacco and cigarette paper and rolled his own cigarette. When he closed the tobacco pouch by pulling on the string with his teeth and twisted the end of the freshly rolled cigarette, Bob was convinced he was indeed an American, for "only cowboys twist the end of their cigarettes."

But as the pressure of more evaders became more intense, Priser and his hosts were faced with a new challenge: finding enough food. It was almost impossible for Madeleine to get food at the market, for the Germans were taking it all, and her small garden was not able to yield enough for three people. She could not shop the black market because it would immediately raise suspicions about where she was getting her money, so the trio had to exist on whatever they could find. Bob could tell the situation was getting very bad when he came back from the cave and could find only strawberries to eat. The situation evidently became too desperate, and one morning Albert told Priser that he was going to move to a nearby house that afternoon. Fortunately, moving was never a problem for Priser because he had only the clothes on his back, a razor, and a toothbrush to take along. At some of his stays he had done a few sketches of the views out of the windows and made other drawings and plans, but these were always left behind with his hosts.

After a rather sparse lunch and an emotional good-bye to Madeleine, Albert and Bob set out for his next home. As they walked along the dusty lane, Bob and Albert talked about the prospect of the Allies' liberating Belgium soon and their plans after the war. Albert said that as soon as the Germans were gone, he was going to dig up his stocks, clip the coupons, and live as he could really afford to live. Priser just wanted to get back to England, his wife, and his squadron. About forty-five minutes later, as they approached a paved road on which could be seen a number of German military vehicles and staff cars, Albert detoured down a little lane that led to the back of a masonry water tower. They continued past the structure to a small farmhouse that Albert identified as Château d'eau. There Priser was to stay. The modest, comfortable house was occupied by a middle-aged woman and her brother. He was a very active member of the underground, so he came to the house only once or twice a week. Before Albert departed, he cautioned Priser that the house was separated by only about an acre of orchard from the main road, so he would have to stay inside and away from the windows. Priser agreed, but realized that would be difficult since he had been used to getting outside nearly every day at his last two residences.

Priser's time at Château d'eau was uneventful and often boring. The lady spoke no English and he spoke little French. They would try to converse through pointing to things and using a few words common to both languages, but Bob missed having someone with whom he could sit and chat. He spent a lot of time drawing pictures of scenes around the house and, since he had majored in engineering at Arizona, figuring out engineering problems. He even designed an airplane that he would someday like to build. There was ample food and the lady was a good cook, so Bob looked forward to meals. Fortunately, there was a radio in the house, and Priser could keep track of the Allied advance across Europe. He could not contain his excitement as the advance toward Brussels continued. And although there was no noticeable evacuation of the German forces as the British neared Brussels, he thought there was more traffic going east than west on the rough cobblestone road in front of the house.

On the morning of September 3, 1944, more than seven months after he had been shot down, Priser was drawn to the window by the sound of low-flying P-47s. He actually yelled out when he saw that they were strafing a junction on the road about a mile away from the house. He knew that the ground forces couldn't be far away, for the rugged P-47 had become the best fighter for close support of ground forces. Its radial engine could sustain hits by small arms fire, whereas one hit in the radiator of the Mustang's liquid-cooled engine would put it out of operation. The P-47 was therefore ideal for attacking concentrations of troops, truck convoys, trains, and buildings where soldiers might be hidden. That afternoon, he also watched a comical sight: two German soldiers trying to get a horse that they had hitched to a wagon to move. "This must be the end," Bob told his hostess, using their system of words and pointing. "They're trying to get away in that wagon and don't have any idea of how to drive a horse." Obviously, the Germans were evacuating by any means possible. Bob's excitement continued when, later that same afternoon, Marcel, his friend who had the cave in the forest, came by and reported that the British spearhead was on the main road to Brussels. He asked that Bob accompany him to capture a collaborator and turn him over to the underground.

After forcing their way into the house where the young man lived and finding him hiding in the bedroom, Marcel and Priser took him and left to find the British forces. Although it was clear that the Germans were evacuating and didn't care a thing about Priser and Marcel as they walked along the road, Bob still found it hard to believe that the British had really arrived and his evasion was over.

When the trio arrived at the main highway, they found a British military policeman directing traffic as Allied vehicles tried to get through on roads that were clogged with military vehicles, civilians, and German prisoners. Bob's initial reaction was to just stand there and stare at the first Allied soldier he had seen since January, but that lasted for only a few seconds, and then he put his mind to finding a way to get to the British headquarters so he could begin his trip home. "I only wish that I could go back to all those people who helped me and thank them personally," Bob told Marcel. "Please thank them for me." With that, the two shook hands and the Belgian departed to turn his collaborator over to the underground. Bob was finally in Allied hands!

When he asked the British MP how he could get to Brussels and the Allied headquarters, the MP told him there was no transportation available. The best he could do was to wait until the MP was relieved and then ride on the back of the Brit's motorcycle to Brussels. When they arrived in the city, the British soldier did not really know where to go to find his unit. And as he and Priser motored through the city, they were stopped time and again by Belgians who insisted on buying a drink for the first British soldier they had seen in over four years. Priser just stayed on the sidelines during the celebrations, hoping that his driver would find British headquarters before he got too drunk to ride the motorcycle. Near midnight, the pair finally stumbled onto the British headquarters, where Priser was given a cot to sleep on for the night, but nothing to eat.

The following morning, a British officer took Priser for a ride around Brussels. He would never forget the sight of the cheering citizens who lined every street and often mobbed the jeep. He was perplexed by the sight of several women with shaved heads and the piles of furniture burning in the street. The officer told him that the women had been collaborators with the Germans and that shaving their hair and burning their possessions were retaliatory measures. The tour ended at a large park where a number of evaders had been assembled. As Priser gazed around the group, he realized that he had indeed been quite fortunate. About sixty of his comrades had been prisoners of the Gestapo and had walked out of prison when the British were on the outskirts of Brussels. They were thin, sick, and generally in very bad shape. Although Bob did not find anyone he knew, several men in the group were Americans. The greetings and stories lasted until the British told them it was time to begin their trip home.

From Brussels, the evaders and former prisoners were put on trucks for the two-day journey to Normandy. There, they were taken to an airfield to await transportation to England. Four days later, Priser was on a C-47 transport for what seemed to be one of the longest flights he had ever endured, even though it was only an hour. On September 9, he again set foot on British soil.

Much to his disappointment, all the returnees were put in a barracks and held in isolation for two days while the American authorities determined that they were actually who they claimed to be. Priser was then allowed to call his wife. The receptionist at the Department of Transportation and Works in Cambridge, where Jill had been employed in January, told him that she no longer worked there. However, he was able to talk to one of her friends, who told him she would contact his wife. For Jill, the situation was quite different. When Bob failed to return from his mission, the squadron adjutant had called and asked her to come over to the base. There, he told her that her husband's plane had been observed going down on fire and that no one had seen him bail out. They assumed that he had been killed. He then proceeded to give her Bob's personal effects and told her that she would be contacted when and if there was some official word about his fate. Shortly after that, Jill had changed jobs and moved to Ipswich. Certainly the shock of a lifetime came when Jill's friend called and said she had just talked to Bob on the phone and he would soon be calling. A few minutes later she heard Bob's voice, the voice of someone she had believed was dead.

After a cursory inprocessing and short debriefing by the intelligence staff, Priser was given a new American officer's uniform and all his back pay, which he took in cash. He immediately got on the train for Ipswich and, in one of the craziest acts of the past months, proceeded to count his money, all in five-pound notes, right there on the train. He later felt bad about his action since most of the civilians on the train had never seen that much money in their lives and had no idea why he had so much. "They probably thought it was just the normal pay of an American," Bob later thought. Priser arrived in Ipswich on September 12, 1944, to be reunited with his wife.

After a month's leave, Priser reported to the departure depot for transportation to the United States. Because of the backup of personnel, there was no slot available, so he was given another month of leave. He was eventually put on a flight to the United States in early November. Because Jill was an English citizen, she could not accompany him. He was able to work through a friend, with whom he had flown in the Fourth Fighter Group, to get the American ambassador to expedite Jill's travel. She left on a ship a few days after Bob and arrived in New York City in late November 1944.

Bob Priser was discharged from the Army Air Forces in the summer of 1945. Although he did not shoot down any German aircraft, he earned the Distinguished Flying Cross, five Air Medals, and the Purple Heart. He worked as an engineer at both Wright Patterson Air Force Base, Ohio, and Davis-Monthan Air Force Base, Arizona, before joining Hughes Aviation as a testing engineer, a position he held until his retirement. He and his wife now live in Tucson, Arizona. They have three children and two grandchildren.

In 1993, Bob and Jill Priser were invited by Jules Rousseau to return to Belgium. They were able to meet some of the people who had aided Priser during his evasion and find out the fate of others. He learned that the Germans had found his leather flight jacket during a search of houses near Horrues, the area where his plane had crashed, shortly after he had departed. The woman who had given him the coat and beret was tortured in an effort to find out where Priser was but she revealed nothing. He met the grandson of one of the mustachioed farmers. He also found out that the teacher who had helped him was betrayed to the Germans and shot for his underground activity. Jules told Bob that shortly after he left the mill, Jules and his wife had been taken to the local church and questioned extensively about the underground. They were tortured quite brutally, but neither one revealed any information. Here again, Jules gave answers that made no sense, which furthered his image as having a mental problem.

The day the Germans left Ecaussinnes, in the face of the Allied advance, Jules and his wife were released from captivity. As Jules departed, the German commander of the garrison told him, "You are the bravest man I have ever known. I know you aren't crazy but everyone thinks you are and that has enabled you to get away with a lot of things. I want to shake your hand." Jules Rousseau was honored for his work with the underground and was exempted from paying taxes for the rest of his life.

Unfortunately, Priser's itinerary did not allow him to return to each of the places where he had stayed, but he did visit a number of them. He had the satisfaction of being able to thank the families of many of the people who had risked so much to help him.

Notes

1. Anne Brusselmans, *Personal Diary, 23 June 1943–9 September 1945,* in Ralph Patton Collection, Escape and Evasion Society, Special Collections Division, U.S. Air Force Academy Library, Colorado.

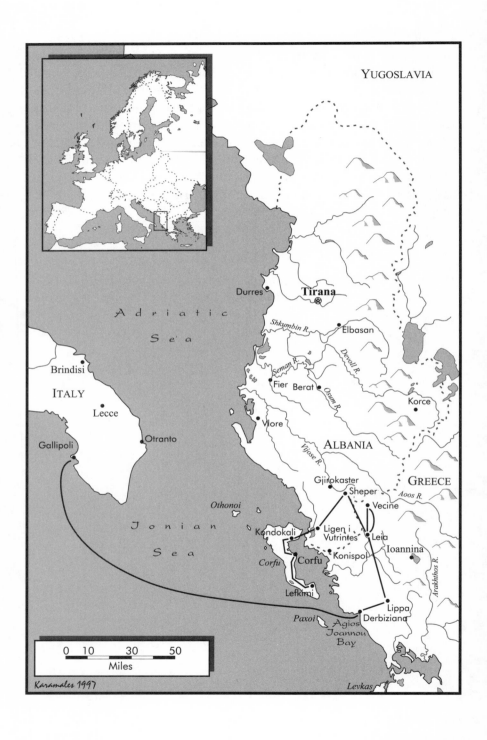

· S I X ·

"All Present or Accounted For"

"**P**ilot, center the PDI [pilot's direction indicator] and give me second station," said the twenty-five-year-old bombardier Ernie Skorheim as he centered the crosshairs of his bombsight on the target of Eleusis Airfield, west of Athens, Greece. The procedure gave control of the aircraft to the bombardier through the autopilot. "Roger, you have it," replied the tall, thin pilot Dick Flournoy over the intercom. The roar of the four engines drowned out any other sound as Skorheim concentrated on the target and waited for the precise moment to release the B-17 Flying Fortress's twelve five hundred-pound bombs on their path of destruction.

This was not a new situation to Skorheim or most of the crew. They had done the same thing, but on different targets, thirty-one times before, and it looked as if this thirty-second mission would also be a success. But not all the men had flown those missions. A week earlier they had crashed on takeoff because of a mistake by the copilot, and he had been replaced. So now Joe Cotton, a brand-new second lieutenant from Rushville, Indiana, on his first combat mission, was in the right seat. For him, the flight was anything but routine. He tried hard to appear calm, but inwardly he was wound so tight that he had scarcely been able to sleep the night before. To make matters worse, the ten-man crew's first airplane of the day had developed engine trouble before takeoff, so they'd had to taxi back and get a replacement. Cotton had finally begun to relax about halfway across the bright blue Mediterranean on the flight from North Africa to Greece. From 26,000 feet, he could see for hundreds of miles and even found himself momentarily lost in the beauty of the sight below him.

In the back half of the airplane, the five gunners—Fred Glor from Batavia, New York; Tom Reich, a tall, lanky New Yorker; the Montana cowboy, Bob Steel; Eddie Novak, a veteran gunner from Chicago (who was also on his first mission with Flournoy's crew); and Russ Leonard, whose home was in the Hudson Valley of New York—as well as the radio operator, Jim Farley, from Oklahoma, were intent on their search for German fighters as their eyes constantly swept the sky. The briefing had been for heavy flak and lots of fighters to oppose the hundred-plane attack, since the target was both the key German air base in Greece and also a major ammunition storage area. Strangely, they had seen no enemy aircraft, and Skorheim had just told them it was only five more minutes to the target. The enemy antiaircraft guns had also remained strangely silent. Maybe there would be no opposition after all.

Every man on the crew heard the bomb bay doors open and felt the rush of ice-cold air into the airplane. Just a few more seconds and it would be time to go home. "I thought we were supposed to break to the right as soon as we dropped the bombs," navigator Jim Wagner, from Hollywood, said over the intercom just after Skorheim announced "Bombs away!"

"So did I," Flournoy replied, "but the lead is not turning for some reason. Who knows?"

Skorheim was elated as he watched the results of the bomb run. There was a huge explosion on the ground and a dense cloud of smoke began to climb skyward. "Take a look at that!" he shouted over the intercom. But at that very instant Skorheim felt the huge bomber lift as if an invisible force had pushed up on it. "Flak!" he hollered over the intercom. Cotton, too had seen and felt the ominous burst as a hole was blown in the side of the B-17's fuselage directly behind him. A moment later a second burst shattered most of the windows in the pilot's compartment and broke a portion of the plane's Plexiglas nose.

Both Flournoy and Cotton struggled to control the big bomber as it veered dangerously and began to roll. "There, there, old girl," Flournoy said to his plane. "Just roll back nice and easy and let's see what damage you have. Joe, check and tell me how the engines look," Flournoy commanded.

Cotton focused on the instruments. What he saw made the new pilot's blood run cold. "Number three and four are both losing oil pressure and

Crew of the B-17 that crash landed Corfu, taken in Nebraska prior to leaving for Europe. Standing are (*from left*): Lieutenant Walker (the copilot who was replaced by Joe Cotton), Dick Flournoy (pilot), Jim Wagner (navigator), Ernie Skorheim (bombardier). Kneeling are (*from left*): Bob Steel (ball turret gunner) Sergeant Troy (waist gunner who was replaced by Eddie Novak), Tom Reich (tail gunner), Russ Leonard (top gunner), Fred Glor (waist gunner), and Jim Farley (radio operator).

Fred Glor

there is a fire light on number three." Cotton spoke in a strangely calm voice to the aircraft commander. A quick look out the window confirmed the instrument readings, as smoke was pouring from both the affected engines.

"Feather number three and number four," replied Flournoy in a very businesslike manner. "Then give me maximum cruise power on one and two." But it was not to be that simple. When Cotton pushed the feather button for the number three engine, the propeller blades promptly moved to the streamline position and the engine quit turning. As soon as that happened the fire warning light went out. But the push of the number four feather button produced nothing, and the propeller continued to windmill wildly as the engine screamed and the aircraft yawed to the right. The windmilling prop was just like a huge hand pushing on the air, and the wounded bomber promptly began to fall behind the formation and descend.

"Navigator, give me a course and estimated time en route to Brindisi [Italy] as soon as you can," the pilot called to Jim Wagner on the intercom as he began to slowly turn the airplane to the northwest. "If both our good engines can stand the strain, maybe we can get to friendly hands there," he remarked to no one in particular. "Fred, how do things look in the rear?" he asked of right waist gunner Fred Glor, who was also one of the crew's engineers. When he received no answer, Flournoy told Cotton to "hold her on a heading of three hundred and thirty degrees for now and try to maintain one hundred thirty miles per hour. You'll have to descend to do that. I'm going to check in back and see how bad off we are." With that, Flournoy unstrapped, got out of his seat, and began to check his airplane. As Cotton took the controls he found it took all his strength just to keep the big plane flying straight because of the drag caused by the windmilling propeller. He had never experienced any damage to an airplane before, and both the work and apprehension had him soaked with sweat in a matter of a minute, even in the ice-cold airplane. He had not been at the controls for more than five minutes when a glance out the space where his side window had been revealed several German fighters. Cotton knew he should say something, but he was so frightened that he just looked, unable to speak. He could only hope that the American P-38s that were escorting the formation were still in the vicinity and had seen the Germans.

Just at that instant, the air crew and their injured plane got their first break. Directly ahead, Cotton saw a cloud deck about a thousand feet below. Carefully, he lowered the nose slightly and, before the Germans could line up for the attack, the solitary and vulnerable B-17 was in the clouds and safe for the moment. It was a mixed blessing for Cotton, however, because it was twice as hard for the new pilot to fly in the clouds on instruments. Within a few minutes, Flournoy returned and reported that, amazingly, no one was injured and that the damage to the plane was not so severe as to cause them to crash if the engines would continue to run.

In the nose, Wagner and Skorheim were busy with their maps and pencils, figuring the time to Brindisi. Finally, Wagner announced that it would take about two and a half hours but that they had enough fuel to make it. Flournoy then told Skorheim to start identifying all the items that might be jettisoned to lighten the aircraft once they got over the water. For the first time since they were hit, things looked like they were under control.

Just then there was a huge thud. Cotton looked out to see that the number four engine had frozen up from lack of oil and the propeller had broken off. A quick check revealed that, luckily, it had not hit the plane. Without the drag from the windmilling propeller, the aircraft felt like a great weight had been lifted from it and the airspeed increased slightly. The crew began to relax a bit for the long flight to Italy.

The flight was fairly routine for nearly an hour. Then, without warning, the number two engine let out the most spine-chilling sound a pilot can hear—a series of backfires that shook the entire airplane. Flournoy immediately retarded the throttle, and the ominous sound and shaking ceased. A quick check of the engine instruments indicated no problem, but the entire crew had felt the great craft almost stop in midflight: it was being pulled by only one engine. The pilot slowly applied power to number two again, and for a few minutes it ran well. Then another series of backfires. The harried pilot repeated the process while Cotton used all his strength to keep the plane flying straight. After three or four repetitions of the same procedure, with the number two engine running well for shorter and shorter periods, Flournoy announced that it was time to start throwing things overboard. Machine guns, ammunition, the bomb sight, about everything that could be detached from the airplane went out. Fortunately, they had crossed the coast a few minutes before, so everything went into the ocean.

But even as the weight was being reduced, so was the power. Finally number two would carry no power without backfiring, so Flournoy told Cotton to feather it as well. The pilot called Glor on the intercom and told him to jettison the escape hatch because he was going to have to bail the crew out. But when Glor looked down at the water, he saw whitecaps and knew there was no way they could survive in the water.

"It looks too rough down there for a bailout," Glor advised the pilot. After studying the water, Flournoy agreed. The ocean also looked too rough for ditching, and it would be impossible to fly the hour or so they still needed to get to Italy. "What is that large island over to our right?" Cotton asked the navigator. A quick check revealed it to be Corfu. Flournoy quickly decided they would crash-land on the shore rather than try to ditch. "After all," he said to Cotton with a wink, "we crash-landed just a couple of weeks ago, so we have practice."

With that, he ordered all the crew members to take their positions for a crash landing while he and Cotton went through the procedure of turning off equipment prior to impact. Skorheim and Wagner immediately left the nose and went back to the radio room, where the rest of the crew was getting in position for the crash landing. They sat on the floor, facing the rear, with their backs against the bulkhead, and deployed one parachute to cover their heads in case of flying glass or other objects. About the time everyone was in position, Flournoy called "Brace yourselves!" over the intercom and the plane's alarm bell began a continuous ring. A moment later the shriek of metal against sand and uncontrolled bumping and crashing announced their flight was over.

As had been the case previously, the pilot had made an excellent landing. After the plane slid to a halt on its belly in the sandy marsh on the southern end of the island, there was a sudden silence. Fred Glor just sat against the bulkhead and heaved a sigh of relief, as did the other nine members of the crew. Instinctively, the navigator checked the time. It was 1:30 P.M., November 18, 1943. Moments later the ten crew members began to exit the aircraft onto the soft sands of their new residence. The aircraft had stopped just short of a row of trees, and an accounting revealed that there were no injuries.

All bomber crews were instructed that, if possible, they should try to burn the airplane or blow it up to deny anything on board to the Germans. Cotton and Wagner were delegated to that job. After Wagner made several attempts to light the ship on fire by shooting at the gas tanks with his .45-caliber pistol, Cotton suggested that they take off the gas caps and try to soak the wings in gasoline. A quick check determined they did not have the screwdriver needed to get the gas caps off, so that plan was abandoned. While Cotton and Wagner were figuring out what to do next, Flournoy was discussing possible plans with the rest of the crew. These activities had not gone on for more than two or three minutes when inhabitants of the island began to arrive in the area. The plan to light the aircraft was abandoned when some of the early arrivals climbed into the big bomber.

About the same time, several other people approached, some carrying clothing. Although none of them could speak English, they made it obvious that the Americans should put on native clothing and follow them away from the area of the crash. The bomber crew had hoped that there would be few, if any, Germans on the island, but the Greeks soon made it clear that there were many—and that some would soon be at the crash site. A young man approached Cotton and led him a short distance to a shack, where he put on a pair of dark pants and a black coat that came down to his knees. Fearing that his shiny new army shoes would be a dead giveaway to the Germans, Cotton exchanged them for a worn pair of Greek shoes. Skorheim, on the other hand, simply took off his flight suit right by the airplane, carefully taking his small survival kit out of the pocket, and put on a gray shirt, pants, and coat that one of the Greeks offered him. After putting his survival kit into the coat pocket, he and Wagner began a brisk walk, following their guide into the surrounding hills. All of the Americans kept their dog tags so they could identify themselves if they were captured. A ten- or twelve-year-old boy came up to the six-foot-four Flournoy and indicated he should follow, on a dead run. They ran until the pilot felt he would collapse. Still the young boy urged him on, and about when Flournoy could go no farther they came to a tool shed near an olive orchard, where he was to spend the next two days. There he changed his clothes for some old blue pants, a shirt, and a black greatcoat that barely came to his knees.

Glor had just begun to run from the area when a young lady who had been hoeing in a field intercepted him and indicated he should follow her. After they had gone about half a mile, she motioned that he should take off his heavy fleece-lined flying pants and jacket, which she loaded with stones and dropped into a small stream. They then continued, Glor in his uniform pants and shirt, to a sheepherder's shack, where he spent the night.

Soon all ten airmen were gone. When the first Germans arrived at the crash site about fifteen minutes later, they found only the local inhabitants climbing over the aircraft, taking anything that was not bolted down. They also discovered five parachutes, which the Greeks had conveniently placed where they would be noticed. The other five had long since disappeared to become clothes, shelter, or whatever else the locals wanted to do with the material. Cotton later heard that when the Germans inquired, they were told that there had been only five men on the plane, which the Greeks suggested might be because American air losses were so great that they were running low on airmen. The five crash survivors, the Germans were told, had taken a boat that was nearby and begun to row out to sea. The Greeks reported hearing them mention Italy. Fishermen would later tell the Germans they had seen a submarine surface and take the crew members on board.

After Skorheim and Wagner had walked and climbed through fields and olive groves for about an hour, their guide pointed to a small shack and indicated they should go inside and wait. When they entered, it was obvious from the odor that the building was primarily used as a drying shed for tobacco. After a short time, a young man entered the shack with a large loaf of bread, a pail with some soup, and another with coffee. After eating, since there was no light in the shed, the two made themselves as comfortable as possible and went to sleep. Sometime during the night, Skorheim awoke to find himself under attack by mosquitoes. Soon both men were fighting their new enemies. By curling up under their coats, they were able to protect themselves from most of the insects, but by morning they were covered with itching bumps. They spent another two days and nights in their cramped quarters before their host thought it safe to move them to the town of Lefkimi, near where their airplane had crashed.

Fred Glor spent a restless night under attack from mosquitoes in the sheepherder's shack. The next morning the young lady brought him some sardines, bread, goat cheese, and a couple of green oranges, and indicated he should wait in the shack until she returned. When it was nearly dark, she came back with some pants, a shirt, and a coat, which Glor exchanged for his uniform, keeping only his small survival kit and his dog tags.

Probably the most exciting experience immediately after landing belonged to Joe Cotton. He was scared to death that he might be caught by the Germans. He desperately searched for ways to destroy his American identity so he could pass himself off as a Greek. In his fear, he forgot the problem of language. He had already exchanged his shoes and gone through his escape kit, putting all the items that might identify him as an American—American money, first aid kit, medicine, chocolate, matches, and compass—into the water bag that was included in the kit. He was trying to figure out what to do about his flying clothes when he heard noises outside the shack to which he had been led. As Cotton tried to hide in a corner, a young boy entered carrying a shirt, some pants, and a short coat. Cotton's hands shook as he put them on over his flying garments. His idea was that if he was caught and identified as not being Greek, he could strip down to his flying clothes to prove he was an American so he wouldn't be treated as a spy. He kept his .45-caliber pistol, which was in a holster on his belt, and a silk map of Greece. He then

A 1996 photo of some of the Greeks who helped the B-17 crew evade on Corfu. Bobbies Koulouris, one of the first to arrive at the crash; Ioanis Koulouris, owner of the property where the plane crashed; Nikos Koulouris, who helped Skorheim; and the couple who helped Flournoy, Alexis Monastiriotis and his wife, Angeliki.

Nick Aspiotis

left the shack with his young guide and, while crossing a small stream, paused long enough to bury the unwanted items from his escape kit in the mud, thinking that he could return for them later if the need arose.

About half an hour later, Cotton entered the town of Lefkimi and was shoved into a store that sold olive oil. The proprietor asked "Americani?" When Cotton replied "Yes," rather than being hidden as he had expected, he was taken to a spot right by the front door, where a pair of mules were walking around and around powering an olive crusher. Cotton's new host quickly put him between the animals and indicated that, should anyone come, he was to act like he was pulling or whipping the mules to keep them walking. Cotton complied, and since he had to look at the ground most of the time, to be sure he wasn't stepped on by one of the mules, no one was able to get a good look at his face. The minutes went by and an occasional customer came into the shop. Cotton did as he was told. An hour or so later, two German soldiers came to the entrance, apparently looking for any of the B-17 crew members that might be hiding in the town. The shop owner indicated that he had seen none, and without paying any attention to the frightened Cotton, walking between the mules, they left. He continued to walk with the animals until dark, when he was given some bread with olive oil and coffee. Soon one of the biggest Greeks he was to see during his entire time on Corfu arrived. His name was Alex, and Cotton followed him to an abandoned Greek Orthodox church a short distance out of town to spend the night. There he joined Russ Leonard, the top turret gunner; Jim Farley, the radioman; Eddie Novak, the left waist gunner; and Bob Steel, the ball turret gunner. Although each had a blanket, they too were attacked by mosquitoes and spent a long and difficult night trying to protect themselves.

The Germans continued to search the towns and countryside in the area of the crash landing but were unable to find any trace of the crew. Apparently believing that the Americans had indeed tried to take a boat to Italy, and bolstered by a report that the survivors had been seen by peasants near the north end of the island, the Germans moved farther north, toward their main garrison, near the town of Corfu. Lefkimi then became relatively safe for the evaders. Thus, after two days in the church, during which the five were confined to a small room, each was taken to a different location in the town.

For Cotton, this meant going to the three-story, white stucco house of Aristotalos Papavalasoplis, known as Harry Pappas, and his wife. Cotton soon found out that Pappas, who looked a lot like Adolf Hitler, had lived in the United States and worked his way from Seattle to the East Coast by washing dishes. Therefore, he spoke fairly good English.

Alex, who guided Cotton to the Orthodox church near Lefkimi, and Harry Pappas.
Joseph Cotton

Unbeknownst to Cotton, Pappas was also the leader of the underground in the area. Cotton slept in a room on the third floor that was reserved for guests and that fronted directly on the street. "That room is OK," Pappas told him, "because the Germans never go above the second floor even if they are searching a house." Cotton never found out why. Directly above his room was a small area to which he was to retreat if any visitors came to the house. Cotton often practiced moving silently to his hideout, just in case there was an emergency. He seldom left his area on the third floor because Pappas thought it was too dangerous. Mrs. Pappas would bring most of his meals up to him, although he was allowed to eat in the kitchen on occasion. Harry did spend many hours in pleasant conversation with his guest, but most of it was upstairs. Pappas also gave Cotton an identification paper with the name Nicos Babis on it. Cotton was instructed to use that identification only as a last resort, because he would have to play deaf and dumb to avoid capture if he were stopped since he did not speak Greek. None of the other evaders were given any false identification papers.

At about this same time, Skorheim, Wagner, Flournoy, and Glor were also brought to town, and each was billeted with a family. Tom Reich was already in Lefkimi. He had been met by George Vallassas and went directly to the Greek's house, where he was hidden in an attic until the initial search by the Germans was completed.

Skorheim and Wagner were taken to different places. There is no record of where Wagner went, but Skorheim soon arrived at the home of Josephus and Tina Montezago. Montezago was the town wheel maker, and he and his wife had a very modest two-story house with an attic. The lower floor was Josephus's shop and the kitchen. On the second floor was a sparsely furnished living room and one bedroom. Skorheim's accommodations were in the attic. He had a bed and little else. The room appeared to normally be used to store dried vegetables, and some hay was placed on the floor for insulation in the winter. Skorheim was allowed to go downstairs for meals and to the living room for attempts at conversation, but, as was the case with Cotton, any visitors meant a quick trip to the attic. One item of furniture that stuck out was an old Singer sewing machine on which Tina made all the family's clothes. During his stay, she even made Skorheim a shirt out of an old sheet.

As with all the Greeks who were hiding Americans, the Montezagos had to do with less so the evaders could eat. Still, Skorheim looked forward to such meals as bean soup, and bread dipped in olive oil. Tina often had fish, since the main industry of the island was fishing, and they occasionally had a small baked bird, which Skorheim was unable to identify. The coarse bread was a combination of wheat and corn, and was served toasted and sprinkled with olive oil. To the always hungry Skorheim, it was delicious. Tina had a silver bowl on one shelf in the kitchen in which she kept the sugar. The way it was stored, Skorheim thought it must be like gold to them. Skorheim's host did not speak English, but soon Skorheim and Josephus were exchanging English and Greek words as each began to build a vocabulary in the other's language. The Montezagos had just lost a son who was in his early twenties, and they took a special liking to Skorheim, who apparently reminded them of their boy. Shortly after Skorheim's arrival, Josephus brought him a piece of plastic from the nose of the B-17. Skorheim used a nail file to fashion it into a cross for his fiancée, Juanita.

Fred Glor had a different experience from the rest. When he was brought to Lefkimi from the sheepherder's shack, under cover of darkness, he found himself entering a large, multistoried stone building that, he soon found out, was the town hotel. He was taken to a room and told he was to stay there. The next morning a young lady brought him a breakfast of cheese, bread, and coffee, and he began the most boring month of his life—with nothing at all to do but sit all day in his room. Since the twenty-one-year-old Glor was the only married member of the crew, his thoughts turned often to his wife, Louise, at their home in Batavia, New York. In the early evening of his second night in the hotel, Ula, the sister of the hotel owner, came in and told him he had to remain very quiet for there were two German officers in the next room. Glor thought surely he would be found out. As he spent the night listening to the officers get drunk and rowdy, however, his fear turned to entertainment. Still, he breathed a sigh of relief the following morning when they left.

Within a week or two of their landing on Corfu, most members of the crew began to have chills that were impossible to alleviate, accompanied by uncontrolled shaking, then a high fever, and finally sweats that left them soaked. Everyone in Lefkimi knew the symptoms of malaria. All combatted it with the same home remedy—bloodletting. For Skorheim and Glor that meant putting leeches on their arms, legs, and backs as they lay trying to stay warm. After the leeches were removed, a small, hot, glass cup was placed over the spot where the leech had been. As the cup cooled, it drew out more blood. Finally, a vinegar-soaked rag was used to close up the wound. Malaria was particularly fearsome for Skorheim's hosts, since their son had died from the disease. So after a week, during which Skorheim continued to go through the cycles of chills, fever, and sweats, and periodic lapses into semiconsciousness, Josephus and Tina decided that they would risk getting the pharmacist to treat him. The obliging, middle-aged man gave Skorheim a shot and left a number of different-colored pills, all of which were quinine. Within a couple of days, Skorheim was out of bed, and by the middle of December, he had regained most of his strength. Glor, on the other hand, was in the same situation as the rest of the Americans who had malaria and simply had to weather the bout with the disease by themselves with no quinine. They were extremely sick for about two weeks and never really regained their strength during their entire stay on the island.

By the time most of the group were strong enough to function fairly normally, they had been in the area of Lefkimi for nearly a month and their presence was an increasing hardship on their hosts. Further, the Germans had become convinced that the American fliers were still on the island, so they still had not given up their search. Periodically, a contingent would return to the town to look for the crew members. During one such visit, Glor had to climb into a crawl space above the kitchen in the hotel when the building was searched. It was also obvious to all the Americans that they had to get off the island soon if they were ever to get back to their unit. Unfortunately, the malaria had forced the Greeks to put any plans to move the Americans on hold.

The situation finally came to a head a week before Christmas. It focused on Dick Flournoy's host. Flournoy was staying with a Greek named Furkine who made his living by smuggling goods between Albania and Corfu. On one occasion, he was caught by a customs inspector who, unfortunately, informed the Germans. They soon came to Furkine's house, where Flournoy was hidden in the attic, to discuss the charges. An argument broke out, and in a fit of passion, Furkine told the Germans they should concentrate their efforts on catching the ten Americans who were in the town rather than worrying about his little smuggling operation. Fortunately, the interpreter the Germans had hired was not particularly fond of them, and he quickly informed the key people in the underground of the conversation. Within hours the Germans were reported to be on their way to Lefkimi, and the Americans had to be rushed to a small shack in the hills above the town. The next day, December 19, 1943, the Germans surrounded Lefkimi and went from door to door, completely searching every building in the town, but to no avail. The Americans had again disappeared.

The mountain reunion was a happy event since the entire crew had not been together for over a month, but hard reality soon set in. Although there was a stream close by, they either had to find their own food in the hills or wait and hope the townspeople would be able to make good on their promise to make periodic supply deliveries. The hut itself was only large enough to sleep six people at a time, so the Americans had to take turns sleeping, standing guard, and hunting for food. Fortunately, the day after the move to the hills, a girl arrived in the morning with bread and a pail of warm liquid that tasted vaguely like tea. Late in the afternoon, she came back again with bread and soup. This ritual was repeated nearly every day as the townspeople sent whatever they could spare to the beleaguered airmen.

A few days after the Americans' flight to the mountains, the girl who brought food to the group also brought a message that Skorheim's hosts, Josephus and Tina, thought the search was over and wanted him to come back down to their house since conditions were so bad in the hut. Despite warnings from the rest of the group, Skorheim went back to Lefkimi. The morning after he went back, the Germans again entered the town. Skorheim spent the day buried under a pile of hay in a goat barn before he could return to the hideout in the hills. Just as he was leaving, Josephus told him that the Germans had threatened to take some of the men from Lefkimi and deport them to labor camps if the Americans were not turned in. Skorheim's experience and the German threat further galvanized the crew in their determination to leave Lefkimi as soon as possible. (In 1996, Cotton found out that ten men were taken by the Germans but were later released.)

The Americans spent Christmas 1943 in their little hut in the hills. In one corner of the building was a small stove that the group had not used previously for fear someone would see the smoke. After much discussion, they decided to light it up on Christmas. None of them would ever forget their feast of wild onions, olives, tangerines, fried fish, and bread dipped in hot olive oil. That evening, they were told by a messenger that a British flying boat would land before dawn between the island and the mainland to pick them up. The euphoric crew promptly evacuated their hut and made their way toward the town and the coast. For unknown reasons, the landing never occurred, if indeed it ever had been scheduled, so the Americans spent the night in a salt factory on the outskirts of Lefkimi and, the next morning, returned again to their camp in the hills. Other rumors of travel emerged periodically, but none seemed practical enough to be authentic. Finally, on New Year's Eve, a sensible plan was communicated to the group. They were told to be ready to move the following morning.

From Lefkimi, it was about ten miles across the Adriatic to Greece. Thirty miles farther north, however, it was only two miles across the water to Albania. The Greeks made the decision that the Americans would go to the northern part of the island and make the crossing from there. The greatest concern with this plan was the necessity of traveling on the main roads and having to go through the outskirts of the town of Corfu, the population center of the island. The road would also take them through a German army camp and next to a major air base. Early on New Year's morning 1944, each member of the group said an emotional thank-you and good-bye to the Greeks who had put their lives on the line for the past six weeks. The Americans were put in five olive carts, each pulled by a donkey, and told to sit on the back of the cart with their feet hanging over the end gate. They were instructed to not speak to anyone and, if they were stopped for any reason, to let the driver take charge. They were also told that if they were stopped by the Germans to act as though they had been arguing with each other and therefore weren't speaking. With that, the five carts began the journey north, keeping about a quarter to half a mile apart.

Not long after departing Lefkimi, the first cart, which was occupied by Flournoy and Glor, was stopped by a tree that had fallen across the road. Several German soldiers were busily sawing it into pieces. The two frightened Americans were sure they would be caught as they sat on the back of the cart trying to act like Greek workmen. In a few minutes, which seemed like hours to the evaders, the road was clear and the cart was given the signal to proceed. Just as they began to move, a German soldier with a rifle slung over his shoulder walked to the back of the cart for no apparent reason. He looked Glor directly in the eyes, not two feet from him. Glor's blood ran cold as he returned the German's look. He was sure he would be recognized as not being a Greek and questioned, in which case both he and Flournoy would be taken prisoner and the driver probably shot. But, as the cart pulled away, the German said nothing and went on with moving logs. It was ten minutes before either Glor or Flournoy could breathe normally.

A few hours later, Cotton and Skorheim also had a close call. Cotton had been the only member of the crew to keep his .45-caliber pistol when they ran from their crashed B-17. As the trip continued, he succumbed to the slow movement of the cart and fell asleep, and his coat moved so that it no longer covered the holster on his belt. The heavy .45-caliber was soon hanging outside the cart for all to see. Cotton was awakened when the cart stopped momentarily to allow a truck to pass. As Cotton opened his eyes, directly above him was a German line crew repairing the telephone wires. If they had looked down, they would have seen the gun and the evasion would have been over. By the time he realized his pistol was exposed, the cart had again begun to move and the danger had passed.

For the rest of the crew, the trip was uneventful. Early in the afternoon, the carts turned off the main road just south of the town of Corfu. The Americans were told to get out of the carts since they could safely go no farther. As the men began to walk down the road, in groups of two or three, they were accompanied by several Greeks who simply walked along saying nothing. Several of the crew were worried about the trek, however, since they were sure that Flournoy would certainly stand out at six feet four. They had only seen one Greek that size in their month and a half on the island. Fortunately, since it was a holiday, many people were on the road.

After a few minutes, the Americans approached their first obstacle, the German army base, which was actually built on both sides of the main public road. No sooner had Cotton and Skorheim entered the portion of the road on the base than they approached a German officer out for a stroll with his wife and two children. Cotton instinctively gripped his gun under his coat as he approached the German. When they were almost abreast, Cotton said good afternoon using his newly learned Greek greeting. The German nodded, his wife smiled, and they passed. As they walked farther, Skorheim said softly to Cotton, "That German doesn't know how lucky we all were." The experiences of the rest of the group were similar as they confronted a number of soldiers enjoying the sunny holiday afternoon.

The next obstacle was the German airfield. It was considerably more dangerous—not only was it fenced and guarded, but also there were no strollers on the road. Cotton moved up beside Flournoy and whispered, "What an opportunity. We could just go in there and steal a couple of planes, maybe fighters, and be out of here before anyone could do anything about it." Fortunately, Flournoy vetoed the crazy idea. "No," he said. "We've been together as a crew for a long time and we're going to return from this experience as one." As Cotton thought about his suggestion, he realized it wouldn't have worked anyway since he had no idea how to start a German plane even if he could have gotten inside one. But he was also impressed with the cohesion of the crew and felt proud to be one of them. Several times during the remainder of the walk, one of the Greeks would say "Off road" and stroll off with one or two Americans in tow. In seconds, all the airmen would be hidden in a ditch or behind the trees. A few minutes later, a German army vehicle or two would pass by, no doubt returning to the main base. The Greek would then lead his charges back onto the road and the walk would resume. The American air crew was constantly amazed at how well organized the Greeks were and how they always seemed to know about a problem before it ever emerged.

It was well after dark when the exhausted group reached their destination, the small fishing village of Kondokali, a few miles north of Corfu. They silently followed their guide to a large, three-story house on the edge of the town near an olive grove. When they entered the warm, cheery kitchen, they were served the best meal they had received since leaving North Africa: garbanzo bean soup, spaghetti, bread, olive oil, and wine. Although their hosts did not speak English, the good food and the cozy surroundings made communication easy, and the meal lasted well into the evening. The tired and apprehensive Americans were then put in a barn for the night. Several of the party were awakened by the wind and rain that swept the island that night. "It's a good thing we're not on the boat tonight," Cotton said to Flournoy. "We probably wouldn't be able to get across the water." Both agreed that fortune was on their side, at least for the time being.

The travelers awakened well after daybreak and, since they would not be attempting the passage to Albania until night, had to remain out of sight and quiet all day. They were told that once the next portion of their trip began, they would be on the move for nearly twenty-four hours, so they should rest as much as possible. None of the group was a stranger to sitting quietly for hours, but it was difficult to sleep as each anticipated the adventure that lay ahead. Harry Pappas had told Cotton that crossing the heavily patrolled water between Corfu and Albania would be the most hazardous part of the trip, and Cotton had been quick to relay that to his companions.

Each of the ten was often lost in his own thoughts as the cloudy day wore on. Fred Glor thought about his wife in New York and the long adventure that no doubt lay ahead before he would see her again. Cotton contemplated the ironic twist of fate that had him completing pilot training just as the need for bomber pilots was so great that he ended up in the B-17 rather than the anticipated fighter. And then to be shot down on his first mission. . . . In contrast, Ernie Skorheim had completed thirty-two missions, one more than the rest of the crew. Maybe thirty-three was his unlucky number.

Late in the afternoon the group had another meal, much more basic than the feast of the previous evening. After dark, the anxious Americans were quietly taken through Kondokali to a warehouse on the edge of the water. They were reminded that the crossing would be long and extremely dangerous. It was essential they do exactly as they were told and be absolutely silent. There were almost continual patrols by the German navy, and if one of their boats was intercepted, the Americans would be taken prisoner and the Greek fisherman probably shot. The only other alternative, if they were stopped, was slipping into the water and swimming, if they were close enough to shore. The chances of surviving such a swim on a cold, black January night were almost nil, however.

With that, the apprehensive group, their hearts in their throats, moved quickly and silently across the short stretch of deserted beach to the edge of the water, where several waiting Greeks carried the airmen on their backs to two fishing boats that had been moved from the pier and pulled up on the sand. The Greek fishermen knew that if the Americans began their journey with wet feet, they might not be able to survive the miles of hiking that lay ahead in Albania. "What caring and thoughtful people these are," Cotton whispered to Flournoy when the two were safely in the boat. "How will we ever repay them?" "I doubt if we ever will be able to," was the pilot's hushed reply. The five passengers in each boat quickly got down as low as possible on the cramped floor, and the single Greek fisherman leaned into the oars to begin his long, dangerous, and exhausting journey.

After they were a safe distance from the shore, the occupants were able to sit up and watch as the trip unfolded. They could see nothing in the blackness of the night except the occasional searchlight of a German patrol boat some distance away. As the hours went by, the passengers were amazed by the stamina of the Greek fishermen and their ability to navigate a small boat and remain clear of the patrols. Although it was almost impossible to get comfortable, each dozed off periodically during the trip. As it began to get light, they could see the coast of Albania a short distance ahead, and everyone's spirits were buoyed at having successfully evaded the patrol boats.

A short time after the sun came up, the two boats went through a narrow strait and into a large bay, Ligen i Vutrintes, which was surrounded by hills and forests. About an hour later they entered a small river, and the fisherman in the lead boat began to call out a word in Greek. Soon the passengers heard a reply, and shortly thereafter the boats were pulled ashore. After having been on the water for nearly twelve hours, the Americans were finally in Albania.

The short, muscular man who met the boats gave the airmen only a moment to express their thanks to the exhausted fishermen who had rowed and navigated all through the night. He then urged them to move rapidly into the tree-covered hills. As the Americans climbed away from the water, they noticed the falling temperature and realized that they did not have adequate clothing for what lay ahead. Still they hiked on—cold, tired, hungry, and miserable—following the stranger who spoke no English but held their lives in his hands. On several occasions their guide motioned the group to move off the small trail into the trees. Apparently he thought he had heard a German patrol or some other threat, although none of the evaders saw anyone.

Late in the afternoon, about the time that the exhausted and famished airmen felt they could go no farther, they began to see terraced hillsides. Soon they arrived at a village. Their guide took them, one by one, to different houses, knocked on each door, and when a door was opened, shoved one of the hapless Americans inside accompanied by a comment in a language none of the evaders understood. Apparently the command was to give the airman something to eat and a place to sleep for the night. Ernie Skorheim was given some corn bread, a little cheese, and a glass of milk. His apparently reluctant host then indicated that he could roll up in the rug on the floor and go to sleep in front of the fire. After his ordeal of the past two days, Skorheim felt as if he were in a luxury hotel.

When the group assembled in the town square the next morning, each said he had had about the same experience the previous night and was ready to face the day. With their guides, they headed north toward a rendezvous point in Yugoslavia, where an American or British plane could fly them back to freedom. But sometime during the second day of their sojourn in Albania, their guide was informed that this plan was no longer possible. Rather, the Americans should be brought directly to a guerrilla camp in Greece, more than twenty miles away through the mountains. So when they reached the Albanian town of Sheper in the middle of the afternoon, the guide did not stop as the evaders hoped he would, but skirted the town, turned almost directly south, and picked up the pace. This was too much for Bob Steel, the ball turret gunner. He was still wearing the soft-soled flying boots he had had on when he left the airplane, and they had worn through to the point where he could not walk without excruciating pain. Cotton's Greek shoes, for which he had unfortunately traded his G.I. shoes, also were worn completely through, and he was putting paper in the soles to keep his feet from contacting the ground. Steel sat down by the side of the trail and told the group to just leave him. He could walk no farther and would just die there. Skorheim, who fortunately had not only good shoes but also two pair of socks, gave Steel one pair and was then able to get him back up and on the trail. But every few hours, Steel would again give up. Unbeknownst to the rest of the group, in addition to his foot problem, Steel had the first of what would be several cases of jaundice.

The trip through the mountains lasted four more days and was certainly the most miserable any of them had ever endured. Every time they would get to the top of a mountain, it seemed there was a higher one in their path. There was also no food or shelter, and to make matters worse, it snowed periodically. Since most of the group had no outer coat except the Greek equivalent of a suit jacket, they were sure that if they had to stop in the open they would freeze to death. So they continued their zombielike walk until evening, when they came upon another small village. There the procedure of the previous day would be repeated—a knock on the door, a brief command, a sparse meal, and a few hours of sleep—then back on the trail again. Not everyone was able to stay in a house, however. One night, Flournoy and Glor found themselves a short distance outside a town with a sheepherder in his hut. Fortunately, they had bread, some mutton, a few onions, and a hot, indescribable liquid. At least the hut was warm, and after their welcome meal, the two sat by the fire and talked about what they were going to do after the war. Both had several ideas, but the main point around which the discussion revolved was making lots of money.

After a short time, the Greek sheepherder with whom Flournoy and Glor were staying departed in the snow. Soon he returned accompanied by a slim young woman who had a submachine gun over her shoulder and wore leather pants, fur boots, and a fur-lined coat. She was also carrying a bag from which she produced a bottle of uzo, a potent Greek liquor. After offering the Americans each a drink, she took off her coat, which revealed a full figure, and began to get very friendly with Flournoy. When he was not receptive to her advances, she started to work on Glor. Both men were too tired and sick to take advantage of the situation, and after a while, she departed, obviously disgusted. When the evaders reassembled the following morning, the two related their experience and rapidly became the envy of the group. They found out later that the word *money* in English sounded very similar to the Greek word for prostitute. The Greek sheepherder had thought that was what the two Americans wanted and had been doing his best to be the perfect host.

Two days after they turned south, the group was surprised on the open trail by three British soldiers, Major Philip Nind, Captain Ian Anderson, and Corporal Ken Smith, all members of the Highland Light Infantry. The trio was one of a number of teams that had been parachuted into the mountains of Greece to help with the underground activity against the Germans, as well as influence the communist-dominated Greek resistance to remain loyal to the English-supported Greek government. (Although Flournoy's crew did not become directly involved in the brewing civil war, they were occasionally passed between the pro- and antigovernment groups as they made their trek, since all were anti-German.) The trio was on their way to the same underground camp as the Americans, so they joined forces. Although the Brits had no medicine or other capability to help the near-desperate airmen, they told them that the camp was only two more days' walk and that an Italian doctor was there who could help get the sick back on their feet. Also of importance to the Americans was having someone to talk to and knowing that they were not the only Allies in the area. "If these men can survive out here working with the guerrillas, then we can sure make it to the camp and out of the country," a confident Flournoy told his crew at one of the infrequent rest stops.

On January 7, 1944, the emaciated evaders arrived at the resistance camp near the town of Leia, Greece. They were indeed a sad sight. Half of the Americans were undergoing another attack of malaria, several had jaundice, all were exhausted from having had little food or sleep, at least two were walking practically in their stocking feet, and six had dysentery. And although the Greeks were friendly, they were also cautious about the Americans. As with every resistance movement, they were concerned that the group might contain German infiltrators. They were also not overjoyed at having ten additional mouths to feed. The first action was to treat the Americans to a small shot of uzo from the camp distillery. As the potent liquid warmed their bodies, they began to forget some of their minor aches and pains. The warming drink was followed by hot lamb stew, freshly baked bread, and coffee, prepared by three female camp cooks. Fred Glor and Tom Reich thought it was the best meal they had ever eaten, and even Bob Steel was able to forget his bleeding feet for a short while.

As the Americans surveyed their surroundings, they were impressed with the location if not the facilities. The camp was comprised of several sheepherder shelters augmented by the ruins of what had been at one time a moderate-sized stone house. The Greeks had added to the facilities by raising several tents, supplied by the British in an airdrop, under the trees, where they could not be seen by the all-too-present German patrol planes. The British had also dropped sleeping bags, clothes, and medical supplies, including quinine. The entire complex was situated near the top of a large hill, and from the observation area, a few hundred feet away, a lookout could see for several miles in any direction. There was a nearby stream that supplied ample water.

For the next week, the Americans concentrated on regaining their health and strength. Although they ate stew at almost every meal, it was always hearty, and the fresh bread was delicious. Periodically those Americans who were strong enough would help gather the wood needed to make the fire for baking. There was even a makeshift shower where the evaders could get clean for the first time in several weeks—if they could tolerate cold water in the winter. As soon as they finished their shower, however, they had to put on the same lice-ridden, smelly clothes, so few took advantage of the facility. But the most important health item was found by Fred Glor. One evening, as he walked past the kitchen, he spied a toothbrush in a small can on a shelf. Glor was desperate, as were all the others, to brush their teeth, so he asked the cooks

The American airmen and British soldiers with members of the Greek resistance near Leia, Greece. (1) Fred Glor; (2) Eddie Novak; (3) Dick Flournoy; (4) Philip Nind; (5) Ian Anderson; (6) Ken Smith; (7) Bob Steel; (8) Ernie Skorheim; (9) Russ Leonard; (10) Jack Farley; (11) Joe Cotton; (12) Jim Wagner; (13) Tom Reich *Ernest Skorheim*

for some salt without divulging why. At the small stream behind the camp, he reveled in the feeling of brushing and having clean teeth. He then replaced the brush where he had found it. Glor was able to keep the toothbrush a secret and continued to make the brushing a daily ritual. It was not until some weeks later that he divulged his good fortune, only to find that nearly every member of the group had also been using the toothbrush secretly.

One of the British soldiers, Ken Smith, had been a well-known and accomplished prizefighter before the war. He was now a radio operator and had installed a very powerful radio that had been parachuted in to him, along with a generator to operate it. Each night, the Americans would gather around him as he talked to his contact in Cairo. This was a huge morale builder for everyone, for not only did they learn the latest news, but they were also reassured that their location was known to the British, who were working on a plan to get them out of Greece.

Ken Smith, a British radio operator with the Highland Light Infantry.   *Joseph Cotton*

On January 20, the radio contact in Cairo informed the Americans that they were to be picked up by a transport plane in Albania. They were to begin the five-day trek on January 23. The plan revolved around a group of nurses who were to be evacuated from Albania. They had been on a plane going from Africa to Italy, but the craft had become lost in the weather and been forced to crash-land in Albania. The nurses had been able to get to an airfield from which they were to be evacuated by a C-47 cargo plane. Still, the Americans could scarcely believe their ears when told that the evacuation point was near Sheper, Albania—where they had been three weeks earlier! Every member of the group retained vivid memories of the trials of that route. Several of the crew even approached Flournoy to express their concern at undertaking the trip again for fear everyone would not survive. The pilot took these concerns very seriously since he had maintained from the beginning that the crew should stay together, so if they were to undertake the trip, it would be as a group of ten. After being assured by Nind and Anderson that the route they would take this time was well established, easier, and had been used a few weeks earlier to evacuate a defecting Italian general, the air crew agreed to go.

In preparation, Smith arranged for a British Lancaster bomber to drop a number of containers with food, clothing, and boots to the resistance camp. When Joe Cotton got his new boots he felt that he could do about anything, his feet felt so good. Unfortunately, Bob Steel's feet were still in such bad shape that he was unable to even get a new pair of boots on. The guerrillas, commonly called *Andartes,* provided several donkeys to aid in the trip and four of their band to accompany the airmen. The group, now with proper clothing, supplies, and footwear, began the long trek. The hazard was significant because they had to travel at night to remain clear of German patrols and avoid being seen by Luftwaffe patrol planes. At times the narrow trail dropped away into a black abyss on either side, and it began to snow on the second day of the journey. Several times, the men had to hold on to a rope that was tied to one of the donkeys just to remain on the trail, for one false step on the wet shale could mean slipping down the side of the mountain and never being found. While the windswept sides of some hills were free of snow, the wind was bitterly cold and seemed to blow right through the weary hikers. When the trail wound through the forest, there were often several inches of snow on the ground. The worst circumstance was having to ford the several small rivers that crossed the trail. After wading through the icy water, the evaders had to take off their shoes, wring out their socks, and continue on with cold, wet feet. Another concern was dogs. Time and again, the group would think they were in an unoccupied wilderness, only to hear a dog bark, alerting anyone nearby to their presence. The Americans often threw stones in the direction of the bark to silence the offending animals, but had little luck.

Despite having supplies and being somewhat stronger than when they had arrived in the camp, the trip soon began to take its toll. Three of the airmen—Steel, Farley, and Leonard—were still suffering from the problems they'd had on the previous trek, so they had to ride on the pack animals. Leonard was in such bad shape from malaria and dysentery that he could not even sit upright on a donkey, but rather had to be draped across the animal's back. Farley, too, was getting weaker all the time. Steel, on the other hand, was able to walk enough that he could keep up with the group on the trail for short periods of time.

The guerrillas sent scouts ahead, often as much as half a day, in order to be sure the route was safe from the Germans. As a result, the Americans were often expected in the towns along the way. On one occasion, the entire population of a remote mountain village turned out to welcome them, shouting in Greek, "Hurray for the Americans! Good victory! The sooner the better!" The food was also far different from that which they had previously been given. The Americans pooled the money from their survival kits and asked how much it would cost to have a leg of lamb dinner. The price was agreed upon, and in a few hours, the hungry airmen sat down to a feast of leg of lamb, some vegetables, lots of fresh-baked bread, and even some wine. The meal, coupled with the anticipation of freedom, kept the group in good spirits despite the weather and the endless walking.

On the morning of January 26, the evaders reached the town of Vecine, Greece, on the Albanian border. From there they were to follow a valley to the vicinity of Sheper, Albania, about ten miles to the east, for their January 28 flight to freedom. Spirits were high as the airmen were once again hidden for the day in different locations. But their hopes were dashed early in the afternoon when one of the Greeks made a hurried trip to each of the places where they were staying and told them they had to depart Vecine immediately to return to Leia and the guerrilla camp. Through broken English and the little Greek various members of the group had picked up, they learned that the scout who had been leading their group had been captured by the Germans the preceding day. Evidently he had been forced to divulge their location, although he'd apparently said nothing about the planned flight or the group of nurses being hidden around Sheper. A number of German soldiers had been dispatched to Vecine to capture the Americans, but the information had been passed through the countryside, and by the time they arrived, the evaders and their Greek guides had departed again to the south.

The spirits of the entire group were lower than they had been at any time during their entire evasion experience as they again began the torturous trek south over mountains and along slick trails. It took only two days to make the return trip, and late in the morning of January 28, about the time they had been scheduled to land in Italy, the Americans straggled back into the Greek resistance camp—tired, hungry, and discouraged. It did not help matters when Ken Smith told Flournoy that there was presently no other plan to evacuate the group.

To make the situation even more demanding, there were seven additional British evaders now in the camp. The Lancaster bomber, commanded by Jack Radcliff, that had dropped the supplies to the camp on January 21 had developed engine trouble right after completing the drop, and the crew had been forced to bail out a few miles away. No one was seriously injured, and they had all been able to find their way to the camp. Although the added men put more stress on the facilities of the Greek resistance and made any plan for escape or evacuation more difficult, they helped in the work of the camp and the activities of the *Andartes*. A New Zealander on the crew, Len Dougherty, particularly stood out as he aided in patrols, tended the sick, and went on dangerous supply missions.

Because of the desire to continue to harass the Germans, particularly in the area of the Albanian border, those Americans who were able to move were divided into groups of two or three and dispatched to various partisan outposts. These small camps, located a few hours' hike from the main camp, were manned by six or seven men, including the Americans, and were charged with both monitoring the Germans and disrupting their activities if possible. The partisans had a number of weapons and explosives, which had been dropped by the British, with which they could blow up trails, bridges, and roads. During the next month, several of the Americans got firsthand experience in this risky operation.

The complexity and danger of the missions varied. The day after Skorheim and Wagner arrived at their outpost, they were detailed to help with a supply mission. In the company of two Greek partisans and two mules, the Americans began a two-day trip through the hills to pick up a number of special weapons and several bags of gold sovereigns with which to buy supplies on the open market. The trust that the guerrillas placed in their new colleagues was demonstrated when the pickup had been completed. The Greeks elected to lead the laden animals and detailed the Americans to guard duty. Each was given a rifle and directions that the money was to be protected at all costs. To the consternation of the two airmen, they were told that Greek outlaws were as big a menace as the Germans, and if they were told to shoot by their Greek compatriots, they needed to follow the order instantly and not ask questions. Fortunately, they saw no one as they trekked through the hills, but they were followed on two occasions by small packs of wild dogs, which would often come up behind them and sniff their legs. Although the Greeks told the two Americans to just ignore the animals, that was all but impossible, and for Skorheim, the dogs became a more serious threat than other people. Fortunately, there were no incidents with the dogs or outlaws, and the small band arrived safely at the main guerrilla camp.

A much more exciting trip was that undertaken by Cotton, Steel, and Glor, who were asked by two of the British soldiers, Nind and Anderson, to help carry the supplies and provide any other assistance needed to blow up a bridge on the road in the vicinity of Sopik, Albania. Remarkably, the bridge was less than ten miles from the town where the entire group had turned around a couple of weeks earlier when the plan for evacuation with the nurses had to be abandoned. The undertaking was a four-day affair, which meant that the group had to carry not only the supplies to blow up the bridge but also enough food to keep them going. It was a heavily laden band that departed northward early on a cold February night. Their Greek guide knew the route well, and the weather cooperated. As the sun began to appear above the horizon, the saboteurs found a small house, probably used by a shepherd during the summer, and there they spent the day. As Cotton lay on some pine boughs on the floor, he reflected on how amazing his adventure was becoming. Who would have thought, when he departed on his first combat mission, that less than three months later he would be hiking through the Greek countryside with two British agents on a mission to blow up a bridge used by the Germans? Late in the afternoon, Anderson produced a sketch of the bridge, made during an earlier reconnaissance, and noted just where they would place the explosives. "The guards will be taken care of," he said, "so we will just have to worry about any German patrols that happen to come along." He also explained that the explosion would be small, designed only to crack the bridge enough that the weight of the trucks would cause it to collapse.

As darkness descended on the mountains of northern Greece, the little band emerged from their hiding place and once again began their trek. The second night was not as difficult since they were following the valley through which the road was laid. Around midnight, their guide motioned that the bridge was a short distance ahead. Warning the three Americans to remain where they were and to be absolutely silent, Anderson and Nind, along with the guide, took the Jellignite explosives, which looked like small jelly beans, and departed into the darkness.

For the trio that had been left behind, the wait seemed forever. Suddenly they heard a muffled explosion and the sound of their companions returning. With only a quick "Let's get out of here!" Anderson led the group quickly back in the direction from which they had come. Shortly after dawn, they were back in the house they had used the previous night. After a sparse meal of bread, cheese, and a little dried meat, everyone settled down for a day of rest and preparation for the long night ahead. Even though he was dead tired from the night's adventure, Cotton found himself unable to sleep as he kept wondering about the explosion and its consequences. He was not sure he liked the life of a saboteur, and he hoped that he wouldn't get called upon to perform another such duty.

They consumed the last of their rations just as darkness fell and were soon on the trail again. After an uneventful all-night hike, the six arrived back at the guerrilla camp. Three days later they heard that the bridge had indeed collapsed and all the truck traffic in that area had been halted. As fate would have it, shortly after the group returned to the *Andartes'* camp, Ken Smith reported that the officials in Cairo had authorized the Americans to remain in Greece and help Nind and Anderson with their underground activities. The enlisted airmen were also offered a commission if they agreed to stay. Each of the Americans had gone into the Army Air Forces because they wanted to fly, and they all hoped they would soon be back in the air, so no one accepted the offer.

On February 15, 1944, Smith's contact in Cairo told him that both the American and the British air crew were to make their way to the town of Lippa, situated in a valley about thirty miles to the south. They would be met there by an American army captain who would direct them to a site from which they would be evacuated by air on February 22. Within a day, the Americans, along with the three Highland Light Infantry troops, the Lancaster crew, and the Italian doctor, again found themselves struggling over snowy mountains and sliding down slick hillsides as they attempted to keep up with the Greeks leading them. Several members of the group led mules laden with supplies and equipment for the partisan group near Lippa. Fortunately, none of the crew was still so sick that he had to ride. As before, most of the travel was done at night.

Because of the animosity between the communist and anticommunist partisan groups, periodic confrontations were quite common. Sometimes the Americans were caught in the middle. Late in the afternoon of the second day of their journey to the south, just as they were beginning their all-night trek, Ian Anderson, leading the first mule, came around a turn on the six-foot-wide trail and found his way blocked by several armed men. The group had to stop since there was a steep hill covered with trees on one side of the trail and a precipitous drop into a streambed on the other. The second mule was led by Flournoy and two more back was Glor, also leading a pack animal. Anderson and the apparent leader of the Greek band, through a Greek interpreter, got into a discussion, which then turned into an argument. At issue was the demand by the band who had stopped the pack train that the Italian doctor be given over to them, apparently because of their severe medical problems. Flournoy and Glor soon joined the discussion, although they really did not know what it was all about. But a few moments later, Glor's blood ran cold when the interpreter told them that there was a boy up on the hill with a .50-caliber machine gun ready to wipe out the entire group on the command of their leader. Neither Glor nor Flournoy had ever been so scared in his life; both could see the machine gun, and there was absolutely no place they could go for protection if the young man opened fire.

Anderson, reputed to be one of the coolest and bravest men in the camp, told Flournoy and Glor to back their mules down the trail and leave him with his adversary. Backing a mule down a six-foot-wide trail is easier said than done, and the two were able to retreat only a few feet. Glor thought surely they were going to be shot. In a flash, Anderson pulled out a knife and held it to the bandit's throat. "Tell him to get his men and that machine gun out of here right now or I'll cut his throat," Anderson yelled at the interpreter. A moment later the hapless Greek made a motion to the machine gun operator, who immediately began to take the big weapon off its tripod and move it off the hill. Ten minutes later the entire pack train moved past the spot with no sign of the gunmen. Anderson later told Glor that the men were members of a rival political faction and would have kept the doctor in the hills with them until the civil conflict was over.

The hours and days became a blur as the exhausted airmen followed their Greek benefactors south through the nearly trackless mountains. Although they had departed the camp at Leia in the early February sun, the pleasant warmth soon gave way to clouds, wind, rain, and snow. Adding to the challenge was their inability to see more than a few feet in the darkness. As the narrow trail wound through the rugged terrain, none of the group even dared to think how far down he would go if he fell off the path. This fear was fueled late the second night when one of the Greek partisans slipped off the left side of the trail. Fortunately, he hit a small tree a few feet down and was able to hold on until the rest of the party could form a human chain to pull him back to the trail. "Did you notice that we couldn't hear the rocks he kicked loose hit the bottom of the canyon?" a nervous Skorheim asked Cotton. "It might be a thousand feet down. Maybe it's just as well that we can't see."

Fatigue also began to take its toll. At one rest stop, Skorheim sat down in a bush and was instantly asleep. Tom Reich woke him after the fifteen-minute stop was over, and Skorheim was convinced he had been asleep all night. Within a couple of days, members of the group also began to again have attacks of malaria. The weakened Farley and Leonard soon had to be put back on mules to continue the trip, which necessitated moving some of the supplies to the backs of the men. The Italian doctor was unable to get the two men back on their feet, but he did have enough quinine to prevent any of the malaria cases from becoming debilitating. Still, the Americans began to openly fear that the entire group might not make it back to freedom alive.

As they approached their objective of Lippa on February 21, Cotton and Flournoy were sent with several of the Greeks to scout out the area and make contact with the American captain. It took the small band most of the afternoon to reach the village of Upper Lippa. Well before arriving, they had seen smoke on the horizon, but they did not know how serious a problem it portended. As the forward party cautiously looked down from the hills on the town of Lower Lippa, they found it was in flames. As the group began their return to camp, they were met by the American officer and a Greek sergeant, who told them that the Germans had learned of the evacuation plan and decided to bomb Lower Lippa as a warning to the citizens of both towns of what would happen if they aided either the partisans or any Allied evaders. The two had been able to flee their hiding place in Lower Lippa just ahead of the Germans, so, like the evaders they were supposed to help, they were now fugitives. It was a devastated band that arrived back in camp late that night to report that any evacuation from the area of Lippa was out of the question.

After considerable discussion and the dispatch of a scout team to survey the area, the partisans decided they would establish a temporary camp in the hills near the village of Tseritsena and await further word on what to do with the air crews. They began to build shelters while Ken Smith reported their precarious situation to Cairo. A new plan to

Joe Cotton and three Greek messengers.   *Joseph Cotton*

evacuate the air crews had to be devised quickly, he told them, for the
new location lacked the facilities of the camp at Leia. Supplies, especially food, would be very difficult to find since there were German patrols operating in the area. Smith also expressed doubt that everyone
would survive the trek back to the main base at Leia and still have
enough strength to make another attempt to get out.

     Until a new plan could be devised in Cairo, the air crew members
had to move to small outlying camps to reduce the chances that the entire group would be found by the Germans. So, in groups of three or
four, the discouraged and increasingly exhausted evaders trudged over
the hills for two or three hours to several small camps, generally a
sheepherder's hut or some other simple shelter, where they were to remain for an undetermined length of time.

     The next two weeks were a boring blur to the evaders and their
Greek companions. There was little to do, and a good portion of their
time was taken up looking for food. The partisans had plenty of money,
thanks to the trip previously made by Skorheim and Wagner, so they
were able to send the women who had come with them from the main
camp at Leia into some of the villages to buy food, often on the black

market. This meant that every two or three days the residents of the out-lying camps would have to make the arduous and dangerous trek to the camp near Tseritsena to get enough food to keep them going for another few days. None of the residents of the small camps was ever able to breathe easily while on these hikes since there was always the chance of being seen by a German patrol. However, arrival at the main camp meant a hot meal and a chance to find out what progress, if any, had been made on a new evacuation plan.

Eddie Novak and Tom Reich often talked about the aborted rescue plans and speculated on the chances of future success. "I really think we're going to be in these mountains until the war is over," the tall, good-looking Reich remarked during one boring afternoon in their di-lapidated hut. "If only we could have kept one more engine running we could have made it to Italy and I would probably be back in New York by now." Novak agreed that the prospect of being successfully evacuated looked pretty dim. "I guess this is just the way war goes," he responded. "After all, this was my first mission with you guys, so I didn't know what to expect. I keep wondering what my folks back in Chicago have been told about me. I sure hope they have just said we were missing since my mom couldn't take having that telegram delivered saying I was dead." And so it went in each of the small camps as the residents whiled away the hours and days.

On March 7, in his nightly radio contact with Cairo, Smith was told that the American and British air crews, and the Italian doctor, should be at Agios Ioannou Bay, about forty miles west-southwest of Tseritsena, for pickup on the night of March 15. The area was considered ideal for the evacuation since it had been controlled for decades by a Turkish clan, the Bal Kamitar, who were noted for their fierce disposition and who were feared by Greeks and Germans alike. The Italian ship that was to pick up the evaders would also be delivering a large load of supplies to Nind, Anderson, and their Greek comrades. Early the next morning, the word was sent out by messengers for the evaders to return to the main camp as soon as possible. Late in the afternoon, when everyone had ar-rived, Smith told them the plan. They were to leave the main camp on March 10 for what was going to be another long and arduous trip through the mountains. The group had to arrive at the Turkish enclave on the coast by the early morning of March 15 for pickup that night.

While the evaders had little to do but start walking, the preparations by the partisans were intense. They had to obtain enough food to sup-port at least five days on the trail for the entire group and the five-day return portion for the partisans. In addition, pack animals were essential for carrying back the supplies that would be off-loaded from the ship. These mules were put to good use on the way to the rendezvous point by those evaders who were unable to walk the entire distance. Ken Smith packed his radio equipment on the back of one animal and covered it with canvas to keep it from the prying eyes of unfriendly Greeks, or Germans, they might encounter along the way. His presence on the trek was essential, for any change in plans had to be communicated to the band in a timely manner.

Spirits were high as the group of nearly forty men set out on the evening of March 10. Most of the Americans were more confident of success than they had been on previous attempts. Not only did the plan make more sense this time, but the Greeks had also made extensive preparations as well. Soon, however, the euphoria was replaced by the all-too-familiar exhausting routine of hiking up and down the often snowy mountains, trying not to slip into the unknown blackness beside the trail, and cringing at the sound of a barking dog. Silence was essential because it was common knowledge that there were German patrols in the area, and they could only be expected to become more numerous as the group approached the coast, which made the dogs all the more of a problem. As had been the routine on each of their other trips, when daylight came the group broke into smaller bands of four or five and went to seek shelter for the day. And although they had enough rations to sustain themselves at a minimum level, there was always the need to find more food. Wild onions were particularly abundant as they neared the coast, and proved a tasty addition to the bread and other basics the guerrillas carried.

On the first day out, Skorheim found himself, along with Glor and two Greeks, in a small hut near the town of Derviziana, looking at a pot of some kind of stew. The meal looked delicious until Skorheim spotted an animal's eyeball floating in the mixture. Much to his relief, one of the Greeks snatched it up, apparently savoring the delicacy. Cotton had been told that one way to really get the Greeks on your side was to show your respect for their elders. An old man, obviously the patriarch of the family, took out his pipe, put in a little very precious tobacco, but could not find a light. On impulse, Cotton reached into the edge of the fire, grabbed a small coal with his fingers, and placed it in the bowl of the pipe. Immediately he was the darling of the camp because of his concern for the old man, but also for his bravery in taking the coal from the fire. Cotton would never forget the warmth of that early evening, sitting around the fire in a strange Greek town but still feeling the comradeship of a group all dedicated to the same cause. The glow lasted throughout the night's journey.

Once again, however, the trip began to take its toll. Glor became ill with dysentery, and his feet, which had become frostbitten on the trek to blow up the bridge, made walking difficult. He was put on a mule, as were Wagner and Leonard. Early in the morning of March 13, the group skirted the town of Vouvopotamon and realized that they were nearly two thirds of the way. Again spirits were high, since Smith had talked with Cairo each night before the band began their hike and was told that all was still in order.

Just as the sun was rising on March 15, the evaders and their companions found themselves less than a mile from the coast. The journey was complete. Now all they had to do was sit and wait. The day dragged by as they sat in a large grove of trees, well up on the side of the mountain. They had been assured time and again that the plan would work, but all had some doubt, given their previous experiences. As darkness fell, the anticipation grew. Every eye was trained on the water as the group silently and slowly made its way down to the narrow beach. The hours passed and still there was no signal. The spirits of both the air crews and the guerrillas began to sink near midnight. Just when the Americans were about to give up hope, they saw a small light blinking on the water. Quickly one of the Greeks took out his flashlight and answered. After another exchange of light flashes, all was once again dark. The minutes dragged by with no sound or sign of any boat. Suddenly, out of the blackness, a large rowboat emerged, followed by another similar craft a few minutes later. Both were heavily laden with supplies. It was all that Skorheim and his fellow crewmen could do to stifle a cheer. The plan had worked and they would soon be back with their units. Several, like Cotton, uttered a small prayer of thanks at having survived.

Although the Americans expected that the supplies would be quickly unloaded and that they would be on their way, that was not to be. Almost immediately, an argument broke out between the Italian sailors who were manning the small boats and the Greeks. The problem appeared to be money. At one point, much to the terror of the Americans, the sailors got back in their boats and prepared to shove off into the surf. Finally the Greeks gave the sailors a bag, apparently containing money, and the unloading began. It was nearly two hours later, around two in the morning, when the ten Americans, the seven-man Lancaster crew, the Italian doctor, and two other men were able to bid good-bye to their Greek compatriots to whom they owed so much. They had decided to give everything of value to the guerrillas when they were ready to leave, so Cotton gave away his .45 and extra ammunition and other members of the group did likewise, giving up maps and other survival gear. "If this

evacuation doesn't work, we are going to be in big trouble," Cotton remarked after giving away his pistol. "I still have the Beretta that they
gave me," Glor replied. "Anderson said not to try to give it to the Greeks
because they would consider it an insult that I was giving a gift back."
About that time, the man to whom Cotton had given his .45 reached out
and handed him a Beretta as well.

Not everyone was glad to give up his equipment to the Greeks, however. Jock, the short, small navigator on the Lancaster crew, was not
about to give his kit bag to anyone. When he had bailed out of his Lancaster, Jock had been very careful to take all of his navigation equipment and carefully stow it in a kit bag that he tied to his waist and held
between his legs during the descent. Thereafter, he guarded it with his
life. "This is the king's equipment, for which I am responsible," he told
the group. "And I intend to return it to the proper authorities when I get
back to England." Within a few days, Jock's navigation equipment became entertainment for the evaders. They would hide all or part of it
during the night, try to give it to the Greeks, or almost anything else to
get him upset. In reality, outsmarting Jock had often kept up the morale
of the group when things looked very bleak. As the two air crews
boarded the rowboats that would take them out to the evacuation vessel,
one of the other crew members of the Lancaster remarked how happy
everyone was that Jock had been successful in saving his equipment.
"Let me have a look at that bag and see just what you've been guarding
so carefully for the past few weeks," he told Jock. The navigator handed
over the bag, which his fellow countryman promptly threw to the guerrillas. It was all the crew could do to keep Jock from jumping overboard
and going after his treasured bag.

The minutes seemed like hours as the rowboats made their way
slowly past the surf to the Italian subchaser anchored some distance off
shore. As soon as all were aboard, the craft began to move, and the
group could finally express their joy at having been rescued. "I knew we
could do it if we just stuck together," a euphoric Flournoy yelled. "We
had faith in each other and it paid off." Later the pilot told Cotton, his
copilot, "I never had any doubt that we could do it. Our spirit was tested
several times, but this crew had so much faith in one another and so
much confidence that we became larger than life. You were lucky to be
with this crew, Joe." Cotton could only nod in agreement during that
emotional moment.

Although it was not a feast, the canned milk and crackers that were
soon set in front of the survivors were consumed with relish. After about
an hour they entered much rougher seas. The Italian doctor told the oth-

ers that they had passed the island of Paxos and were now making all possible speed toward his homeland, nearly a hundred and fifty miles away. As the minutes passed, the rough seas, confining quarters, and having drunk too much milk took their toll, and one after another, the passengers succumbed to seasickness. Even the moping Jock forgot his lost navigation equipment as he lay moaning on the floor. To make matters worse, no one was allowed on the deck for fear he might be swept overboard into the darkness, so the stench continued to build. Just after dawn, the seas subsided somewhat and the new arrivals were allowed to go out on the deck. For most, that was just what they needed to shed their seasickness, and some even began to enjoy the ocean air and the endless sea.

About ten in the morning, on March 16, 1944, their Italian companion, his eyes glistening with emotion at seeing the coast of Italy, told them that the land they saw to their right was the Cape of Santa Maria di Leúca and that they would arrive at the port of Gallípoli about noon. The Italian ship entered a packed harbor and was soon tied up at the wharf. The passengers stepped ashore on rubbery legs, trying to fathom the hustle and bustle all about them. They were a sight—dirty, bearded, lice-infested, ragged men looking about, several with tears in their eyes, as the reality of freedom slowly sank in. A moment later, Skorheim saw an American flag on the stern of one of the ships, and as he pointed it out to the group, every member knew he really had successfully evaded and made it to safety.

No sooner had their emotions begun to subside than both the British and American air crews were invited aboard a large British merchant ship for lunch. As the ragged entourage entered the captain's dining room, he must have had second thoughts. Nonetheless, he offered them some scotch, which Flournoy likened to "nectar from the Gods," and told them how proud he was to be able to host them on his ship. After another round of scotch and what was a sumptuous feast to the former evaders, the captain told them good-bye and sent them out into the afternoon sun. The Americans then bade farewell to the crew of the Lancaster and were immediately loaded into the back of a waiting British army truck and driven the thirty miles to the city of Lecce. There they sat in an office and waited several hours for a truck to be dispatched from the U.S. Army base at Bari, nearly one hundred miles to the north. While the truck was en route, the crew passed the time by reminiscing about their experiences on Corfu and in Greece. "The one thing that kept emerging as the common thread of all the conversation," said Joe Cotton later, "was each person's admiration for the courage, cleverness, imagination, and vigilant protection given us by the Greeks. No matter the danger or the challenge, they were ready to do whatever was needed to see to it that we survived. Each of us would be eternally indebted to them for that." It was well after midnight when the ten airmen were loaded into the truck to begin the final leg of their journey back to American hands.

About midmorning the group arrived at the American 36th General Hospital in Bari. The corpsman in charge immediately ushered them into a large shower room for delousing. They were also provided with razors, toothbrushes, and clean clothes, albeit hospital pajamas. No one wanted to leave the hot showers, their first in four months, and they reveled over being able to shave and brush their teeth. It was a very different-looking group that was ushered into the doctor's office an hour later for a cursory physical exam. Their conditions varied. All were weak from malnutrition and suffering from malaria, but several had other maladies as well, the most common of which were dysentery and jaundice. After the physical exam, all of the crew members were confined to the hospital for various tests and treatment. "This isn't such a bad deal," Wagner told Skorheim. "The beds are soft, we have sheets, a genuine American female brings us three meals every day, and we don't have to walk anywhere." And none of the group would soon forget nurse Gudrun Stenoien from Mayville, North Dakota, who took personal charge of them. The tenor of the entire stay was set the afternoon of the first day in the hospital when she told them that anytime they wanted anything to eat, just call. And if they woke up in the middle of the night, there were Post Toasties, milk, and sugar in the ward. They were to help themselves.

After resting for the day and having an uninterrupted night's sleep, they were taken to a small room in the hospital where several intelligence officers interviewed them for several hours. The first objective was to establish the identity of each member of the crew. This was not difficult since all ten had remained together for the entire time. Then the questions about their experience began. The inquiries took all morning. Before the officers were finished, the items of discussion had ranged from the actual evasion experience to the details of their crash, how they used their survival equipment and training, and observations they had about German installations and equipment on Corfu and the Greek mainland. Then the personnel department got its time with the crew. Its purpose was to officially put them back on their unit's roster as present for duty, figure their back pay, make arrangements for uniforms, and, most important, notify their families that they were again safe. The exhausted airmen gladly returned to their hospital rooms late in the afternoon. Officially, the crew was listed as returning on March 18, 1944, four months to the day after their crash landing on Corfu.

The following day, medical treatment began in earnest. While Skorheim and Wagner were released back to their units within a week, several, including Leonard, Cotton, Flournoy, Steel, and Glor remained in the hospital. Time and again, as he recuperated, Cotton reflected on the miracle of the entire crew's surviving and returning together. "But maybe it wasn't a miracle," he told Glor one day. "I have never seen such a spirit of comradeship and self-sacrifice for the group as I did during our evasion. I never realized that people had so many different talents or the ability to stand up under hardship that I saw in our crew." Glor was less amazed than Cotton since he had been with the crew so much longer. "We would not even go on sick call unless we were on death's door," he told Cotton, "for fear that someone else would be assigned to our position on the crew and we would never get back with the group. This was a special crew." As each member of the group was discharged from the hospital, he was sent to their unit, the 49th Bomb Squadron, which had moved from North Africa to Foggia, about seventy-five miles north of Bari. They were given orders and assigned transportation back home. Unfortunately, it was while Cotton was living in a tent at Foggia that his diary, which he had kept during the entire evasion, was stolen—along with his Beretta pistol.

All the crew members were returned to the United States within two months of their arrival in Italy. Skorheim and Wagner flew from Foggia to Casablanca, to the Azores, and on into New York. Cotton, one of the last to be released from the hospital, also flew home from Foggia. Flournoy, Glor, and Steel flew to Casablanca and then spent ten days on a Liberty Ship sailing to New York. Shortly before the ship arrived in the United States, everyone was briefed that they would be in trouble if they tried to bring any firearms into the country. Glor, anxious to avoid any trouble so he could get home to his wife, threw his Beretta pistol, which he had carried with him during the entire evasion, overboard.

Several members of the crew, including Cotton and Wagner, were given extensive intelligence debriefings in Washington, whereas Glor and Flournoy recounted their experiences to army officials in New York City. All were given a recuperation leave when their work with intelligence was finished. Cotton went to Miami Beach for a month, Flournoy and Steel went to Atlantic City, and Glor took a train to Batavia, New York, and a reunion with his wife, Louise. Skorheim, after looking all over the United States for his fiancée, Juanita, who was in the Spars (the women's reserve of the U.S. Coast Guard), found her in Paducah, Kentucky. They were married, and Skorheim then took his leave in Atlantic City as a honeymoon.

After their recuperation leave, each of the crew went on to various other duties and assignments, but none served together again. In 1985, Flournoy, Cotton, Skorheim, Reich, and Glor attended a reunion in Sacramento, California. Bob Steel could not attend. The whereabouts of the remaining four members of the crew were unknown.

Dick Flournoy, the pilot, left the Army Air Forces after the war and joined Trans World Airlines as a pilot. He retired in 1982 after thirty-seven years, which included a term as TWA's master executive chairman to the Air Line Pilots Association. He and his wife, Iris, had five daughters. Flournoy died in 1991. Mrs. Flournoy presently lives in Princeton, New Jersey.

Joe Cotton, the copilot, stayed in the Army Air Forces and then the Air Force for twenty-six years, retiring as a colonel. During his Air Force career, Cotton was a premier test pilot, making the first flight of the XB-70, and serving in key positions in both the B-58 and B-52 test programs. After retiring from the Air Force, he was an engineering flight test pilot for United Air Lines in San Francisco for thirteen years. During his flying career, he flew eighty-four different types of aircraft for a total of over 15,800 hours. He and his wife, Rema, live in Atherton, California, and are the parents of one son and two daughters. Cotton and his wife returned to Corfu in April 1997 for the first time since the war.

Ernie Skorheim, the bombardier, also remained in the Army Air Forces and then the Air Force, from which he retired in 1964 as a lieutenant colonel. He was in Training Command and Strategic Air Command his entire career, where he logged over 4,500 hours of flying and was designated a master navigator. Skorheim was on the crew of one of the B-52s involved in the 1957 record-breaking nonstop flight around the world. After leaving the Air Force, he worked for the U.S. District Court Clerk's Office in Sacramento, California, until his retirement in 1979. In 1989, Skorheim and his wife, Juanita, returned to Corfu where they revisited the site of the crash, the town of Lefkimi, and had a reunion with several of the people involved in his survival experience. He visited again in 1997. The Skorheims now live in Sacramento.

Thomas Reich, the tail gunner, went back to Tarrytown, New York, after the war and entered the hotel business. He remained in contact with the crew periodically and attended the reunion in 1985. Reich died in 1994.

Robert Steel, the ball turret gunner, returned to Montana and was in charge of the tourist service bus system at Glacier National Park. He died in 1987.

James Wagner, the navigator, went to pilot training after his return to the United States but did not remain in contact with the group. He is now deceased.

Russell Leonard, the top gunner, died of Hodgkin's disease shortly after the war.

Eddie Novak, the left waist gunner, and James Farley, the radioman, did not remain in contact with the crew after leaving Italy.

Fred Glor, the right waist gunner, left the Army Air Forces after the war and returned to his home in Batavia, New York. He was employed by the federal government, Bell Aircraft, and Niagara Power and Light Company after the war and still lives in Batavia. Glor and his wife, Louise, had three sons. They returned to Corfu in 1988 and were able to visit several of the people who helped him, as well as see the site where his B-17 crashed. While visiting the crash area, Glor saw a woman hoeing a field nearby. On a chance, he walked over to talk with her through an interpreter. She was the same woman who, forty-five years earlier, had been hoeing the same field and had helped him escape.

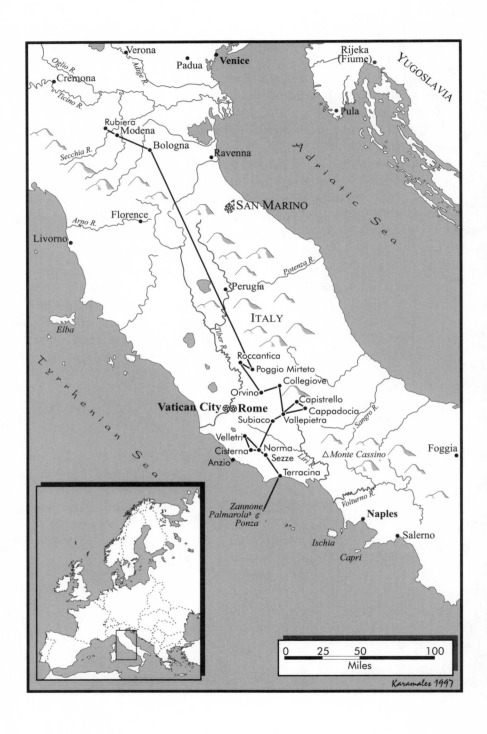

Verona

Padua

Venice

Rijeka (Fiume)

YUGOSLAVIA

Oglio R.

Cremona

Adige R.

Ticino R.

Pula

Rubiera
Modena

Bologna

Ravenna

Secchia R.

Adriatic Sea

◈SAN MARINO

Arno R.

Florence

Livorno

Elba

Potenza R.

Perugia

ITALY

Tiber R.

Tyrrhenian Sea

Roccantica

Poggio Mirteto

Collegiove

Orvino

Capistrello

Vatican City◈◈**Rome**

Cappadocia

Subiaco

Vallepietra

Sangro R.

Velletri

Cisterna

Norma

Anzio

Sezze

Liri R.

△*Monte Cassino*

Foggia

Terracina

Zannone
Palmarola⌖
Ponza

Volturno R.

Naples

Ischia

Salerno

Capri

0   25   50   100
Miles

Karamales 1997

· S E V E N ·

"I Was So Close"

"**S**onny" Fassoulis had always loved the culture and history of Europe. The son of a Greek immigrant, he had grown up in Syracuse, New York, hearing of the ancient architecture and monuments of Greece and Italy, and wanted someday to take a trip to the Mediterranean and see it all for himself. In some ways, he had already visited that part of the world as he looked down on the blue Mediterranean from the Plexiglas nose of his B-17 bomber. Fassoulis was making his fifteenth mission as the navigator on Flying Fortress 42-30396, piloted by Lieutenant John G. Caraberis. Sonny was always doubly careful as he charted the course for the big bomber because a mistake could mean bombing the wrong target and possibly destroying some building of great historic value. Because he was always exact with his navigation, he had been selected as lead navigator for the 346th Bombardment Squadron, so all twelve B-17s were now flying in formation behind Caraberis's airplane.

September 2, 1943, had begun as just another flying day. Fassoulis had been awakened at four-thirty in the morning, and after a quick breakfast and cup of coffee at the mess hall, he joined the rest of the crew in the briefing room. While drinking their second cup of coffee, the airmen were briefed by the group commander. There was nothing unusual about the mission, and Fassoulis had even told Caraberis as they were leaving the briefing that it "looked like a cinch." Out of habit, Fassoulis made a quick detour by the squadron mail room on his way to the airplane. He had a bonanza of eight letters, but since it was against regulations to take any mail on a flight for fear that it might fall into enemy hands and be used against prisoners, he gave the packet of mail to the crew chief, Sergeant Huska, to hold until the flight returned to Tunis that afternoon. Sonny wondered briefly what was in all his letters as he looked down on the blue water and double-checked the course from Africa that would take them between Sicily and Sardinia, over Florence, and finally to the city of Modena for the start of the southeasterly bomb run on the railroad marshaling yards at Bologna.

Fassoulis had never intended to be a navigator. Although the work was extremely important, he still wished he were flying the bomber. That would have been the case had he not been caught in the forbidden maneuver of flying down the Colorado River in the depths of the Grand Canyon while he was at advanced pilot training in Mariana, Arizona. Despite his pleas and assurances that he had learned his lesson, he was eliminated from pilot training and found himself graduating from navigator school at Mather Field, California, in May 1943. He immediately volunteered to go overseas and into combat, so a few weeks later he was listening to the drone of the engines of an Army Air Forces C-54 transport as it winged its way toward Rabat, Morocco. Crew assignment followed, and by July 1943, Fassoulis was stationed in Tunis as part of the 99th Bombardment Group.

About two hours after takeoff, Fassoulis informed the crew over the intercom that they were passing to the right of Sardinia and the tension in the bomber began to increase noticeably. The gunners tested their guns while Fassoulis and the bombardier, Lieutenant Edward Hooper, checked their maps and calculations once again. Less than an hour later, Fassoulis noted in his log that they had made landfall about halfway between Rome and Florence. The intelligence briefer had told the crews to expect some flak and maybe a few German fighters, but overall the opposition was supposed to be light. The formation had been over land only a few minutes when they encountered the first flak. It was inaccurate and caused no damage. Over Florence, the antiaircraft fire increased, but the crews were more intent on looking for German fighters. They were less than twenty minutes from making the right turn over Modena that would begin the bomb run when a sudden lurch of the heavily laden bomber and the accompanying explosion made every crew member's heart skip a beat. They realized they had been hit by the burst of an antiaircraft shell.

A quick check by the copilot, Lieutenant Clayton Dean, indicated that no one had been seriously injured by the blast, but both reports from

Sonny Fassoulis in 1942.   *Maria Couvaras*

the crew and a glance out the windows indicated that the aircraft was seriously damaged. There were holes in the wing and in the nose. Fassoulis and Hooper had been showered by broken Plexiglas and a storm of blowing paper. As they looked at the riddled and broken Plexiglas, both were amazed that they had not been seriously wounded or killed. But the men had no time to think about the blast as they struggled to retrieve maps, logs, target photos, and the other material blowing about the nose compartment. Hooper immediately began to check his Norden bombsight to determine if they could still make the bomb run. Fassoulis finally retrieved his map and again checked the heading to Modena. Then, as he listened to the various members of the crew reporting aircraft damage to the pilot, he began to chart an emergency course for Switzerland—just in case the pilot called for one.

For Caraberis and Dean, the reality of the problem was much more graphic. Three of the four engines had been hit. Number one was smoking but still running fairly smoothly, as was number three. The number two engine, however, was on fire, and when Dean tried to feather the propeller, it would not respond. The result was so much drag on the wounded aircraft that it was impossible to stay with the rest of the squadron. By the time the formation turned over Modena, it was obvious that 42-30396 could not make the bomb run. Caraberis asked Fassoulis to find a place where they could jettison their bombs without hitting a concentration of civilians. Hooper dropped the bombs a short distance north of the highway between Modena and Bologna, and with the bombs gone, the plane was able to maintain altitude. It even began to look like they might be able to keep up with their formation at a lower altitude. But as the rest of the bombers continued to pull farther and farther away, that hope vanished. Rather than try to fly nearly four hours over five hundred miles of open sea to get back to Tunis, Caraberis asked Fassoulis for his course to Switzerland.

The prospect of making it to that neutral country was not good, either. Although both the number one and number three engines were still running, they were not producing their full power. The drag from number two's windmilling propeller was tremendous, and the bomber continued to lose altitude. To make matters worse, the dreaded German Me-109s had finally made their appearance, and several pounced on the wounded Flying Fortress. In the ensuing melee, the gunners on the bomber were able to shoot down two of the fighters, but the German aircraft departed leaving pieces coming off the bomber's cowling around the number two engine, number one so badly damaged that it had to be feathered, and bullet holes all over the aircraft. Amazingly, none of the crew members was seriously wounded. There was nothing that Caraberis could do but alert the crew to prepare to abandon the plane. No sooner had he given the order to bail out than the propeller on the number two engine finally feathered and the fire went out. Hope returned to the crew that they might make it to Switzerland. That expectation proved hasty within the next fifteen minutes, as the big bomber, flying on only two engines, was unable to maintain altitude. Caraberis knew that he was too low to clear the Alps. One by one the crew went out the escape hatches into the bright noon sunlight of northern Italy.

The bailout began as a disaster for Fassoulis. His heart was racing as he looked out the open hatch at the countryside over 10,000 feet below. He had been briefed many times on the proper procedure to follow, but when he went out the hatch, his chute caught on the door and he was stuck with his legs hanging out of the aircraft, being buffeted so hard by the wind he thought they would break. Try as he might, he could not get the rest of his body out of the airplane, nor could he get hold of anything to pull himself back inside. The copilot was to follow him out the hatch. Because Fassoulis was blocking everyone else in the front of the plane from bailing out, Dean was able to exert a superhuman effort and pull the one-hundred-and-fifty-pound navigator back into the bomber for a second try. This time Fassoulis cleared the hatch and the smoking bomber.

Time and again, all flight crew members had been told to count to ten before pulling the rip cord so they would be sure they were clear of the aircraft. Scared out of his wits by his traumatic exit from the plane, Sonny counted faster than he ever had in his life and breathed an audible sigh of relief as he felt the terrific jerk that indicated his chute had deployed. He looked up to check his parachute and saw only two other chutes some distance above him. Fassoulis wondered about the rest of the crew, but that concern soon left his mind as he began to look at the ground to see what might be in store for him when he landed. Although he was too high to know where he might come down, he marveled at the beauty of the Italian countryside. As he got lower, it became obvious that he was going to land in what appeared to be a vineyard. Fassoulis prepared to make his long-awaited visit to Italy.

Fortunately, he landed between the rows of grape-laden vines. He rolled over a couple of times and his six-foot frame came to rest against a small tree. Before he had time to even think about what to do next, he was surrounded by the Italians who were working in the vineyard. In less than a minute, they were elbowed aside by a small group of German soldiers. A young German, apparently in charge of the detachment, approached Fassoulis with leveled rifle and asked in English if he was injured. "Something seems to have happened to my side," Fassoulis answered, pointing to the spot where he had rolled against the tree. The Germans were evidently unconvinced, and less than fifteen minutes after he had landed, Fassoulis was loaded into the back of a truck with several German soldiers.

As the Italian countryside slid past, the airman wondered about the rest of the crew and tried to devise a plan to escape. He assumed that he was really on his own, since he had seen no other members of his crew land. What he did not know was that the intercom system in the plane had been damaged, so the members of the crew in the back of the bomber had not received the command to abandon the airplane. By the time the intercom problem became evident to Caraberis, the copilot, bombardier, and navigator had all bailed out. It took some time for the pilot to finally get word to the gunners to leave, and then he bailed out himself. The result was that the crew was spread over more than one hundred miles of Italy.

Sonny had always been a very self-confident person, and despite the fact that he was alone, he was surprisingly calm. He knew that if he could get away from the Germans and stay clear of the cities, he could evade and eventually return to his unit and get back into the fight. Certainly his fluency in Greek would help. Unfortunately, there was no chance to even try to escape, since the trip was short and the truck never stopped. About midafternoon, the vehicle entered a city, which Fassoulis assumed was Modena, since they had been nearly over that city when the order was given to bail out. The vehicle stopped in front of an old building that resembled a small fortress. Sonny was led from the truck and past a small group of onlookers, through a small doorway, into the ancient building. He was taken aback by the smell of mold and dampness that permeated the structure. His German guard moved him directly to an area with several small cells, pushed Fassoulis into one, and locked the door. In the dim light, Sonny could make out a bare board along one wall about eighteen inches above the floor, and a bucket in a corner. There was nothing else. He was not very concerned with his surroundings since he assumed he would shortly begin the journey to Germany and one of the prison camps there. Surprised that he had not been searched by the Germans, he sat down on the board and began to think of the different ways he might be taken to Germany and how he might escape from each.

A short time later, a young German officer was admitted to the cell and greeted him in excellent English. "Where do you come from in the United States?" he asked. Fassoulis replied that he was from Syracuse, New York. "And when do you think the war will be over?" the German continued. "In about a year for you," Fassoulis answered. "I agree with you, but it has been wonderful," was the surprising reply. After confirming that the prison was in Modena and that Fassoulis had landed near the village of Rubiera, about ten miles northwest, the German departed and left Sonny wondering about the purpose of the conversation.

He did not have to wonder long. About an hour later he was escorted to the prison office and there was confronted by the commander, a short, heavyset man with thick glasses and a short haircut. Several medals were prominently displayed on his uniform. Using the lieutenant who had visited with Fassoulis as an interpreter, the commander asked Fassoulis where he was stationed, the number of men in his unit, what type of plane he had been flying, the size of the crew, the target they were attacking, and several other specific questions. To each, Fassoulis simply answered that he could not give that information. Apparently the commander soon tired of the one-way conversation, and Fassoulis was taken back to his cell. Sitting on the board once again, his thoughts turned from escape to the necessities of life: food and water. His parched tongue and gnawing stomach reminded him that he had received none of either necessity since morning. As night fell so did his spirits when it became obvious that he was not going to get anything to eat or drink. The lonely, frightened airman said a short prayer and then, with no blanket, curled up as best he could on the board.

It was very dark when Fassoulis was awakened by someone opening the door of his cell. Without uttering a word, someone pulled him roughly to his feet and led him down a winding stairway to a waiting car. He was shoved inside and the vehicle immediately moved off at a brisk pace. Soon the city was left behind. When the two guards in the back seat finally spoke to him, it was obvious that he was in the custody of Italians. They were well outside the city before the vehicle slowed and one of the occupants of the front seat offered him a drink of water. The car soon turned off onto a side road and stopped near a truck with a canvas-covered back. Fassoulis was led to the truck and loaded into the back, which was already occupied by several Italian soldiers. As they drove, one of the guards apparently wanted to know more about the United States, for he kept asking Fassoulis questions, but because neither spoke the other's language, he got few answers.

About an hour later, the truck entered the gates of a military complex. It soon stopped by a large building on top of which Fassoulis could see a lighted wind sock. It looked like he was going to be flown to Germany—a contingency he had not planned for and from which escape appeared nearly impossible. He was led to the second floor of the building and locked in an office. In the corner was a bed with sheets and blankets. The confused airman immediately flopped down on it and closed his eyes. A few minutes later, a young Italian entered the room and asked in broken English if Fassoulis would like something to eat. The emphatic "*Si*," the extent of Fassoulis's Italian at that time, apparently impressed the young man, for in about twenty minutes he returned with a large meal of cold cuts, cheese, pasta, bread, and coffee. Fassoulis thanked him, ate with relish, and went back to bed.

When Fassoulis awoke the following morning, he anticipated a breakfast in keeping with the meal of the preceding evening, but that was not to be. No one came to his room all morning. When he looked out the window and saw a number of training planes sitting on the ramp, he thought about trying to steal one and making a break for freedom, but the two guards posted outside his door ended that scheme. He also wondered why there was no transport plane in sight if he was going to be flown to Germany. About noon, Fassoulis was taken to another building and questioned by an Italian officer. When he refused to answer the

Italian's questions, he was finally searched and relieved of his watch and his escape kit, but he was allowed to keep his American armed forces identification card. The officer then told Fassoulis that he was going to be taken to a prison where he would be with other Americans. With that, he was led back to his room.

September 3, 1943, dragged by as Fassoulis sat on his bed and once again thought about escape possibilities. He also wondered if the remarks of the Italian officer indicated that he was going to be kept in Italy rather than being given back to the Germans. What neither he nor the Italians at the prison knew was that Italy had concluded an armistice with the Allies that day. Fassoulis's entire situation was soon to change.

Early in the evening a famished Fassoulis was again loaded into the canvas-covered back of an Italian army truck with several guards to begin the next leg of his journey. Nearly four hours later, they entered a city, and through a seam in the canvas, Sonny was able to read the word "Bologna." The truck stopped at the railroad station and Fassoulis was taken under guard to a small room, where he was finally fed. About midnight, he was put on a train with three Italian guards. As he made his way from the room to the rail car, he noticed the destruction to the tracks and the rail facility in general. "I guess the raid was a success," he said to himself when it became apparent that there was only one track in operation.

Late the next morning, the train stopped in another bombed-out marshaling yard, and Fassoulis was taken from the car. After a wait of several hours, he was placed in the back seat of a small automobile and began a long drive into the Italian hills. As the towns became smaller and farther apart, the apprehensive Sonny realized that his chances of escape might be better, but his ability to survive on his own would be less.

It was late evening when the car finally pulled into the small, walled front court of a convent that had been converted into a prisoner-of-war camp. Fassoulis later found out that it was the St. Valentino convent, located about a mile above the tiny town of Póggio Mirteto, about thirty miles northeast of Rome. He looked up at the three-story stucco structure and wondered how long it would be home to him. He was taken directly to the office of the camp commander, where the questioning procedure was repeated once again. When he refused to answer the questions, he was curtly dismissed and led to his second-floor cell, a five-by-ten-foot room with one large, barred window, which had apparently been the living quarters of one of the nuns. The only furnishing was a straw mattress on the floor. A small blue light burned in the ceiling.

St. Valentino Convent near Póggio Mirteto, Italy. Fassoulis's room was on the back side of the building.

St. Valentino Convent

After a meal of watery soup, Sonny lay down, and for the first time since he had landed in the vineyard, he was afraid. He didn't know where he was, there was no one to talk with, and he could not see any way he could ever escape from his cell. At least the prisoners in Germany were with other Americans in their compound. As he lay in the darkness, his thoughts turned once again to his letters and home. He wondered what news his mother would get about him. She had always encouraged his pursuit of a military career. When he had tried to get into West Point she'd supported him, and when that failed, she agreed to his enlisting in the army at Fort Belvoir, Virginia, in June 1941. She had been excited when he was accepted for aviation cadet training in the summer of 1942 and was always anxious to hear about his flying adventures. Now here he was, lying on a straw mattress in a small room in the hills of Italy, and no one probably had any idea where he was. It was hard to keep back the tears.

The world seemed a much brighter place to Sonny when he awoke on September 5. He looked out his window into a tree-covered, walled courtyard and saw several prisoners taking their thirty-minute morning walk. Most, he noted, were airmen; they were still wearing their flight suits or jackets. Beyond the wall he could see the beautiful green hills that surrounded the convent. Breakfast was only a piece of bread washed down with a cup of black coffee, and lunch was again watery soup with a little pasta floating about in it, but at least the sun was shining and he was not alone. He spent most of the day looking from his window, and his spirits soared when, about the middle of the afternoon, he saw John Caraberis being led across the courtyard. Amazingly, the captured pilot was put in the adjoining room. Both men realized they could not let the Italians know they were from the same crew since that might help with the questioning. The guards also prohibited any talking among the prisoners while they were in their cells. They did not forbid singing, however, and soon Caraberis and Fassoulis were singing songs in Greek, which both had learned as children, and passing all sorts of information to each other. For Sonny, this best day since bailing out was capped by the delivery of a Red Cross parcel late in the afternoon. It almost felt like Christmas as he saw the chocolate, butter, canned meat, milk, jam, sugar, sardines, oatmeal, cigarettes, hardtack, and soap. After augmenting the evening's watery soup with some of the precious rations, he found it much easier to sleep.

The routine at the prison varied little during the following three days. However, on the evening of September 9, there was a different mood in the air. First, the sound of the church bells ringing down in

Póggio Mirteto wafted up to the hills. This was soon accompanied by the guards' yelling that Italy had declared an armistice with the Allies. Since none of the prisoners understood Italian very well, they could not believe what they thought they were hearing. Still, they stayed awake most of the night waiting for some official news and wondering what it meant for them. Early the following morning, it was obvious that something had indeed happened. The inmates awoke to find practically no guards around, and when several prisoners broke open the doors of their rooms, there was no Italian opposition. As the inmates gathered in the courtyard, the commandant appeared and announced that there was indeed an armistice, and that the Allies had landed at Salerno the previous day. "Since we are no longer at war with the United States and Great Britain," he told the prisoners, "the situation is entirely different. However, this territory is occupied by the Germans, they know of this prison, and they will be coming to take you somewhere else. It is important that you leave and go into the mountains as soon as possible." Surprisingly, the camp commandant concluded his remarks by offering to find his former prisoners a guide and supply them with provisions for their trek into the mountains. With that he departed. It was clear that he was trying to be on the good side of the Americans and British since he was now their ally, so the former prisoners were confident he would help them.

The unexpected armistice had actually been signed on September 3, but the news and implications of the action were very slow in being transmitted to such out-of-the-way places as the small prison in which Fassoulis and Caraberis were housed. The prisoners were also unaware that the agreement with the Allies threw Italy into two battles: one with the Germans on the one hand; and another between the fascists and the Italians who wanted to end the war on the other. The Germans were quick to pour reinforcements into Italy and secure the portion of the country north of Rome. Benito Mussolini, the leader of the Italian Fascist Party, fled from Rome to Milan and from there continued as a puppet of the Germans. The Italians in the south were generally pro-American and pro-British, but there was also a significant Communist element—and a large number of fascists who still supported Mussolini. The Allies landed at Salerno, south of Naples, and at Reggio di Calabria, across the Strait of Messina from Sicily, on September 9, and with the support of the Italians, were expected to move rapidly the length of Italy. The German resistance was much greater than expected, however, and it was not until June 4, 1944, nine bloody months after the initial invasion, that Rome was liberated.

The inmates busied themselves with gathering all the food and survival equipment, Red Cross packages, guns, ammunition, and explosives they could carry on their backs and on the two donkeys found at the prison. By early afternoon they were ready to travel but still had no guide. No sooner had they begun to discuss how to find their way by themselves than the commandant returned accompanied by a brute of a man whom he introduced as Nazarene Franchescino. The group was taken aback by their new helper. Nazarene was at least six feet, six inches tall and built like a brick. He wore a big smile that exposed teeth that looked like parallel clamps. As he was introduced to each of his charges, he twitched his mouth and his handlebar mustache waved back and forth. Although he could speak no English, everyone liked him and a bond of trust instantly developed between him and the group.

It was obvious that Nazarene was in a hurry to get out of the convent and back into the mountains from which he had come. Although the commandant urged the prisoners to leave, they decided that it would be better if they waited until night so the inhabitants of the small nearby towns would not see them going and be able to report their route to the Germans. Since all the Italian guards, as well as the commandant, had departed, the group posted lookouts and busied themselves preparing their evening meal. There were plenty of supplies in the convent kitchen, and the former inmates were soon sitting down to a dinner of spaghetti, day-old bread, and slices of ham. Most then went to bed in the guards' former rooms to get what rest they could before night.

It was nearly midnight on September 10, 1943, when Sonny Fassoulis's evasion experience and that of his twenty comrades began. The heavily loaded men turned right out of the convent gate and began walking up the narrow, rocky road. It was reasonably level for the first half mile and the trek seemed easy, but very soon the road narrowed into a path. The climb became slower, and after an hour the evaders began to tire and the supplies on their backs seemed to double in weight. Nazarene continued his brisk pace, however, and soon his followers were literally falling by the wayside. Fortunately for Fassoulis and Caraberis, they were still in good condition, since they had been prisoners for only a week, but several, whose only exercise for the past several months had been a half-hour walk in the convent courtyard twice a day, were not up to the task. As rest stops became more frequent, Nazarene became more impatient. The situation got more complicated when the big Italian turned off the path on which they had been hiking and began climbing a narrow trail up the steep hills. The Apennine Mountains, which run the length of central Italy, are characterized by their steep, rugged, rocky surfaces, vegetation that ranges from nearly barren to dense forest within a few miles, and valleys that are often several thousand feet deep, the result of millennia of erosion by the rivers that flow in their floors. It is possible to hike up and down for days and cover only a few miles as the crow flies. It was into this hostile terrain that Nazarene led his exhausted charges. The darkness, the exhaustion of many of the climbers, and the increasingly steep climb soon made it impossible to continue.

Nazarene Franchescino during World War II.   *S. G. Fassoulis*

By using a few English words and a lot of sign language, Nazarene finally made it known that those who could continue on should do so and that the others could stop and find any shelter that was available for the night. He would return for them in the morning.

When those who were able to continue on finally reached the camp, about five miles from the convent, they too were exhausted, for the trek had taken nearly five hours. There was nothing to do but feel around among the trees, find a comparatively soft spot, and roll up in a blanket on the ground. It seemed that Fassoulis had just fallen asleep when the sun beamed into his face and he awoke with a start. It took him a few moments to realize where he was, but he was soon up and exploring the area. It was a very isolated spot, and he marveled at Nazarene's ability to find the area in the dark. Since most of the supplies had been left with the portion of the group farther down the mountain, breakfast was blackberries, watercress, and a rabbit that Nazarene had snared. The big Italian then departed to go down the mountain and get the rest of the group.

It was not until early afternoon that the remainder of the evaders struggled into the camp, having spent a miserable night in the open. Most had slept little because of their concern that the Germans might be following them, and all had been relieved when Nazarene arrived and they could continue their hike up the mountains. Actually, it would have been nearly impossible for the Germans to have tracked the group without a local guide in the densely forested hills around Póggio Mirteto and its companion town, Roccantica. Apparently the Germans couldn't find one in the hostile little village.

For the next few days, the airmen did little but sit around in the sun, take turns guarding the approaches to the area, and generally enjoy their freedom. Since Fassoulis and Caraberis were in the same group, they were able to talk about their experiences since bailing out and speculate on the fate of the rest of the crew. When Caraberis had finally bailed out of the crippled bomber, he had been only a few miles south of Switzerland. He had landed near the town of Domodossola, northwest of Milan. Captured almost immediately after he landed, he had endured an experience similar to that of Fassoulis. He too, had been spirited away in the night by the Italians and had gone by train and automobile to the area of the convent turned prison camp. He didn't know what happened to the other members of the crew. (All of the other crew members of Caraberis's aircraft were taken prisoner by the Germans as well, but they were sent to Germany and spent the remainder of the war in prison camps there. Neither Fassoulis nor Caraberis ever knew why the Italians took them from the German prison camp.)

All had been quiet for over a week, and apparently the Germans were not going to be a problem, but food was beginning to become scarce and water was a concern. Nazarene also believed that their hiding place had become known and so he suggested they move to a new location farther up the mountain. This was not welcome news to anyone since they were used to their present surroundings, several had built crude shelters in which to sleep, and the area seemed very difficult to find. They were also concerned because September was about gone and it was getting noticeably colder at night. Being farther up the mountain would only exacerbate the situation. Nonetheless, Nazarene insisted.

Early the following morning, Nazarene appeared in the camp with two friends, Primo Poulino and Gildo DeSantis. It was hard for the evaders to keep a straight face when they saw the less-than-five-foot Primo walking with the huge Nazarene. Primo also had a dog that went everywhere with him. Gildo was about five-feet-six, very well built, and fairly well dressed, which indicated to the group that he was not a mountain man. Each man carried a pistol—despite the German decree that any Italian carrying a gun would be shot. The group soon learned that Primo had a passion for guns and often carried several. With the aid of the three Italians, the difficult and taxing climb was completed by late afternoon. Although the new location was ideal in that it commanded a view of every trail coming up the mountain, the site was extremely rugged and there was no water available. Nazarene told them that it was over two miles to the nearest water source but that he would see that they had water. That meant carrying it up the mountain every day. That evening, as the group discussed their situation and what course of action they should take, all marveled at the willingness of Nazarene and his two friends to not only put their lives on the line to help the Allied airmen but also to make the trip for water each day. Sometimes Nazarene's fourteen-year-old son, Fernando, also helped with the supplies. If anything happened to the three Italians, however, the airmen would be unable to survive in their location.

This situation also brought the first argument about what to do next. Several evaders were confident that the Allies would soon take the area and that the wisest thing to do was to sit tight, survive, and wait for them. Others, Fassoulis and Caraberis included, thought they should start planning how to get farther south and try to cross the lines to the American side. They finally decided to wait a few more days before making any decisions since they really didn't know what the Allied situation was. Nazarene also told them getting food was becoming a more serious problem. As October progressed, there were few crops still in the fields, and the local people had to be able to feed themselves through-out the long winter. In addition, the Germans had become much more active in the area, often visiting Póggio Mirteto, only five miles away from the evasion site. The German army was spread the length and breadth of Europe, and with the war's tide turning against them, there was simply not enough food or transportation available to adequately supply their force in Italy. Thus, the Germans were putting pressure on the local populace for food. Finally, Nazarene decided he would go to town and get some civilian clothes for several of the evaders so they could accompany him and make a personal appeal for food, thinking this might make it easier to get.

During the next two weeks, several members of the camp made the trip to Póggio Mirteto for food or water. They always went at night so they would not be seen, but still, the first venture for each was not soon forgotten. Fassoulis's turn came about five days after his pilot had made the first trip. As he followed Primo down the rugged trail, he was re-minded of just how far into the hills they had really gone. He also had some second thoughts about the pack of food and the five-gallon can of water he was to carry back. Fassoulis had been in the hills for so long that he had almost forgotten the sounds of a town, even at night. But when the first dog barked, every nerve in his body was on edge. As they made their way as quietly as possible down the deserted streets toward Primo's home, where the food was hidden, they heard German voices and the click of boots on the pavement. Sonny was absolutely petrified. In a flash, Primo was lying flat in the gutter next to the street. Fassoulis followed suit and tried to make his six-foot, one-hundred-fifty-pound frame as small as possible. He dared not even breathe as the Germans approached. Fortunately, it was a dark night and the Germans walked on past, enjoying conversation among themselves, unaware of the men flat-tened in the gutter not more than three feet away. The food pickup was done quickly, and the two started the long and torturous journey back up the mountain. "I don't know how you can make this climb every day," Fassoulis said to Primo in his beginning Italian. "It is for a good pur-pose," was the only reply. Just as it was beginning to get light, the two men arrived back at the camp. Primo dumped his load and immediately turned around to make the trek back to his home while the exhausted Fassoulis fell asleep on the ground.

As more of the evaders made the trip down to Póggio Mirteto, they came to realize how difficult the food situation really was. They could only imagine how it would be if they were still in the mountains when it began to snow, for then the trip could often be impossible. The decision of what to do was made for them near the end of October when they heard gunfire down the mountain. Late that night Nazarene and Primo came into the camp announcing that the Germans had come to the foot of the mountain, intent upon climbing to search for the evaders' camp. They had evidently been told about the old camp, Primo said, and also knew the general area where the present camp was located. It would be impossible to bring supplies up, except by a very circuitous route, because the Germans were looking for anyone who was helping the evaders. The threat was that if the Italians were caught, they would be shot.

Late the next afternoon the group was galvanized into action when they heard rifle and machine gun fire very close to their location. They grabbed what they could and went as deep into the trees and bushes as possible. For the next two hours they lay among the branches, scarcely daring to breathe. Finally they heard Nazarene give an owl call and they all went out to meet him. He was accompanied by his son, Fernando. For the first time since they had known him, he had no grin on his face. The Germans had entered his home and taken him and his family prisoner. They had machine-gunned everything in his house and carried away all the food they could find. He and his son had escaped in a hail of bullets. The gunfire the group had heard was a battle between some partisans and a group of Germans who were searching for the evaders. "The Germans are just wandering around the hills firing into the bushes, but they know you're up here," Nazarene told them. It was time to leave.

Again, a debate ensued as to what to do. Finally they decided to break up into small groups that would go their own way. Those who wanted to remain in the mountains and wait for the Allies departed to find another hiding place in the area, while the remainder finalized their plans to go south and try to get through the lines. Caraberis, Fassoulis, and another B-17 crewman named DeLouche decided they would try to find a better hiding place in the area until they could get some maps and make a workable plan for getting to the Allied side of the lines. So, with good-byes, agreements to meet in New York after the war, and expressions of good luck, the men split up and went their separate ways into the wind and rain of late October.

Earlier in their stay, Fassoulis and Caraberis had heard of an ancient grotto about ten miles to the northeast of Póggio Mirteto, quite near the old mountain town of Roccantica, and they decided to search it out as a temporary hiding place. But before they even began their trek, following sketchy directions that Primo had given them, they were soaked to the skin and absolutely miserable.

It took all day and most of the night to find the ancient cave. It was very dark when the trio stumbled onto the entrance, so they couldn't see the interior at all. It felt so good to get out of the rain that they just lay down on the dirt floor and fell asleep. The next morning they gathered some dry sticks from under the brush and built a fire. With everything hung up to dry and the grotto getting warm, they were able to look at the old sanctuary. Primo had told them it was very old, and the religious Fassoulis was filled with awe as they looked at the small altar and the stone walls that were covered with paintings that must have been there for centuries. Although most were badly faded, some color and images could still be seen. The cave had recently been used since there were photographs of Italians in uniform on the altar. The grotto had been dug into a stone cliff and could not be seen from the trails. "Maybe the ancient builders were hiding just like we are," Fassoulis remarked to Caraberis.

Although there was a spring nearby, food was an almost insurmountable problem for the trio. They were literally down to their last piece of hardtack when they heard a rustle in the bushes near the entrance to the grotto. Immediately, they retreated as far back into the cave as possible and waited. In a moment a familiar figure stood in the doorway. It was Gildo, who they had known at the previous hideout. "I wanted to be sure you were here," he said. "I will return tonight with food and some civilian clothes for you." "When you get the civilian clothes," Caraberis had warned the others earlier, "be sure to keep your uniform and identification card, because when we try to cross the lines, we'll be shot if we're captured in civilian clothes carrying weapons and can't prove who we are."

Life in the grotto settled down to the daily trip to the spring for water, taking turns acting as the lookout, and accompanying Gildo to nearby farms and villages to find food. All three members of the group were now able to speak quite a bit of Italian and were confident they could fool the Germans. The only thing they feared was being stopped and asked for some type of Italian identification, which they did not have. Gildo was also able to get a fairly good map of the area so the trio could decide on a route to the south and where they should try to cross the lines. Visitors to the grotto also included Primo and Nazarene and his son, who were also hiding in the mountains. Nazarene said that his family had been taken to Rome and he had no idea what had happened to them. Each brought some food as well as news of German activity in the area. On one trip, Primo reported that all of the group's former hiding places had been discovered by the Germans and it would only be a matter of time until the cave was found as well.

Reluctantly, in the snow of mid-November, the trio once again began to trek. Leading them was a new Italian partisan, Gervasio Leti, the son of a wealthy Italian farmer who owned a number of coal mines in the area of Roccantica. Leti was good-natured with a ready smile, about five-feet-eight, and like all the other Italians who had helped the evaders, built like an ox. He, too, sported a mustache, but unlike Nazarene's, it was neatly trimmed. Leti had brought a mule loaded with supplies his father had obtained, since they were going to a cabin high up on Mount Pizzuto, well above the grotto and a long day's hike from Póggio Mirteto. The journey was a miserable one for Fassoulis. It was snowing, he was cold and soaked through, and his shoes had holes in the soles that put his feet directly on the freezing ground.

The small band had hiked all day and well into the evening when Leti confessed that he did not know just where they were going. They were supposed to meet a workman at an intersection in the trail, and he would guide them to their destination. "I think this is the end," a discouraged Caraberis said to Fassoulis. "There are hundreds of square miles on this mountain, so how can we have any hope of meeting one man? We'll be lucky if we don't freeze to death." Fassoulis's feet had lost all feeling long before and he certainly had no reason to disagree. Still, the miserable airmen continued to find the strength to put one foot in front of the other on their seemingly endless climb.

It was dark when Fassoulis heard the sound of an owl hooting. It immediately got his attention since it was similar to the sound that Nazarene used to identify himself. Leti answered it, although his noise didn't sound like an owl at all, and within a few minutes, the hikers were greeted by a short, dark man dressed in a big fur coat. Rather than take a rest, the four did their best to follow his brisk pace. In less than ten minutes, they came upon a cabin that was so well hidden it could not be seen from any direction. There was no furniture inside except for two huge wooden beds with small branches as cross pieces, covered with hay; there was one bed at each end of the one rustic room. And even though there was no fire, the shelter seemed like a luxury hotel to the exhausted hikers. They soon had devoured bread, cheese, and a few small pieces of meat from their precious supply and, stripped of their wet clothes, burrowed into the warm hay for the night.

Morning dawned crisp and clear. Leti built a fire of charcoal, and by noon their clothes were fairly dry. Fassoulis ventured outside to get a better look at their location. The cabin itself had mud sides and a tar paper-covered wooden roof. An hour's climb to the top of the mountain revealed an absolutely spectacular view. In the far distance Sonny could see Rome and, if he used a little imagination, the ocean. And on the horizon in every direction were the small towns and cities that populated the hills. He climbed to the top of the mountain each of the nine days the group was in the cabin, just for the view. While he was climbing on the fourth day, he heard the rumble of aircraft engines in the distance. No sooner had he arrived at his lookout point than he saw a formation of B-17 bombers. As he watched, they passed directly over his head, and his heart was in his throat as he yearned to be up there with them. It wasn't until after they had gone that he realized he had been holding his breath.

On Thanksgiving morning 1943, one of the Italian partisans arrived with the news that the group was to leave the cabin and go to the Letis' house in Roccantica, about five miles to the west. Apparently the Letis had heard of Thanksgiving from relatives in the United States and wanted to make the evaders feel as much at home as possible. The group set out in order to arrive at the outskirts of Roccantica about dark. A welcome bath followed at the Letis', although the group had to share the heated water since fuel was scarce. After shaving to look like Italians, the airmen were treated to a feast Fassoulis would never forget.

Obviously the Letis were quite wealthy, for their cook prepared a meal that began with hors d'oeuvres, then minestrone, gnochi, spaghetti, fish, pork chops, chicken, and lamb. Each course was washed down with glasses of local wine, and the evening ended with toasts to everything imaginable. Needless to say, the evaders were in no condition to go any-where, and since they had no desire to return to the cold of the moun-tains, they stayed at the Letis' for three days despite the presence of a German garrison in the town. Mr. Leti assured them that they looked so much like Italians that the Germans would never know. Still, since the Leti house fronted on the main road and was directly adjacent to the town square, the fugitives stayed inside the house during the daylight, playing cards and working hard on their Italian. Early in their evasion, several of the Americans and British, including Fassoulis and Caraberis, had determined that their chances of successfully evading and eventu-ally getting through the lines would be greater if they were relatively fluent in Italian. Although they had no hope of being able to learn the language well enough to convince an Italian, it was not very difficult to fool a German. Planning the trek to the south and through the lines also occupied a great deal of their time.

Early in the evening of November 28, 1943, the group departed the Letis' home to return to the cabin in the mountains. This was the first step in finally starting south. Mr. Leti had given them as many supplies as they could carry, so the trek was slow. When they got to the foot of the trail that would take them to the cabin, Gervasio Leti left the group. He had been informed somehow that there were two British servicemen at a point about twelve miles north of Póggio Mirteto who were also trying to get through the lines and who would like to make the try with Fassoulis, Caraberis, and DeLouche.

The next day was spent dividing the supplies into quantities that each could carry and making packs out of parachute material that the Italians supplied. Each of the three evaders was too excited about finally beginning their trip to freedom to be able to fall asleep easily, and the trio talked well into the night, until fatigue finally won out. The next thing they knew, Gervasio Leti was walking through the door, and out of a snowstorm, with Charles Nicholas, a bomber crewman, and William Morris, an engineer on a submarine that had been sunk. Their new British comrades said they knew of two South African airmen who would also want to come along, so the departure was delayed for a few more hours while the Englishmen went to find their friends.

Finally the group of seven was assembled, along with two guides, Giovanni Bargelini, the man who had brought them food when they were at their first hiding place after leaving the convent, and Pucho Conforzi, who was the son of a wealthy Italian who owned several tea plantations in South Africa but had lost most of his fortune when the fascists came to power in Italy. Pucho truly hated the Germans and, along with his father, was ready to do anything to help the Allied cause. Although Nazarene had not trusted him, Giovanni had proved to be a friend, and he now led the way as the seven evaders began to climb to the top of Mount Pizzuto. Spirits were high, but it soon became evident that neither the Englishmen nor the South Africans were in anywhere near the physical condition of the three Americans, and they began to drop behind. "I'm not sure it was such a good idea to bring those guys along," Fassoulis confided to Caraberis as they hiked. "We're only going five miles today and they're already having trouble. What will they do when we really have to make time?"

The mountain was not the only obstacle to be dealt with. The Germans, too, were scouring the area for food. Each time the group would come to a main road, Giovanni would have them hide in the bushes while he and Pucho went to find out where the Germans were. This way there were no close calls, and the evaders arrived at a farm owned by one of Bargelini's friends at about dusk.

The farmer must have been expecting them, for his wife had prepared a large meal of pasta and tomato sauce, with bread and cheese, which the famished hikers soon devoured. Although the three Americans were tired from their day's trek, their host kept asking them questions about the United States far into the night. This situation was repeated at nearly every stop. It seemed that every Italian they met either had relatives in the United States, had been there themselves, or had false and often fantastic ideas about the country that they wanted to have verified.

Everyone was up before dawn the next day to begin the long hike to the small mountain town of Orvínio. The route was particularly dangerous because they would have to cross the main road connecting Rome and Rieti, which, as the only hard-surfaced road through the mountains in that area, carried a large amount of German military traffic. As with most roads through the hills, there were few straight stretches, so the evaders could easily be surprised by vehicles rounding a corner. When they reached the road, Giovanni once again had the seven fugitives hide in the brush. This time he stopped two women who were walking with baskets on their heads. After determining they were not fascists, he convinced the women to carry the evaders' packs across the road under the blankets they were wearing as coats. This way, if they met Germans, they would not be suspicious. The evaders then crossed in pairs. Fassoulis, Pucho, and Giovanni were the last to cross.

Just as they reached the middle of the road, a German army truck coasted slowly around the corner and rolled to a stop less than ten feet from the trio. The occupants got out and opened the hood. Sonny was petrified! He knew his Italian was not good enough to get him through the situation if one of the Germans happened to speak the language, and he had no Italian identification. If he was searched, the Germans would find his American identification card. Fassoulis just stood there, scarcely able to breathe. "Turn around and go back where you came from, and don't run, just walk slowly," the also frightened Giovanni told him in hushed tones. "Act like you have forgotten something." It took a superhuman effort for Fassoulis to make the seemingly endless walk back across the road without breaking into a run. Finally he was out of sight in the trees and bushes. Once there, he hid and watched and waited.

Giovanni and Pucho walked up to the Germans and asked if they could be of help. Evidently they were useful, for in a few minutes, the truck's engine roared to life and the Germans drove on down the road. "That is about as scared as I've ever been in my life," Fassoulis told Caraberis when he was safely on the other side of the road. "I thought my trip through the lines was over before it got started." The remainder of the trip to Orvínio was uneventful, and after another delicious meal, the group was put in a large hayloft for the night.

Their next destination was the town of Collegiove, about eight miles to the east. The journey would require crossing yet another major road and some very rugged terrain. To make matters worse, the evaders needed to cross a bridge over a large river. Fortunately, there was much less traffic on that road, so it was possible to pair up and walk down the road and across the bridge carrying their own packs. Fassoulis was concerned when his turn came to make the two-hundred-yard trek since he knew that any observant German would stop a man carrying a large pack. Each time he heard a vehicle approaching, he held his breath, but all of them simply passed by, the drivers evidently intent on navigating the snowy road rather than paying attention to Italians carrying packs. After a hike of fifteen hours, the group reached Collegiove early in the evening. To Fassoulis, the scene was out of an Old World storybook. As they walked down the narrow stone streets of the ancient mountain village, the air was filled with the mouthwatering aroma of roasted chestnuts, which, the group found, tasted as good as they smelled. Giovanni said that the Germans seldom visited the town, and there were few fascists there, so the evaders received a boisterous welcome.

Still another surprise awaited the evaders. One of their former prison mates, Dave Parlett, who had gone with a different group when they had separated in the mountains near Póggio Mirteto, came running from one of the houses to greet them. He had been left behind, they learned, because of severe blisters on his feet. These were now healed and he was anxious to make his try to get through the lines. He reported that the group he had been with had not been heard from but the rumor was that they had been recaptured.

Mile after mile and town after town, the little group continued its trek to the south, sleeping in barns, eating with friendly families or going hungry, and each day having some sort of dramatic brush with the Germans. The evaders' objective was the tiny town of Vallepietra, which clung to the sides of steep, rugged hills near the bottom of a small, beautiful valley nearly sixty rugged miles south of Póggio Mirteto and about forty miles east of Rome. There they were to rest, get resupplied, and when the time was right, make their move to cross the lines in the area of Monte Cassino Abbey, another fifty miles to the south.

They were almost stopped well short of Vallepietra early in December. In order to continue south, it was necessary for the ten to cross the main highway from Rome to Pescara. Because of the British offensive to the south, the road was the most heavily traveled in Italy, with almost continuous German military traffic. In addition, neither Giovanni nor Pucho was as familiar with the area as he had been near their homes in

Póggio Mirteto. As they looked down on the road from a mountain nearby, it appeared that the trip to the south would soon end in failure. The continued overcast skies had kept any Allied fighters and bombers from attacking the highway, so it was saturated with vehicles and men. In order to get to the mountains on the other side of the road and continue their trip to Vallepietra, the hikers first had to cross a railroad that paralleled a river in the valley and that was policed by German guards for its entire length. They then had to get to a bridge, cross the river, and finally walk along the heavily used highway for nearly three hundred yards before there was a place to get off on the other side.

"Boy, oh boy, if we make this I'll believe in Santa Claus," Fassoulis remarked.

"I think there is a tunnel for the railroad going through the mountain right next to the river," Giovanni told the group. "We'll go down the mountain and over the tunnel so we won't have to cross the tracks."

"But the guards may see us on the hill above the tunnel," Caraberis muttered.

"If God will only blind the guards, we may make it," Fassoulis whispered to Caraberis.

No sooner had he uttered the words than Parlett whispered, "Do you see what I see? God has answered your prayer. Look, fog is settling in."

Sure enough, in the nick of time the visibility became so poor that the guards on the railroad never knew of the evaders' presence as they moved silently across the shallow, barren hill above the tunnel and down the side toward the river.

The challenge was not yet over, for the bridge still had to be crossed. Dividing into pairs as they had done many times before, they went across in the heaven-sent fog, one pair at a time, until all were across the bridge. Unfortunately, the fog was much less dense as they approached the road. "It would be best to wait until early morning to cross the road," Pucho said. "The traffic should be lighter then." They spent the night burrowed into hay in the stalls of a nearby farm.

Early the following morning, the evaders approached the road in their usual pairs. Every time there were no vehicles in sight, a pair would cross to the bushes and trees on the other side. The process was repeated without incident until Fassoulis and Pucho started across. They were in the middle of the road when they noticed a German truck a short distance away. Once again, Sonny could feel the sweat break out on his neck as they continued across the road. "Why does this always have to happen to me?" he asked Pucho. "Maybe I should try crossing with someone else." However, the Germans paid no attention to the pair.

Because of its isolation, over ten miles from the nearest village by a tortuous narrow road that was often carved out of the side of the sheer cliff of the mountain, the town of Vallepietra was an ideal place for the group to rest. The area was often visited by German soldiers in search of crops and livestock they could confiscate, so the population was friendly and willing to help the evaders. There were also a number of grottos, caves, and shepherds' huts in the neighboring hills where they could hide. Giovanni had earlier taken another small group of evaders as far as the town and instructed them to remain in the hills in the area until he brought the Fassoulis group in. Unfortunately, when Fassoulis arrived, there was no trace of the previous evaders and no one seemed to know what had happened to them. Giovanni decided they had gotten tired of waiting and, when their supplies got low, decided to try to make it through the lines without a guide. Fassoulis later learned that their situation had become so desperate that they had to take extraordinary risks to get food. As a result, they had been captured and sent to Germany to a prison camp.

Fortunately for his present charges, Giovanni had made an arrangement for them to use a one-room cabin about two miles from the town. It belonged to a wealthy family and was frequented periodically by a caretaker who had lived in Boston. He not only brought the fugitives supplies but would spend hours talking to them about the United States. He also carried the unwelcome news that the Allies had made little progress and that people were giving up hope for an early liberation from the Germans. Among other things, he let the evaders know that any food he was able to get for them had to be purchased and that he was about out of money. At that juncture, Giovanni offered to go back to Roccantica to get more money from his father. In the meantime, the group would simply get supplies wherever they could. When Giovanni arrived in Roccantica, he learned that both his and Pucho's fathers had been taken into custody by the Germans on suspicion of helping the American evaders. Although they were later released, most of the rest of their property was confiscated, so they were unable to finance the evaders further.

With Giovanni gone and supplies short, Fassoulis and Caraberis decided they would leave the rest and try to make it through the lines on their own. Fortunately, Pucho volunteered to help them go as far as possible, but said he would have to abandon the fliers when they neared the actual lines because he wanted to be able to return to his family, which would be impossible if he was across the lines. Although they decided to take no money or equipment with them, Fassoulis and Caraberis did need some better clothes. A day later, Pucho miraculously showed up with newer outfits for both, including such luxuries as overcoats, a pair of field glasses, and a bottle of cognac "in case things get too hopeless." He also suggested that they go to the home of the butcher, Signor Graziosi, that evening so they would have a better rest and a good breakfast before they started out. The Graziosi house, a two-story stucco structure that had the store on the street level and the living quarters upstairs, had become a familiar place to Sonny and Pucho during their stay near Vallepietra. The second-story window looked directly across to the ancient town fountain and clock tower, so it was an easy place from which to keep track of anyone coming into town. Signor Graziosi had two very attractive daughters, and any excuse to walk to town would generally result in a good meal and some friendly conversation.

Once again, they spent a nearly sleepless night. Sonny tossed and turned on his narrow cot, thinking of his family and wondering what they thought had happened to him. It was his worst case of homesickness yet. In an effort to counteract it, he prayed for hours that God would grant them success and that he would be able, once again, to be with his family. Fassoulis's family had no idea of his real fate. On September 22, three weeks after he bailed out, they had received what was always a dreaded telegram for those who had loved ones in combat: "I regret to inform you that the Commanding General North African Area reports your son Second Lieutenant Satiris G. Fassoulis missing in action since 2 September. If further details or other information of his status are received you will be promptly notified." It was common knowledge that most of the men in this category had actually been killed, but Fassoulis's mother refused to believe this. She knew in her heart the entire time that her son was still alive.

The butcher's house in Vallepietra was a beehive of activity at three-thirty the next morning as the trio prepared to depart. From her meager resources, Signora Graziosi cooked a delicious breakfast of eggs and meat rolled inside bread. With warm good-byes, especially from the daughters, and heartfelt thank-yous, the next phase of the adventure began. As the gray light of dawn began to permeate an overcast sky, the trio was tramping through the mountains on one of the countless small trails.

"If we did not have Pucho as a guide, we would already be lost," Caraberis observed.

"That's for sure," replied Fassoulis, "since this compass doesn't want to indicate north, no matter what I do."

Remarkably, Pucho seemed to know exactly where they were, and they continued on through the day at a good pace—with far too few rest

Photo by the author

Sonny Fassoulis in front of the former Graziosi home in Vallepietra, Italy, in 1996.

stops to suit the Americans. On top of that, it was getting bitterly cold, especially for the hikers' feet.

As the sky began to darken, Pucho pointed to a valley ahead and told them the village they could see well below them was Capistrello, about fifteen miles east of Vallepietra. Capistrello was the home of a garrison of nearly five thousand German soldiers. The trio would have to sleep in the open. Fassoulis knew that he would surely freeze to death. Pucho finally agreed that they would go down the mountain in the twilight, far enough that it might be warmer, and maybe find shelter. About halfway down the mountain, they came to an area that was sheltered by a grove of trees and had much less snow on the ground. The trio ate most of the bread the butcher had given them and drank the bottle of cognac, which, combined with exhaustion from the nearly ten miles of mountain hiking, produced a fitful sleep.

It was light when the trio awoke, but the hills were blanketed in a thick fog. Fassoulis felt chilled to the bone and was sure he would never get warm again. They were soon on their way. It did not take long to realize they were making almost no progress in the deep snow. They decided to go down the mountain toward the Liri River, where the hiking would be easier—but much more dangerous because of the large number of Germans about. As they descended, it got a little warmer and the fog began to lift. They had just entered a forest when Pucho grabbed the other two, hissed "Sh-hhh!" and motioned them to crouch in the snow. The trio forgot the cold as they listened to the sounds of boots in the snow, and Fassoulis almost stopped breathing. Less than a hundred feet away was a column of at least fifty German soldiers climbing the mountain. Long after the Germans passed, the evaders remained motionless and silent for fear that another platoon might be following the first. Finally, Pucho motioned for them to move, and the trek down the mountain continued.

Although they encountered no more Germans during the day, it began to rain about noon, and by dusk the trio was soaked. "You make a shelter from some branches and I'll go into the town and try to find food and a place we can stay," Pucho told the Americans. The shivering fliers huddled together under a few branches and waited for what seemed like hours for him to return.

"Well, I got us a place," he announced when he finally arrived. "An old woman, living with her only son, will take us after dark, give us some food, and let us dry our clothes by the fire. Her son knows of a hayloft where we can sleep." Fassoulis could not refrain from asking Pucho how he worked this kind of miracle all the time. "I just say I'm a refugee, and find out what the people's feelings are towards the Germans. If they are favorable to our cause, I ask them for help. The people in this town are wary because about a month ago a British airman was caught here and the Germans took twenty-four hostages from the town. They warned the townspeople that if another Allied man was found in the village, they would take away every man, including the village priest."

After getting their soaked clothes partially dry in front of the woman's small fire, the trio were taken to a hayloft, where they settled in for the night.

Their objective the next day was the small hill town of Morino, which was sited on a river about twelve miles to the south. If they could successfully cross the river near that town and continue their trek, Pucho figured they could be through the lines in about five days. As the trio progressed toward the front, they found there were so many Germans that it was impossible to stay clear of them. Pucho suggested they simply act like three Italian peasants and see what happened. During the day they passed several small groups of soldiers. Each time they drew near the Germans, Pucho would begin talking excitedly in Italian to Fassoulis and Caraberis. Although the Americans were shaking with fright, they would answer with an excited *"Si, si."* To everyone's relief, the Germans paid no attention to the three men.

By late afternoon, they neared Morino, and Pucho once again left the two Americans hidden in the trees. This time their Italian guide returned with bad news: there were practically no civilians left in the town and it was crawling with Germans. There was no way to get any food or shelter. But even more discouraging was his analysis of their situation. "The only way we have of crossing the river is either to go over the heavily guarded bridge, which requires identification papers, or swim across. If we swim the guards on the railroad will surely see us, and the river is so swift and cold I don't know if we could make it anyway. Once we get to the other side, we will have four days in the mountains without food, since the Germans have taken everything. With miraculous luck, we may be through the lines by that time."

"In the shape we're in we'll never make it," replied Caraberis. Fassoulis agreed. There was no alternative but to turn back toward Vallepietra.

The decision to turn back was heartbreaking to Sonny. He had waited so long for this journey and had laid awake so many nights planning and hoping that he found he had tears in his eyes as the three turned to the northwest. The trek that followed was the most difficult the downhearted Sonny had yet endured. As they hiked, the mountains got steeper and the snow began to fall. Soon they were walking in a blizzard. There was no shelter, no food, and the trio was getting water by eating snow. To make matters worse, they were not sure where they were. With no place to stop, they continued to hike through the long night of December 21, 1943. Occasionally, one of the group would break through the crust of the snow and sink chest deep. The other two would have to use their precious energy to pull their companion out. Caraberis had developed terrible blisters on his feet, but they were so near freezing that he did not feel the blood in his socks. It seemed that the nightmare would never end.

It was a sorry group of evaders that crowded into the warm kitchen of a sympathetic lady in the town of Cappadocia the next day. There was delicious bread, and the pasta cooking on the stove made their mouths water. They looked forward to having a good meal and being able to sleep for twelve hours in the hay. After such a respite, they would be ready to hike the rest of the way to Vallepietra.

Suddenly a man rushed into the kitchen crying, "Quickly, go. The Germans are making a house-to-house search for food and there is no place to hide you." Throwing some loaves of bread into a sack, the trio struggled into their soaked shoes and coats and once again found themselves out in the snow, walking as fast as they could out of the town. Their wonderful meal and long sleep had turned into a twenty-minute rest and a panicked departure back into the nightmare of survival.

Time ceased to exist as the three followed the maze of paths that led through the mountains to Vallepietra. Again, they walked all night, and it was afternoon the next day when Pucho led them up a familiar trail to the cabin from which they had departed five days before. Pucho banged on the door, but there was no answer. The door was locked and the cabin was deserted. It took the trio less than a minute to break into the shack, and they soon had a fire started. After eating the bread that remained from their rest stop in Cappadocia, they curled up on the mattresses and slept until nearly noon.

The trio awoke on December 24 in the freezing cabin, without food and with one of Caraberis's legs swollen and red. The days of walking with open blisters had taken their toll. Pucho knew the doctor in Vallepietra, so he and Caraberis departed to get some medical treatment. Fassoulis remained behind and sulked. He was cold and famished, and discouraged because their attempt to get through the lines had failed and nearly been fatal. The only possible bright spot would be the Graziosi's house in Vallepietra, so he set off for a Christmas Eve visit. The dinner he found waiting, a glass of wine, a warm fire, and the company of the butcher's family made him forget the trials of the previous week and realize he did indeed have much for which to be thankful.

Two days later, Caraberis, his foot and leg having healed enough so he could walk, and Fassoulis were taken to another home in Vallepietra, where they were reunited with the other members of their group. The pair were in the middle of telling about their adventures when Pucho burst in with the news that the Germans knew they were in the vicinity and were going to mount a search early the next morning. Once again, it was time to leave and return to the cabin in the mountains. The cold shack and lack of food were in sharp contrast to Christmas in Vallepietra, and every member of the group was down in the dumps when they arrived at the cabin. It was in that context that Fassoulis suggested they build their own hut in a well-hidden area a short distance from the cabin. There they could wait out the winter.

In less than a week the log hut was finished, and the evaders began moving their supplies from the cabin to their new home. There was enough room for eight or nine people in the hut, and a fairly small fire could keep it warm, but the first snow showed that a log roof covered with mud was not waterproof. Pine boughs helped solve the problem, but the roof always leaked. Once the structure was completed, the Americans again had time to consider their plight and soon realized that they were in a desperately hopeless situation. The last news they had heard about the Allied offensive in Italy had indicated that there still was little progress. They might be in their new hut for a year. And although the news of the American landing at Anzio in January lifted their spirits, the lack of progress by that force soon added to the winter's gloom. To make matters worse, the people of Vallepietra were finding it nearly impossible to feed the evaders.

After spending a month hibernating in the hut, Sonny could stand it no longer. Taking Pucho aside, Sonny said that he was going to try once again to get through the lines, this time at Anzio. Sonny believed he would have a better chance with only Pucho and Caraberis along. Pucho agreed to join him, but Caraberis was not ready to endure another trek, so he declined to go. Early the next morning, the American and his Italian guide once again bade their comrades good-bye. Fassoulis would never see any of the group in Italy again. The rest of the evaders remained in the area of the hut and were all captured by the Germans in April 1944. They spent the remainder of the war in prison camps in Germany.

The first stop for Sonny and Pucho was, as before, the Graziosis' house in Vallepietra to get a good departure meal and a few supplies.

While there, they were told of two Englishmen, an Italian officer, and an Italian woman who were also planning to get through the lines near Anzio. The two groups met at a house on the edge of town. Although the larger group had planned a route almost identical to that of Fassoulis and Pucho, each group decided to go its own way. Following the meeting, Sonny and Pucho returned to the butcher's house for the night. Sonny was unable to sleep, and he went over the plan in his mind time and again, trying to determine if there was any flaw that might cause them to fail. Regardless of what happened, he vowed that this time he would not turn back.

After a lavish breakfast and a tearful farewell, with the Graziosi daughters again shedding most of the tears, the two departed shortly after sunup into the February cold. They planned to cover nearly twenty miles and get to Route 6, the main highway from Rome to Naples, by dark. Not long after leaving Vallepietra, they overtook a farmer with a donkey. Pucho divulged their identities, and the farmer let them put their supply packs on the animal. They had not gone more than a mile when, rounding a bend in the road, they were faced, as they had been on their previous trek, with a stalled German truck. An officer stood beside the vehicle while the driver worked under the hood. As the trio passed, the mischievous Pucho said "*Que bella machina!*" to the officer. He either did not understand or decided to ignore the three ragged Italians, but when the trio had gone some distance farther, Sonny told Pucho not to do something like that again because his heart couldn't stand the strain.

About noon, the farmer left the road, and the two evaders decided it would be safer to travel in the hills, carrying their own packs. They were able to get a meager lunch at a monastery high above the village of Subiaco, but at midafternoon they came to a narrow valley and realized they would have to use the road. Again, Pucho thought that the best course of action was to simply walk down the road. "The Germans are too busy to pay any attention to two Italians," he told Sonny. So, with the familiar feeling of having his heart in his throat and with sweat pouring out of every pore, Fassoulis again followed his Italian friend down the road and past column after column of German soldiers. The road was bordered by vineyards, and both men knew that escape was impossible if they were stopped, but when the Germans continued to ignore them, their confidence grew. Soon they were again in the fields and hills, approaching the strategic highway.

When they were a few miles from that critical highway, Pucho began to look for shelter for the night. The Germans had imposed a curfew of six o'clock for all Italians, so trying to travel farther would be pushing their luck too far. Besides, it was already dark. Luckily, he found a farmer who would sell them some food and let them stay in his hayloft for the night. The next morning, the farmer again sold them some bread and told them that there were two large German garrisons in their path, right by Route 6, but that there was no way around them without going through several villages that also had a number of Germans living in them.

Luck had been with them so far, so the two decided to try to pass the large garrisons without being seen. That was not to be, however. Just as they approached Route 6, they saw a large formation of German troops marching down the highway, probably going to reinforce the defensive positions around Anzio. The evaders' timing was such that they would reach the point where the path intersected Route 6 at the same time as the Germans. They had been seen, so they could not turn back. Retreating would be a dead giveaway that they were not peasants.

A few weeks earlier, Fassoulis would probably have panicked in that situation, but he calmly followed Pucho. "Throw your pistol into the bushes," the Italian quietly instructed. "If you are caught with a weapon, you will probably be shot on the spot." Fassoulis did as he was told and continued to walk toward the line of troops. As Pucho and Fassoulis stood on the side of the highway watching the Germans march by, they could scarcely breathe. At any moment they expected to be asked for their identity papers. But the Germans evidently dismissed the two as harmless Italian peasants and marched on past. Fassoulis and Pucho quickly crossed the road and were soon in the fields and hills again, minus their weapons.

After crossing one of three mountains that lay in the path to Anzio, they arrived at the village of Segni. Pucho made his usual inquiries with his habitual luck, and soon the pair were sitting in the kitchen of a large farmhouse eating bread and pasta and washing them down with delicious red wine. The next morning they departed for the town of Norma. By noon the two were still climbing Mount Lupone in the throes of a blizzard for which they had been unprepared. Numb with cold and exhausted from climbing, the pair stumbled onto a small house early in the afternoon and, without knocking, entered the structure. The two inhabitants were paralyzed at the sight of the two strangers emerging from the snow. It took Pucho only a few seconds to tell the man and woman of their plight. As soon as the man found out that Fassoulis was an American, he threw his arms around him and treated him like a long-lost brother. The owner of the hut, Gustave, had lived in New York City for fifteen years and was overjoyed to see an American. He had been hoping the

Norma, Italy. Taken in 1996, this photo shows the strategic position of the town.
Photo by the author

Americans would liberate the area soon, but they were still making little progress, he reported.

Two days later, when the blizzard finally stopped, Gustave led Pucho and Sonny through the snowdrifts down Mount Lupone and out of the snow. He stopped at the base of the final mountain they would have to conquer before getting to the front near Anzio. "Stay on this path," he told them as he departed, "and in about four hours you will be at the summit. You will be able to see Norma and Anzio." The flat plain that extends from the ocean to the east south of Rome is bordered on the east by a range of sharp, steep, rocky hills that rise hundreds of feet almost vertically out of the absolute level land. The ancient village of Norma sits high on the side of one such hill nearly a thousand feet above the surrounding countryside.

Sonny was so excited that when the pair finally neared the top of the mountain, he ran the last hundred feet. He stood in awe at the top as he looked down on the miles of flat land below him. He could clearly see the huge invasion force in the harbor and he could watch the shelling and strafing of the German positions. Sonny could hardly contain himself as he realized he was only a few miles from the Americans. His ringside seat made him all the more excited, and he could not sit still during the afternoon as he watched the action. "I can't wait to get that cablegram off to my mother," he kept thinking.

That night the two went into Norma. Because of its location high above the flat plain, the town was used by the Germans for strategic observation and directing gunfire. Pucho persuaded a man named Giuseppe Borticelli, whom he met on the street, to help them. Giuseppe showed them a hut above Norma where they would be safe. "The Germans are no problem in the hills or in the town," their new benefactor told them. "They are too busy fighting to worry about people they meet on the roads." He also told them he had heard that the Englishmen and Italians Fassoulis and Pucho had talked to in Vallepietra had tried to make it through the lines in the vicinity of Norma and been caught. The Englishmen were taken prisoner and the Italians were shot.

During the evening, as they sat by a small fire in the hut Giuseppe had shown them, Pucho told a dumbfounded Sonny that he was leaving to go back to Póggio Mirteto. He was anxious about his father and could not go through the lines since he was responsible for his family. "I can be of no further help to you," he told Fassoulis. "You will have to make it the rest of the way by yourself."

The next morning was one of the hardest Sonny had ever had to endure. He and Pucho had become closer than brothers, but neither could find words to express his feelings. The two hiked to the top of the mountain, where they simply said "Good-bye and good luck" to each other and turned to go their own ways. But as Sonny walked down the mountain, he had the most empty feeling he had ever experienced.

The news of the unsuccessful attempt to get through the lines by the Englishmen and Italians, the loss of his guide and adviser, and his observations from the vicinity of Norma, all convinced Sonny that he would have to go farther north. Referring to the maps he and Caraberis had received weeks before, he decided to try to get to the Allied side of the lines in the area of Cisterna di Latina. He hoped to make the seven miles to the town of Cori during the day and then go to Cisterna di Latina and through the lines that night.

It was late in the afternoon when Fassoulis arrived in the vicinity of Cori. When it was dark, he left the hills and began the treacherous trek to the front lines. Without Pucho beside him, he jumped at every sound he heard. It was a dark night with no moon, and several times he was saved from running into a German position only by hearing the inhabitants talking. After he crossed the Appian Way, the ancient Roman highway that connected Rome with Brindisi, on the Adriatic Coast, the still night was interrupted by ear-shattering explosions. Fassoulis found himself in the middle of a firefight. The small arms fire seemed to be coming from all sides. In panic, he dove for cover in a ditch. The bullets whizzing over his head and the ground-shaking artillery explosions were terrifying. There was no place to go and nothing he could do, so he just hugged the ground and waited for what he thought was certain death. Miraculously, the fire finally subsided. He cautiously retreated, abandoning any idea of getting through the lines that night and just glad to be alive. His only choice of action now was to pose as an Italian and, using the tactic Pucho had taught him, boldly take the road back toward the mountains to formulate another plan.

Fassoulis was dejectedly trudging down the road near Cisterna di Latina at dawn when a group of German soldiers approached him. With his heart in his mouth, he continued at the same rate of speed, trying to look nonchalant. But luck was not with him. He was ordered to stop, and his heart stopped too. "*Documenti*," one of them demanded. "My home has been bombed by the damned Americans," Fassoulis answered in his best Italian, "and my papers were all burned." Nonetheless, they searched him and found his U.S. Armed Forces identification card. Nearly six months after he had bailed out of his stricken B-17, Fassoulis was again a prisoner.

The heartbroken Sonny was numb. Tears welled in his eyes as he was marched back to the village of Cori and loaded into the back seat of a car. The Germans made no effort to question him as they started toward Rome. No sooner had they gotten under way, however, than the driver slammed on the brakes. An American P-51 was about to strafe the road. The car skidded to a halt, and everyone dove into the roadside ditch. Fortunately, Fassoulis was not hit, but neither were the Germans or their car.

This time the drive was short, and Sonny was put into a small room in a nondescript building in Velletri, about twenty miles south of Rome.

Sonny couldn't sleep during that night. He kept thinking about home, about the Graziosi family, and about countless other Italians who had literally put their lives on the line to help him. He had walked through snow and rain, gone days without food, covered hundreds of miles on foot, been close enough to hear American voices, and here he was, back where he'd started—a prisoner. Wave after wave of despair washed over him. He felt no better the next morning when he was again loaded into the car and taken to Rome. He was kept overnight in a building somewhere outside the city, and the following day was put on a train going north. Sonny knew that every mile he went put him closer to the prisoner-of-war camp in Germany that would be his final destination.

The train moved at a snail's pace because of the bombed-out tracks and the threat of attacks by Allied fighters. About three hours after they started, everyone got out of the cars and ran for their lives as the train was attacked by bombers. Fassoulis just kept on running. He'd never dreamed he could run so long and so fast, but he was soon far enough away from the train that he could no longer hear the shouts of the guards as they tried to round up the prisoners. As suddenly as he had been taken, he was again evading the Germans.

Fassoulis walked south, staying clear of the road, until dusk, when he was too exhausted to go farther. Without food and water, there was nothing to do but lie down in some bushes and sleep. In the morning, he started to walk along the road toward Rome. He was again using Pucho's idea of acting as if you belonged. Fassoulis had been walking for about an hour when a German truck pulled up beside him and stopped. "I knew it was too good to be true," he thought. But the Germans apparently assumed he was an Italian peasant and offered him a ride. They told him to sit in the back on several large barrels of gasoline and watch for Allied airplanes, a common practice for the Germans. The soldiers needn't have worried about his keeping a sharp eye for any attackers, since the last thing he wanted was to be sitting on gasoline drums when the bullets began to fly.

The Germans drove through Rome without stopping, and at Velletri, where three days before Fassoulis had been a prisoner, the driver stopped to prepare something to eat. He sent Fassoulis to find water and once again, the American just kept on going until he was well into the countryside to the west of the town. After dark, he went back east, crossed the Appian Way, and by late that night was back in Norma.

Giuseppe Borticelli couldn't believe his eyes when he opened his door to the late night knock. He quickly took Fassoulis in and fixed the starving airman something to eat. They spent most of the night talking about the American's adventures and deciding what he should do next. "I know a hiding place where you can go while you think about what to do," Borticelli said. "Maybe by the time you decide, the Americans will have come this far and you will not have to try the dangerous trip again." In the morning, he took Fassoulis back into the mountains to an area where several men from the town were hiding their livestock from the Germans.

A few days later, when he was out for a walk, Fassoulis ran into two of his friends from the prison camp near Póggio Mirteto. They had been making their way south as well, and had also been unable to get through the lines to the American side, so they had decided to wait for the Allies to capture the area. Also with the group was an RAF lieutenant, John Hall, with whom Fassoulis struck up an immediate friendship. He, like Fassoulis, was not content to wait and wanted to try to get through the lines as soon as possible.

For the next six weeks there was no appreciable change in the situation around Anzio, so the small group was confined to the area between Norma and the small hill town of Gorda, about twelve miles to the east. They remained in the mountains, staying in whatever shelters they could find and going into a town for food and to stay overnight on the few occasions when the Germans were not in the area. Their evasion site offered excellent views of the entire Anzio beachhead, and Fassoulis spent many hours recording the location of German positions and facilities, and any other information he thought would be useful, on small pieces of paper. He planned to carry these through the lines for use by the Allied forces despite the fact that he would have been shot as a spy had he been caught with the notes.

Fassoulis was getting more anxious to try a third time to get to the Americans, and he and Hall talked often about trying once again. Spring had come, and with it a new Allied offensive. It also appeared that the German forces were becoming increasingly poorly organized under the pressure of the Americans at Anzio. A few days after a wonderful Easter dinner in Gorda, Fassoulis and Hall decided it was time to go. They left the rest of the group and made the familiar trek to Norma. After a day there getting a few supplies and any intelligence they could about the best place to try to get through the lines, they set out. The two had decided that the most logical place to try to cross to the Allied side was near the city of Terracina, a port about twenty-five miles south of Anzio.

Their plan was to get to the coast, steal a boat, and then sail to the island of Zannone, which they had heard was held by the British. As they departed Norma, Fassoulis told Giuseppe that he would not be back as an evader. He was either going to get through the lines or spend the rest of the war as a prisoner.

The pair made good progress the first day. Although they stayed in the countryside and hills as much as possible, their route made some travel on the roads essential. Hall was concerned about the possibility of capture while walking on the roads, but Fassoulis believed they had nothing to lose. Despite having been captured once, his travel on the roads had been generally successful, and he believed that the Germans

John Hall, the RAF pilot who escaped from Italy
with Fassoulis.   *John Hall*

were in such disarray that they would pay no attention to two Italian peasants among the hundreds who were walking down the roads. "Just act like you belong here and there will be no problem," Fassoulis told Hall. By the time the sun was setting they were near Priverno, halfway to their destination. Fortunately, they happened upon two farmers on the trail. After learning who they were, the Italians agreed to provide them with food and directions to a haystack where they could spend the night. As they went through the familiar routine of burrowing into the hay, both knew that the most dangerous day of their trek lay ahead.

The first obstacle of the next day was a heavily guarded railroad. As Fassoulis and Hall approached the road that would lead them to the railroad bridge, they were able to join a group of Italian refugees, made homeless by the fighting, walking in the same direction. Since there was no way the German guard could stop or question each member of the group, he simply let them go across the bridge. The area in which the two now found themselves, however, was occupied almost completely by Germans.

When it was nearly dark, Fassoulis and Hall came upon a small settlement of improvised grass huts. Taking a big chance, Fassoulis, in his now fairly fluent Italian, asked a man who was sitting in front of one of the huts about the situation in Terracina. He told them that the city had been badly bombed and shelled. "The Germans have made it a restricted zone," he added, "and no one is allowed in the area who does not have a pass. Most of the people here are from Terracina." Fassoulis and Hall were disheartened by this news, since it eliminated still another possible point at which to cross the lines. As they searched for a place to hide for the night, the pair came upon several Italians who were roasting a lamb. They welcomed the two strangers, and after eating their fill of the delicious meat, the evaders found another haystack in which to spend the night.

The following day was one of trial and error for Hall and Fassoulis as they went down one road and then another in their attempt to get to the sea. Each time they were thwarted by a German force in the area, an artillery barrage, or some other unforeseen obstacle. Although the new map they had been given in Norma was fairly accurate, it did not depict the German emplacements that continued to impede their progress. It was late in the afternoon when they finally were able to make their way to the Sisto River and begin to follow it the few miles to the ocean. Surprisingly, there were no Germans along the small river, and by late in the afternoon the evaders were within a stone's throw of the ocean and freedom—except they did not have a boat and had no idea where to find one. A retreat up the river led them to a landing where an Italian was pulling a boat from the river. He told them that it was impossible to sail down the river and into the sea since the mouth was always guarded by several German sentries and an artillery battery. Their only hope was to find a boat that could be carried the mile to the coast so it could be launched at a relatively deserted part of the beach.

As darkness fell, Fassoulis and Hall realized they had eaten nothing all day and that, if they were to make an effort to get to the sea the next day, they had to be physically prepared. Taking a chance once again, they made themselves known to a boy who was walking down a lane near the river. They told him who they were and promised him a big reward after the Americans took the area if he would help them. He agreed, put them in his boat, and rowed through a flooded area to his house. A great deal of the flat plain had been flooded by the Germans to prevent any Allied invasion, so much of the local farmland was under water. After sitting in the boat for a few anxious minutes, the evaders were welcomed inside. Although their meal was meager, it was all the beleaguered Italians could afford. After dinner, Fassoulis and Hall went into a neighboring vineyard, where they spent the night in the open.

The evaders spent the next day hiding in the vineyard as well. The sister of the boy who had helped them, Amalia, brought them breakfast and later some bread for lunch. She also agreed to find two or three men who would help the pair if they needed it. Amalia was about twenty-five, a widow, and very pretty. For at least one brief instant, Fassoulis was tempted to abandon the idea of crossing the lines just to stay with her, but as night began to fall, he again turned his mind to escape and the trial that lay ahead. He and Hall planned to steal a boat from the Sisto River, row it across some flooded areas they had seen the previous day, then carry the heavy wooden craft, with the help of the men Amalia said she would find, a few hundred yards across the large dike and road on the top, down the steep sandy side, and across about one hundred feet of beach to the sea. Fassoulis and Hall would then be off to the island of Zannone, one of the Ponziane Islands. The journey meant rowing across nearly twenty-five miles of open sea and finding a small island. They realized their chances for success were not very good.

It was well after dark when the group set out. With the aid of the Italian men, the pair found what appeared to be a suitable boat and were able to row silently across the flooded portions of land to the point where they had to carry the boat. They then discovered that the craft was too heavy to carry very far, so they had no choice but to return it and wait until the next night to try again. Still, Sonny was euphoric when they got back to the vineyard. "We can make it," he almost yelled to Hall. "All we have to do is get some help and find a lighter boat and we are on our way." Hall didn't share Fassoulis's enthusiasm. He knew that the rugged Italian boats were all very heavy and that a group large enough to carry the boat would attract the attention of the Germans stationed all along the coast. Fassoulis was not to be discouraged, however, and went to sleep again thinking of how to word the cablegram to his mother saying that he had survived.

The following day, the pair once again remained hidden in the vineyard. By nightfall, they were ready to try again. Fassoulis wanted to get going as soon as possible, but Hall cautioned that they had to wait for the moon to go down so they would have complete darkness. It was after midnight when the two airmen, along with their Italian helpers, found a smaller boat and once again began the trip. This craft was lighter, but still nearly impossible to carry down the path. They had covered only a fourth of the distance when they heard a German patrol approaching. It was a struggle to get the boat into the bushes, but they managed with the help of their Italian allies, and after the patrol passed, they resumed their journey.

In a matter of minutes they could hear the surf, and the group rushed to get the boat under way. As soon as they were in the water, Hall and Fassoulis began rowing madly. Their Italian helpers ran in the opposite direction, toward their homes. Although the two evaders expected to hear bullets whining over their heads any second, none materialized as they continued to row. Fortunately, Fassoulis was a trained navigator, so he was able to chart their direction by using the North Star as the pair took turns rowing through the early hours of the morning. It was not long until they realized that they should at least have brought drinking water with them. On the map, Zannone had not looked very far away, but as the sun came up and there was nothing to be seen but open water, the pair realized their survival experience was far from over. Nonetheless, they continued to row hour after hour.

By midday both Fassoulis and Hall thought they could row no farther. Their shoulders and arms screamed for relief and their parched mouths were crying for water, but still there was no land in sight. Sonny could feel the panic gnawing in his stomach. In the early afternoon, a formation of B-25 medium bombers came over the two sailors at a fairly low altitude, but the crews gave no indication that they had seen the frantically waving pair. A couple of hours later a small American liaison airplane passed very close to them. Again the two waved. In response, the small craft dipped its wings as a signal that they had been seen. Apparently having taken them to be Italian fishermen, it soon disappeared to the south. "I'm sure that the air-sea rescue folks will soon be here," Sonny said enthusiastically. "I don't care who comes, Allies or Germans, I'll be glad to see them and get some water," was Hall's reply. But as the afternoon wore on there was no sign of any rescue craft, so the pair continued their weak rowing.

By late afternoon, any hope they had of finding Zannone or even of surviving their ordeal was starting to wane. They had seen no more airplanes or any boats, and both men began to have illusions of drifting in the Mediterranean for days until they perished from thirst. But in the early twilight of May 1, 1944, Hall thought he saw land ahead. Using what little strength they had left, the two rowed as hard as they could. A short while later they stumbled from their boat into gentle surf and crawled onto a beach. Their hands blistered, their hair matted from sweat, and their bodies crying for water, they lay on the sand. Sonny silently thanked God they had made it to land.

But as the two finally sat up and looked around, there was little to be thankful for. There were no houses or signs of any life. As far as they could see there was nothing but sand. "I know Zannone is populated by Italians," Fassoulis told Hall. "Maybe we didn't hit the right island." Still, the two began to stumble along the beach in a life-and-death search for water. As they rounded a point, they saw the most welcome sight in the world, a lighthouse. Staggering in the direction of the building, they spotted a man pulling a small fishing boat up on the shore. After giving them a drink of water, the fisherman assured the two that they were on British-occupied Zannone. They had made it!

The Italian fisherman took the two evaders to the lighthouse, whose keeper was taken aback to see such scraggly, filthy visitors at his door. After hearing who they were and what they had done, he told them that a high-ranking British official was on the island hunting. He was staying at the lighthouse and would be returning shortly. Fassoulis and Hall cleaned up as best they could and were soon seated in the living room of the lightkeeper's home talking to the Englishman. After a meal of C rations, the two exhausted airmen were shown to real beds with sheets. In seconds they were asleep.

Late the following morning, a motor launch took the pair to the island of Ponza, from which they embarked the following day for Naples. At RAF headquarters in Naples, Hall and Fassoulis said an emotional good-bye. The two had been through a great deal together, and their bonds were tight. Fassoulis was then taken to an American prison camp for delousing and a general cleanup before getting a new uniform. He then sent a cable to his mother. On May 5, 1944, he arrived at Fifteenth

Air Force Headquarters in Bari, Italy, for an intelligence debriefing. His information on gun emplacements, where units were billeted and ammunition was stored, and the other facts he had gathered during his weeks in the hills around Norma proved to be immensely valuable to the Allies.[1] Fassoulis was then given orders to go back to the United States, but he asked to have them rescinded so he could remain on General Ira Eaker's staff to give briefings about escape and evasion as well as help with intelligence estimates of the German situation.

After southern Italy was liberated, Fassoulis was able to return to several places where he had been helped when he was evading—among them Norma, Roccantica, and Póggio Mirteto, where he again visited with Pucho. In each location he gave those who had helped him as much food and other supplies as his jeep would hold. In return, he was wined and dined by his Italian friends. But his greatest satisfaction was being able to thank his benefactors.

In October 1944, Fassoulis requested a transfer to the China-Burma-India theater of operations as a navigator. After a month in the United States, he was assigned to the Fourteenth Air Force in China; he arrived on January 3, 1945. Six weeks later, on February 25, 1945, he was forced to bail out of his C-47 transport because of engine failure. He landed in a rice paddy and for the next twenty-five days evaded the Japanese as he made his way back to friendly hands.

Fassoulis was discharged from the army after World War II. He then went into international business, specializing in trade with China and Latin America. He also served on several government commissions concerned with China and the Far East. He is presently the immensely successful founder and president of CIC International Ltd. and lives in New York City.

In September 1996, Sonny Fassoulis, in the company of the author and the author's wife, returned to Italy for the first time since World War II to visit some of the sites of his adventures. The first stop was at the small mountain village of Vallepietra, where Fassoulis immediately identified the butcher's house. Together we retraced the route he and Pucho took into town. Although none of the Graziosi family still lived there, Fassoulis was able to locate two people who helped supply him and his comrades and had an emotional reunion with them. We then went south to Norma. The strategic location of that town and the view it gives of the plain all the way to the area of Anzio is remarkable. Signor Borticelli had died about four years before our visit, but we were able to locate his daughter and spend some time in her home talking about her father and the aid she and her family gave to Fassoulis. From Norma we traced the route Fassoulis and Hall took to the sea and were able to find the spot where they carried the boat and launched it for their trip to Zannone. When Fassoulis asked a young man for directions to the proper area of the beach, the young man said he knew the story of Fassoulis and Hall and told us it was his grandfather who had helped them with the boat.

Fernando Franchescino and Fassoulis in September 1996. Fernando, Nazarene's son, remembers bringing supplies to the evaders after they left St. Valentino convent.

Photo by the author

The final portion of our visit took us north to Póggio Mirteto and Roccantica. In Póggio Mirteto, we visited St. Valentino, where Fassoulis was confined by the Italians. It is still a convent. We saw the view that he had from his room, and were able to walk the road out of the area of St. Valentino that he and his fellow prisoners took when they were released. Nazarene Franchescino had died about three years before, but we were able to find his son, Fernando, who had also brought supplies to the evaders. He immediately realized who Fassoulis was, and they had a long visit about their adventures during the war. They later had a reunion dinner where Fassoulis also met Nazarene's daughter, Pauletta, again. We were unable to find anyone who knew what had happened to Pucho. At Roccantica, Fassoulis hoped to find Signor Leti. Much to his sorrow, he learned that there were no members of the Leti family still in Roccantica and that Signor Leti had died in poverty after using much of his money to aid evaders and others in need and because most of his assets had been confiscated by the Germans. We were not able to go inside the Leti house where Fassoulis and his comrades spent a memorable Thanksgiving and on several other occasions were fed and kept overnight, but neither the house nor the town seemed to have changed at all. At a restaurant in Roccantica, we were put in touch with a local citizen who knew the entire story of the evaders, recognized Fassoulis by name, and spent an hour talking to us about the evaders and the fate of many of the Italians who had helped them.

Not only was the trip a nostalgic visit for Fassoulis, it gave me a much deeper insight into his adventures, especially the enormity of the physical challenge he and his comrades had faced. The most memorable part of the trip was the enthusiasm of the Italians when they found out who Fassoulis was and their willingness to help us. People would lean out of windows or stop what they were doing to take us to find someone just because they had such vivid memories of World War II and the evaders who were in their community. Even the young people in the small mountain towns were familiar with the stories of the war and the role the people in their towns played in it. In every case, high on the list of important contributions to the war was helping the evaders.

Notes

1. Letter, Lieutenant General Ira C. Eaker to Lieutenant General Barney M. Giles, 11 October 1944. Copy in the author's files.

The Art of Evasion and Survival

There is a very close relationship between evasion and survival. The adventures of the airmen in this book graphically illustrate the reality of the evasion and survival situation. Although evading the Germans was the primary objective of each man, most found themselves in a situation at least once—and for Eric Doorly, Bob Smith, D. K. Willis, and S. G. Fassoulis, several times—when evasion had to take a back seat to survival. In those circumstances, the airman was so desperate for food or water that he was willing to risk capture in order to get those necessities of life. Thus, knowing how to survive and being able to do so are essential to successful evasion. There are a number of characteristics that were shown time and again by the evaders in this book and by most other evaders during World War II. These include the will to evade, the ability to trust, courage, patience, self-confidence, stamina, resourcefulness, optimism, perseverance, adaptability, sound judgment, and the capacity to cope with loneliness. To these must be added the abilities to remain calm, to think a situation through, and to rely on one's own common sense. The particular circumstances in which the evader found himself determined which of these and other traits were the most important at the time, but to at least some degree, each of these qualities was displayed by all of the men who are the subjects of this book.

For each, the will and desire to evade was paramount after he had successfully bailed out of his airplane or crash-landed. Eric Doorly began running almost immediately and remained motionless and covered with leaves for hours while the Germans walked within feet of him. Likewise, D. K. Willis made his way through a crowd, stole a bicycle, and watched from only feet away while the Germans searched for him. It took only a few moments for all ten of the airmen on Corfu to disappear into the hills with unknown strangers.

No characteristic was more essential to each of the evaders in these stories, or exercised more often, than trust. As soon as they were on enemy-occupied soil, Bob Smith, Bob Priser, and Joe Cotton's B-17 crew had to trust those who were there almost immediately to help them. That same B-17 crew, to a man, had to trust the Greeks when they were stricken with malaria, and their guides as they made their way through the trackless mountains of Greece. D. K. Willis went into the back room of a restaurant in Belgium with a perfect stranger to get food, and Oscar Coen sat in the back of a truck as it went toward the German base at St. Omer with a German soldier riding in the front seat. Sonny Fassoulis and his companions camped in the Italian mountains were completely dependent upon strangers for both food and water, and Eric Doorly followed the lead of the Ranson boys as they walked through the streets of Paris, elbow to elbow with German soldiers. Every day, in some way, each demonstrated his trust in a complete stranger—with his freedom, and often his life, at stake. But trust is a two-way street, for those who helped the evaders also trusted that they would not be turned in, that the airmen were indeed who they said they were, and that the cause they represented was worth dying for.

Few men are asked to display the courage and optimism of Eric Doorly: hiding in the leaves, contacting a complete stranger at a bridge, lying on what everyone thought was his deathbed in Lourdes, spending days in the Pyrenees, languishing in horrible conditions for over a month in a Spanish jail in Barcelona, and then spending nearly three months in conditions that were beyond imagination at a Spanish prison camp. A very different type of courage and the ability to think on your feet can be seen in the story of Oscar Coen when he detoured into the French bistro early in the morning so he wouldn't have to face several Germans at a railroad crossing. And several times during his evasion he was face-to-face with German guards and able to bluff his way past them.

Bob Priser was the master of patience. He stayed in one room or one house for weeks, moving from place to place within a short distance of Brussels for months on end, most of the time knowing that he was not going to be able to get back to England and his wife until Belgium was liberated. And Sonny Fassoulis was willing to spend months in the Apennine Mountains just waiting for his chance to try to cross the lines. When he failed, he persevered until he finally succeeded on the third try.

Few evaders demonstrated the degree of self-confidence of Oscar Coen as he walked past the German guard at the railroad crossing and on the bridge going into Abbeville. D. K. Willis set off for Brussels on his own and in the dark of night, confident that he would somehow find the underground and be able to get back to England. Bob Priser had enough confidence in himself to drink beer in the same bistro as the Germans in Petite Espinette.

Physical stamina, the ability to endure hardship, and the will to evade successfully stand out in the stories of D. K. Willis and Bob Smith as they struggled through Spain after crossing the Pyrenees. Both nearly succumbed to hunger and exposure before they realized they had to have help or they wouldn't survive. But had they not been willing to endure the physical hardship, they would have been captured and would never have reached eventual freedom. Sonny Fassoulis walked hundreds of miles through the mountains of Italy, in all sorts of conditions, often without food or shelter, just to get to a position from which to cross to the Allied side of the front lines. Fred Glor, Ernie Skorheim, Joe Cotton, and their crew were often at the end of their physical resources during their trek in Albania and Greece, yet they optimistically kept going, confident that Dick Flournoy was right in his determination to bring his entire crew back.

When the German soldiers lined up in the square in front of D. K. Willis, he had to think of a solution to the situation in seconds. In a similar vein, had Oscar Coen not been thinking on his feet when he was confronted by a German guard in the city square, he might well have panicked rather than just continuing to walk. When the Germans seemed to be too close for comfort, Bob Priser used the cave he had been shown to hide in, and D. K. Willis's trek to Brussels could well have been stopped by a river had he not been resourceful enough to join a group of local workers carrying logs across the bridge or to take food from the farmworkers in the fields.

Bob Smith had to adapt to his circumstances when he slept in a culvert under a road and later almost froze sleeping in the trees while crossing the Pyrenees. Haystacks became beds for nearly every one of the evaders at one time or another. Ernie Skorheim and Fred Glor let the Greeks on Corfu put leeches on their bodies to suck out blood when they had malaria. The ability of their entire crew to adapt to the situation was tested when they were individually shoved into Greek houses to eat whatever there was and sleep on the floor. Sonny Fassoulis never knew where he would find food or if he could get shelter for the night as he and Pucho Conforzi hiked the Italian mountains toward the Allied lines.

Often one of the best indicators of whether an idea is a good one or not is one's own judgment or "gut feel." This certainly was true for evaders during World War II. When Bob Smith was left in the little hut after the chain came off his bicycle, he had the feeling that he had been abandoned and so set out on his own. Oscar Coen didn't trust Paul from the moment he came into the Blanchard's kitchen; Paul turned out to be a double agent. Almost as soon as Eric Doorly entered the Ransons' home in Aumale, he had the feeling that everything was going to work out.

Among the most difficult conditions with which an evader, or any-one in a survival situation, must deal is being alone. Spending nearly a month in one hotel room with nothing to do and no diversions, such as reading, certainly taxed Fred Glor to the maximum. Sonny Fassoulis came very close to letting loneliness get the best of him after he was cap-tured near the American lines. For each evader, loneliness became a se-rious problem on several occasions. As Joe Cotton said, "When you are hungry and weak and sick, it is very easy to let loneliness become over-whelming. If that happens you lose hope, your desire to evade, and sometimes your desire to survive." Bob Smith remarked that "just a drink of water, a person's voice, a crust of bread can often break the spell of loneliness and give you the will to go on another day." But for each of the evaders, the time alone was also an opportunity to think through the situation, make plans to cope with various scenarios, and remember those things such as home, family, the mission, prisoner-of-war camps, friends, and what might come after the war was over—things that were essential to the airman for keeping his hope alive and his spirit strong.

Many of these characteristics are not unique to the successful evader or even to World War II. Some would be just as valuable, for example, to a person lost in the mountains or to an airman forced to abandon his aircraft over the desert. But the World War II evaders' situation was much different from the experiences of downed pilots in later wars. These air crews did not have survival radios, and there was no specially trained force to make rescues behind enemy lines as was the norm in Vietnam. The Allied airmen evading in Europe were also in the midst of a friendly population that, by and large, wanted to help them if it was possible. Nevertheless, the fundamentals of using your head and having a strong will to survive are as vital today as they were for the young, courageous men who are the subjects of this book.

A Note on Sources

The primary sources of information for this book were the accounts of the participants and whatever information they had retained over the years. Although I augmented that information in many cases, each story is still as the evader remembered it and lived it. The information available varied considerably from person to person, so I have made a brief note of the sources I used for each chapter.

Oscar Coen and Eric Doorly were in the RAF during their evasion experience, and were not required to complete any evasion report when they arrived back in England. Although Bob Smith was flying an RAF aircraft, he was actually in the U.S. Army Air Forces. However, I was unable to find his evasion report. Therefore, their stories are based primarily on many hours of personal interviews with each man. I was also able to use interviews with members of their squadrons in Europe in my accounts of their experiences. I did obtain a copy of an intelligence report that Smith completed after his return, noting German troop and aircraft positions that he observed during his evasion and the dates he made the observations, which helped account for his movements and, to some degree, those of Eric Doorly.

D. K. Willis died in 1977, so I have no interview records with him. I spent many hours talking with his widow, Pat, who is intimately familiar with his entire evasion experience. She also made all of her husband's records available to me, and these proved invaluable. Her information was augmented by the evasion report that Willis prepared for the U.S. Army Air Forces after his return, the Missing Air Crew Report of the mission, and the maps drawn by the other members of his squadron showing where he went down. Pat Willis also gave me a copy of the German report of the incident. In addition, a Dutch author, Hans Onderwater, has written a very well researched and documented history of the Comète Line, *Reis Naar De Horizon* (*Journey to the Horizon*), in which D. K. Willis plays a key part. (Unfortunately, it has not been translated into English.) It was useful in supporting Pat Willis's recollections and providing additional information about Willis's experiences after he left Brussels.

Robert Priser's story relies primarily on many hours of personal interviews. Since he was not released until the Americans occupied Belgium, he was not required to write an evasion report. I did obtain a copy of the official accounts of his being shot down that were written after the mission by Priser's squadron mates. I also obtained the Missing Air Crew Report relating to his ill-fated flight. His recollections were aided immeasurably by his return trip to Belgium in 1993. He also wrote a very long summary of his experiences a number of years ago that was useful in augmenting the interviews.

The account of the B-17 crew that crashed on Corfu is based on personal interviews with Joe Cotton, Ernie Skorheim, and Fred Glor, the only three members of the crew still living. Fortunately, the crew remained in contact with one another while the others were alive, and I had access to a tape of their 1985 reunion, during which they talked about their evasion experiences for over two hours. In addition, I was able to obtain the evasion reports written by Joe Cotton and Jim Wagner, as well as the Missing Crew Report and Casualty Report for AGO for the entire crew. In 1996, Nick Aspiotis, a businessman who has relatives on Corfu, made a trip to the island, where he was able to talk with several Greeks who had aided the Americans. Their accounts were useful in ensuring the accuracy of the story.

In 1947, Sonny Fassoulis wrote a very detailed account of his adventures in Italy. This account, combined with my many hours of interviews with him, forms the basis for his story. I also obtained the Battle Casualty Report, Missing Crew Report, and Individual Casualty Questionnaires for his entire crew. He made a number of documents and letters available to me that were useful in checking details. Of inestimable value was the trip my wife and I made in September 1996 with Sonny Fassoulis to the area of Italy where he evaded. We were able to see where he went, talk to people in the villages where he stayed, and watch his reactions to the towns and people as we visited.

I also had access to the files of the Escape and Evasion Society, which are in the Special Collections Division of the U.S. Air Force Academy Library. This archive contains hundreds of items pertaining to all aspects of escape and evasion from personal accounts of evaders to records and recollections of the Europeans who aided the Allied evaders.

Finally, I used my many years of experience in survival training. This proved of considerable value in determining if a story or comment really made good sense and could have happened the way it was explained by the participant.

In the final analysis, however, the stories in this book are those of the men who lived them many years ago, as told by them. They are as accurate and factual as the records that exist and the memories of the participants can make them.

Index

About the Author

Philip D. Caine is a retired U.S. Air Force brigadier general and a pilot with more than 4,500 hours of flying time in various military aircraft. In his final military assignment as Deputy Commandant of Cadets at the Air Force Academy, he was responsible for all cadet military education and training including SERE (survival, evasion, resistance, escape) training. Previously, he was the acting head of the Academy history department. A former professor of international studies and a senior research fellow at the National Defense University, he holds a doctorate from Stanford University. General Caine's previous books are *American Pilots in the RAF: The WWII Eagle Squadrons* and *Spitfires, Thunderbolts, and Warm Beer: An American Fighter Pilot over Europe*, both published by Brassey's. He and his wife, Doris, live in Monument, Colorado.